THE
CLUBCULTURES
READER

THE
CLUBCULTURES
READER

Readings in Popular
Cultural Studies

edited by
Steve Redhead

with Derek Wynne and Justin O'Connor
photographs by Patrick Henry

 BLACKWELL
Publishers

Copyright © Blackwell Publishers Ltd 1998.

Editorial matter and arrangement copyright © Steve Redhead, Derek Wynne and Justin O'Connor 1997. Photographs copyright © Patrick Henry.

First published 1997
Reprinted 1997
Reissued 1998

Blackwell Publishers Ltd
108 Cowley Road
Oxford OX4 1JF
UK

Blackwell Publishers Inc.
350 Main Street
Malden, MA 02148
USA

British Library Cataloguing in Publication Data

A CIP catalogue record for this book is available from the British Library.

Library of Congress Cataloging-in-Publication Data

The clubcultures reader : readings in popular cultural studies / edited by Steve Redhead,
  with Derek Wynne and Justin O'Connor.
    p.   cm.
  Includes bibliographical references and index.
  ISBN 0–631–21216–7 (pbk.)
    1. Popular music–History and criticism.   2. Music and youth.
  3. Mass media and youth.   4. Popular culture.   I. Redhead, Steve, 1952–   .
  II. Wynne, Derek.   III. O'Connor, Justin.
  ML3470.R42   1997
  306.4'84—dc20   96–43521
                                                                              CIP
                                                                              MN

Typeset in 10½ on 12pt Bembo
by Grahame & Grahame Editorial, Brighton

Printed and bound in Great Britain by MPG Books Ltd, Bodmin, Cornwall

This book is printed on acid-free paper

Contents

About the Authors

Steve Redhead is Research Director of the School of Law at the Manchester Metropolitan University. He is also Director of the Centre for Law, Culture and Society, which incorporates the Unit for Law and Popular Culture (ULPC) and the National Heritage Research Unit (NHRU), in the School of Law at the Manchester Metropolitan University, where he is Reader in Law and Popular Culture. He was co-director of the inter-faculty Manchester Institute for Popular Culture (MIPC) at the Manchester Metropolitan University until March 1995.

Derek Wynne is Senior Lecturer in Social Science in the Department of Sociology and IDS at the Manchester Metropolitan University. He is also Research Director of the Institute for Popular Culture in the Department of Sociology and IDS. Until March 1995 he was co-director of the inter-faculty Manchester Institute for Popular Culture.

Justin O'Connor is Director of the Institute for Popular Culture in the Department of Sociology and IDS at the Manchester Metropolitan University. Until March 1995 he was Senior Research Fellow at the Inter-faculty Manchester Institute for Popular Culture.

Jon Savage was Visiting Fellow at the Manchester Institute for Popular Culture, the Manchester Metropolitan University, 1992–3. He is the author of the best-selling book on punk rock, *England's Dreaming* (Faber, 1992), and editor, with Hanif Kureishi, of *The Faber Book of Pop* (Faber, 1995). He is a freelance writer on pop music and popular culture.

Simon Frith is Professor of English, University of Strathclyde, where he is also Director of the John Logie Baird Centre for Television, Film and Popular Music. He gave the first Manchester Institute for Popular Culture annual lecture in 1993. He is author of *The Sociology of Rock* (Constable/Sage, 1978) and *Sound Effects* (Constable/Sage, 1983), and author and editor of numerous other books and articles on popular music, youth culture and cultural theory.

Beverly Best is a former postgraduate student in the School of Communication, Simon Fraser University, Vancouver, Canada, and participated in the postgraduate seminar group when Steve Redhead was Visiting Professor at Simon Fraser University in 1994.

Will Straw is Associate Professor in Communications, McGill University, Montreal, where he is director of the Centre for Research on Canadian Cultural Industries and Institutions. He is author of numerous articles and papers on cultural studies, film theory and popular culture. He has spoken at the MIPC seminar.

Cressida Miles is a postgraduate student at the University of Lancaster. She attended the MIPC seminar from 1992 to 1995.

Adam Brown is a former postgraduate student at ULPC and researcher at MIPC, and author of a number of papers in democratization and the regulation of pop music and football.

Simon Reynolds is a freelance journalist who has spoken at the MIPC seminar. He is author of *Blissed Out* (Serpent's Tail, 1992), co-author with Joy Press of *The Sex Revolts* (Serpent's Tail, 1995) and author of *Generation E: Music, Drugs and Technology* (Picador, 1997). He writes for many different journals, including *Village Voice*, *Artforum*, *Melody Maker*, *The Wire*, *Rolling Stone* and the *New York Times*.

Sarah Champion is a freelance journalist who has spoken at the MIPC seminar. She is author of *And God Created Manchester* (Wordsmith, 1990) and many other articles and reviews on popular music and pop culture.

Hillegonda Rietveld is Lecturer in Media and Cultural Studies at Goldsmiths College, University of London, and a former postgraduate student at ULPC and researcher at MIPC. She is author of *This is Our House* (Arena, 1996).

Marek Kohn is a freelance writer who has spoken at the MIPC seminar and has written *Narcomania* (Faber, 1989) and *Dope Girls* (Lawrence and Wishart, 1992) among other books and articles.

Ted Polhemus is a freelance writer and broadcaster who has spoken at the MIPC seminar. He is author of many books, including *Streetstyle* (Thames and Hudson, 1994).

Kate Milestone is Lecturer in Cultural Studies in the Crewe and Alsager Faculty, the Manchester Metropolitan University. She is a former postgraduate student at ULPC and researcher at MIPC, and author of a number of papers on pop production, consumption and regulation.

Dave Haslam is internationally known as one of Britain's top DJs, running *Freedom* and *Yellow* nights at the Boardwalk, Manchester. He is a freelance writer on culture, music and the city, and his book *Manchester, England* will be published in 1997. He has spoken at the MIPC seminar.

David Muggleton is a postgraduate student at the University of Lancaster, and has attended MIPC seminars since 1993.

Steve Jones is Associate Professor and Head of Communication, University of Tulsa, and author of many articles on popular music and communication and the book *Rock Formation* (Sage, 1992). He is editor of a collection of essays on cyberculture called *Cybersociety* (Sage, 1995). He has spoken at the MIPC seminar.

Lawrence Grossberg is Morris Davis Professor of Communication Studies, University of North Carolina, Chapel Hill. He is author and editor of numerous cultural studies books, articles and journals, especially *Cultural Studies* (Routledge, 1993) and *We Gotta Get Out of This Place* (Routledge, 1992). He gave the second annual Manchester Institute for Popular Culture lecture in 1994.

Patrick Henry is a freelance photographer who has worked with ULPC and MIPC on exhibitions, seminars and other projects since the early 1990s. His photographs have appeared in many books and magazines, including *Melody Maker* and *New Musical Express*.

Introduction
Reading Pop(ular)
Cult(ural) Stud(ie)s

Steve Redhead

This book is a collection of essays on the theory and practice of what has come to be labelled as 'popular cultural studies', with particular emphasis on ethnographies of contemporary 'sub' and 'club' cultures. The book has been designed as a 'reader' to complement another forthcoming Blackwell book (Redhead, 1997), and has been produced by a series of inter-faculty post-graduate seminar working groups, including visiting speakers, at the Manchester Metropolitan University between 1992 and 1995. An earlier seminar group in the Unit for Law and Popular Culture at the Manchester Metropolitan University produced two books (Redhead, 1993a; 1993b) which have been widely used across a variety of undergraduate and post-graduate courses focusing on youth and popular culture. We hope the present reader will be similarly used.

The vehicle for promoting 'popular cultural studies' in the early to mid-1990s was the Manchester Institute for Popular Culture. As a postgraduate research centre, the Manchester Institute for Popular Culture at the Manchester Metropolitan University was intended to begin to reorient cultural studies. It was created in May 1992 as a federation of two pre-existing research units: the Unit for Law and Popular Culture (in the School of Law) and the Centre for Urban and Cultural Analysis (in the Department of Social Science). It was set up as an inter-faculty unit managed by a business board from the Faculty of Humanities and Social Science and the Faculty of Community Studies, Law and Education. In March 1995, with faculty and departmental reorganization, the work previously done by the Unit for Law and Popular Culture was separated from the work of the new, redesigned Institute for Popular Culture in the Department of Sociology and Inter-Disciplinary Studies. The Unit for Law and Popular Culture, which had been situated in the School of Law since its inception in 1990, became part of a new unit, the Centre for Law, Culture and Society, incorporating the National Heritage Research Unit, formerly known as the Sports Law Unit.

The seminar groups which produced the present book were originally deemed necessary by the Manchester Metropolitan University to consolidate a long tradition of work by its participants in the emerging interdisciplinary academic field of 'popular cultural studies' of youth and 'pop' culture since the 1970s. The groups' well-received 'Popular Cultural Studies' book series, published by Ashgate's Arena/Avebury imprints, and a single-authored book (Redhead, 1995) have begun to define the theoretical, political, cultural, social and historical underpinnings of the process by which 'popular cultural studies' has come to differ from what emerged as 'contemporary cultural studies' in the Centre for Contemporary Cultural Studies (CCCS) at the University of Birmingham in the 1960s and 1970s. The readings in this present collection further help to distinguish 'popular cultural studies' from some aspects of the theoretical work of 'contemporary cultural studies', while consolidating and extending the important ethnographic work associated with CCCS cultural studies traditions of youth and popular culture research, and applying them to 'accelerated culture' in the 1990s. The seminar groups were given a brief of promoting theoretical and empirical work in the broad area of regulation/consumption of popular culture, both within the university and in conjunction with local, national and international agencies. They comprised many postgraduates, including those registered in the separate research units in the School of Law and Department of Social Science collaborating on various funded research projects from 1992 to 1995. However, many postgraduate students from other universities also attended and contributed to the development of the work. As far as the specific focus of this book is concerned – its work on sub/club cultures – the collective research project was originally set up to continue the ethnographic traditions of the 1960s and 1970s CCCS, but in the very different theoretical and political environment of the 1990s. This book, then, is a collection of chapters from those working at, and associated with, the seminar groups until 1995. It is self-consciously modelled on the CCCS book from the 1970s (Hall and Jefferson, 1976) first published as *Working Papers in Cultural Studies* 7/8 in the mid-1970s. Like that formidable and long-lasting earlier volume, it is designed for use as a student book across a variety of disciplines from cultural studies to criminology.

The present volume begins with a chapter by Simon Frith and Jon Savage, first written in 1992. Their essay was originally submitted to the *London Review of Books* which – incomprehensibly – refused to publish it. The Manchester Institute for Popular Culture swiftly published it as a 'samizdat' working paper, and *New Left Review* subsequently made it more widely available. It is an important warning against the wave of cultural populism, from right and left, which pervades so much analysis of popular and youth culture today. The neo-right *Modern Review* – a prime target for Frith and Savage's withering attack – eventually met its demise in 1995. Frith and Savage's chapter is followed at the beginning and end of the book by largely theoretical forays into what popular and youth culture have come to mean at the end of the twentieth century. The remainder of the contributions are 'commentaries' on these themes. They variously discuss such wide-ranging themes as Northern Soul, house and rave music, the soccer/pop crossover, DJ culture, fashion styles and clubnights. Marek Kohn's essay (taken from his earlier book published by Lawrence and Wishart) is an archaeology of the moral panics surrounding drug use and youth culture so prevalent around 'ecstasy' and dance culture in Britain in the 1990s. The 're-placing of popular culture', as Lawrence Grossberg refers to it, is now manifestly on the cultural and political agenda, particularly in terms of where it fits into the wider theoretical and political perspectives of cultural studies and cultural politics at the end of the millennium. This present collection goes some way towards 're-placing' the 'popular' in cultural studies.[1]

Note

1   Michael Berube (1994, ch. 5) discusses the explosion in popularity of what he calls 'cult. studs.' in the USA in the early 1990s. I have added the 'pop'. 'Pop' here in my usage marks out a 'low modernism' or a 'modernism in the streets' (Lash and Friedman, 1992) which the seminar groups producing the essays in the present book embraced.

References

Berube, Michael (1994) *Public Access*, London: Verso.

Hall, Stuart and Tony Jefferson (1976) *Resistance Through Rituals*, London: Hutchinson.

Lash, Scott and Jonathan Friedman (eds.) (1992) *Modernity and Identity*, Oxford: Blackwell.

Redhead, Steve (ed.) (1993a) *Rave Off: Politics and Deviance in Contemporary Youth Culture*, Aldershot: Avebury 'Popular Cultural Studies'.

(ed.) (1993b) *The Passion and The Fashion: Football Fandom in the New Europe*, Aldershot: Avebury, 'Popular Cultural Studies'.

(1995) *Unpopular Cultures: The Birth of Law and Popular Culture*, Manchester: Manchester University Press.

(1997) *Subculture to Clubcultures: An Introduction to Popular Cultural Studies*. Oxford: Blackwell.

THEORY 1

1 Pearls and Swine:
Intellectuals and the Mass Media

Simon Frith and Jon Savage

For those of us in the academy who have been urging people for twenty years or more to take popular culture seriously, Jim McGuigan's *Cultural Populism* (McGuigan, 1992) is a sombre read. A lucid account of how cultural studies took their place in the university curriculum, it pinpoints the ways in which studying popular culture has become a method of uncritical celebration.

Among other things, it makes clear how much Raymond Williams is missed. McGuigan takes Williams' 1958 essay 'Culture is ordinary' as the beginning of his story, reminding us of Williams' radicalism, his roots in an 'unpopular' working-class politics, his sense of history, and his dogged suspicion of the weasel word of commerce. Williams, you can only conclude, would have been dismayed by contemporary cultural studies' cheerful populism, by academics' new-found respect for sales figures, by the theoretical pursuit of the joys of consumption.

The problem of cultural populism has resonance outside the academy too. In the second edition of his book, McGuigan might well consider the curious case of the *Modern Review*, a magazine dedicated to taking popular culture seriously by defining itself *against* academic cultural studies. In sales terms, the *Modern Review* is not significant, but it exemplifies (both within its own pages and through its contributors' obvious impact on general press coverage of pop culture) the dominant voice of lay cultural populism. Describing itself as providing 'low culture for highbrows' it furnishes a knowing middlebrow consumer guide.

For both academics arguing about the curriculum and journalists arguing about the arts pages, what is at issue is 'popular culture' – how we should think about it, how we should study it, how we should value it. And two further points should be made about this. First, the questions are not only of concern to rival groups of academics and journalists. Popular culture is equally an issue for the political and cultural establishment. It is at the centre of the debates about the BBC's future, for example: what is the 'higher ground' of broadcasting to which the BBC may (or may not) now be committing itself? It is at the centre of the debates about the Arts Council's Charter for the Arts: what is the state's responsibility to amateur or commercial art forms? And it features, in a different way, in discussion of the National Curriculum, as our heritage is defended against soaps and reggae.

It follows, second, that the questions of popular culture are not new. The education system since Arnold, the BBC since Reith, the Arts Council since Keynes, have all made cultural policing in the light of the perceived *threat* of pop and commerce. What is new, then, is not the problem but its formulation. It is as if the ghosts of Adorno and Leavis, ghosts who haunted discussion of popular culture for fifty years, have finally been laid. McGuigan traces the rise of academic cultural popularism to the demise of the 'dominant ideology thesis', the assumption that one could map culture from the top down, from capitalist manoeuvre to audience response; the *Modern Review* reserves its greatest scorn for cultural do-gooders, those people who witter on about discrimination and taste. For cultural populists of all sorts, the popular is to be approached with new, modern assumptions – assumptions about the creativity of the consumer.

For our perspective, though, what is revealed in both McGuigan's book and the *Modern Review* is a crisis of critical language: how can we talk about (or evaluate) popular culture *without* reference to its ideological effects? What does it mean to treat popular culture *aesthetically*? How, now, does the relation of high and low culture work? What authority does either a teacher or a critic have to assert that his or her reading of a popular text – *Single White Female*, say, or *Civvies*, or Madonna – is any more important than anyone else's? Is popular culture just a manner of style and sale?

The unstated premise of McGuigan's book is that the postwar cultural settlement is at an end. The Keynesian consensus, embodied in the Arts Council, was that there is a congruence between two lines of cultural demarcation – the high versus the low, the state subsidized versus the market driven. The state supports the high (and, implicitly, unpopular), whether through the Arts Council, the BBC or the education system; the popular arts are defined in terms of commercial success.

But this equation was never really so clear cut, and over the years it had been rethought in terms of a kind of pluralism, the state being given the responsibility to support a range of cultural groups. At the same time, the equation of the commercial with the low has also become problematic, as certain commercial performers (most obviously in rock music) have sold themselves as artists. The resulting confusion is perhaps best exemplified in

John Peel's BBC radio show, hard to categorize as either low or high culture, as driven by either state or market forces.

The *Modern Review*'s reading of this situation is inevitably populist. Inevitable because populism has long been the only English alternative to Arts Council authority on the one hand, and left cultural progressivism on the other. In the same way, McGuigan shows how cultural studies academics had nowhere else to go when they became disillusioned with Marxism.

The encrusted nature of the populist position was clear in the critical response to another recent book, John Carey's *The Intellectuals and the Masses* (Carey, 1992). The locus of the skirmish was perfect: the (over)expanded feature space in the quality end of Fleet Street. The arguments too were perfect with their familiarity, harking back to the 1950s populist tropes. It is not hard to see why the book got so much coverage: these tropes fit exactly with the way that the once left liberal centre has moved to the right.

Bashing snobbish intellectuals is an old English sport and there are traces, even in Carey's own cool pose, of the nervy, man-at-the-bar *bonhomie* familiar from the work of Kingsley Amis and Philip Larkin. Intellectual-bashing has always rested on a bluff defensiveness about the commonness of common life, on a celebration of small horizons and smaller ambitions which ill conceals its own uneasy violence.

In this discursive world, Britishness becomes Englishness, and Englishness describes a people by nature content in their allotments – and thus defiantly dull. Against this recurring conservative ideal – a pleasant fantasy of Little England: a nation of moderation, tolerance, harmless desire and the sharp snap of common sense – it is easy enough to measure the arrogance, snobbery and sheer silliness of the intellectual. Carey's view of the literary modernist in this respect echoes Larkin's view of modern jazz.

But what concerns us here is less the position of the modernist intellectual in cultural history than the peculiarly English notion of the masses, the common people, which is used to lay down a norm of behaviour – domestic, heterosexual, suburban, middle-class – such that any departure from it becomes abnormal. In this discourse, abnormality is overdetermined: to be an intellectual is to be by definition queer, depraved, *foreign*. (Note the reporting of the recent Jacques Derrida fuss at Cambridge.)

The defence of the masses against the intellectual depends, in other words, on a particular kind of nostalgia. The commonplace acts as a bulwark against all sorts of social change, against a permanent fear of unrest at the margins. Out there aren't just strange ideas, but also strange people – you, female, foreign, homosexual. The cultural question becomes where, precisely, do these people live? The political question is how to keep them there – out of sight, at the margins.

The terms of the ideological debate between the modernists and the masses were overlain from the start by an institutional distinction. By the beginning of the century, the material bases for intellectual life (replacing politics and the church) were education and the press. The twentieth-century career of the modernist writer, composer or artist has been, to a large extent, dependent on an academic position and an academic audience; the twentieth century career of the non-academic intellectual has meant reaching the readership put together by newspapers and magazines. The resulting hostility between academics and journalists has its own history, but what is taken for granted nowadays is not only that academics, in their jargon-patrolled cloisters, don't understand 'life' – as if they did not themselves have parents and children, disappointments and debts – but that journalists do. In practice, of course, most journalists live more sheltered lives than most academics: the Fleet Street agenda remains rooted in a particular sort of metropolitan provincialism.

'Understanding life' – in other words, appreciating 'the ordinary' – is a matter not only of experience, but also of style. Experience turned into moral authority – the newspaper columnists' trade – reflects most significantly an attitude to one's readership. If the academic's task is to tell people what they don't already know, the journalist's is to tell them what they do. In this respect, as McGuigan shows, cultural populism is more a journalistic than an academic project – which helps explain the uneasy symbiosis between cultural studies and the *Modern Review*.

Journalists Eclipse the Academics

We have been describing a tradition of debate, the way in which the particular entanglement of education, the media and the masses in Britain has shaped recurring arguments about culture, its meanings and significance. The question we want to turn to now is how these arguments (and the conditions for them) changed over the last decade.

To begin with, it seems clear that the effect of the Thatcher decade was not simply to widen the intellectual gap between journalists and academics, but, more importantly, to increase the importance of journalists as cultural ideologues while undermining the cultural authority of educators.

The first part of this process can, in fact, be traced back to Harold Wilson and the development (learned from Stanley Baldwin and Winston Churchill) of a populist approach to party politics, in which a direct appeal to the voter (via the media) became more important than an indirect one (via party support). This was automatically to raise the status of journalists, not only as the channel through which politicians established their popularity (with the rise, for example, of the personality interviewer) but also as objective voices of the people which could be contrasted to the self-interested voice of the non-establishment activist. (Of subsequent prime ministers, only Edward

Heath has not worked in such a populist fashion.) The press was particularly significant for Margaret Thatcher's radical ambitions, as her intellectuals (and hers was a determinedly cultural project: she wanted to change how the British people *thought*) were operating in right-wing think tanks that lay outside the intellectual establishment. Their challenge to academic common sense was conducted in the name of some deeper, instinctive popular knowledge.

The eighties thus brought to the fore a variety of right-wing intellectual accounts of the masses, varying from the considered conservatism of Roger Scruton or Ferdinand Mount, in which 'ordinary Englishness' is embedded in the tapestry of the English language, the organic community and historical tradition, to the anti-toff populism of Norman Stone or Andrew Neil, in which a kind of basic British common sense is expressed through market forces, to the buffoonery of Woodrow Wyatt, Paul Johnson and Auberon Waugh, for whom 'the people' are mobile signifiers, now sages, now idiots.

The combined effect of these various populist poses (which certainly helped sap liberal self-confidence) was to construct 'the people' as a mythical site of authority. The political object was not exactly to mobilize popular support (none of these writers was much interested in muddying his or her mind with democratic activism), but rather to articulate it, to 'read' the people through theories of history or concepts of the market, so that raw sales or voting figures could be interpreted in terms of a broader transformational process. Thatcherism was thus defined, to a large extent, not in specialist journals or élite forums, but in newspaper columns and in well-publicized reports and position papers; it represented a well-thought-out (and effective) strategic use of the media by intellectuals. This was, ironically, to introduce a rather un-English approach to the dissemination of ideas, but by the end of the Thatcher decade struggles for power and status within the professions – health, education, broadcasting – were being conducted in the light of media rather than academic support.

At the same time, the eighties saw a boom in newspaper and magazine publishing – itself a consequence of free-market policies. This boom increased media space to breaking point, but not revenue (from sales and advertising). There were not the resources to spread the jam of reportage or investigative journalism (increasingly confined to public-service television, as Andrew Neil, for example, enfeebled the *Sunday Times* 'Insight' team) over the white bread of the new supplements. Rather, the *Sunday Times* section 5, 'The culture', the *Guardian* 'Weekend', the *Independent* magazine, and so forth, depend on the 'feature', a type of writing in which the journalist's style elevates individual opinion to the level of social commentary.

The spread of single corporate ownership across various media –

newspapers, magazines, broadcast and satellite TV advertising companies, publishing companies – also created what Umberto Eco calls 'media squared': a PR-led agenda in place of reportage, soap opera treated as reality, reality treated as soap opera, endless media stories about media. Coupled with the diaspora from Fleet Street (as a distinct location), this has resulted in a crisis of confidence for editors and journalists, only exacerbated by the recession. Competition means a constant jockeying for market position, for the right 'demographic'; newspaper agendas are increasingly organized around assumed consumer tastes (and ever-expanding lifestyle pages), rather than by their readers' supposed interests as citizens.

This was the context in which style culture, developed in the early eighties by magazines like *The Face*, made its Fleet Street impact. Here were a group of writers who might not know much about social issues, but who surely understood shopping. The rise of the journalist as the voice of political common sense, in other words, coincided with a rewriting of political common sense in terms of free trade, as Margaret Thatcher translated social relations into market relations, and John Major redefined the citizen as the consumer.

The Tory challenge to educational authority had both a material and an ideological base: the systematic lowering of the status of teachers and teaching at all levels; the replacement of quangos of the 'great and good' by political placemen and women whose cultural expertise is measured not by any scholarly credentials, but in straightforward tests of political correctness. The first effect of this policy was on modes of argument. If Labour Party policies have to be seen to be reasonable, to rest on surveys and reports, to embrace the virtues of the Fabians and the LSE (we were rarely allowed to forget that Harold Wilson had been a don), the Conservative Party has never justified itself in these terms – ministerial prejudices are taken to be quite adequate to see off the self-serving arguments of so-called 'experts'.

In these circumstances, newspaper columnists, armed with the power of anecdote, take on a particular sort of importance, valued not for their intellectual independence, but for their ability to articulate common sense, to translate the prejudices of politicians into the commonplace of daily discourse and vice versa. Their importance in the competition for newspaper sales is exactly that of the DJ in the competition for radio audiences: their 'we' gives the reader/listener a sense of community. This has always been the role of the columnist in popular papers, of course, but the last decade has seen an obsession with columnists in all sections of the press, columnists whose job is less to make readers think than to save them from thought, less to make them see events anew than to ensure a breakfast-table conversation that is held in clichés.

The Snares of Experience and Openness

In broader cultural terms, the effect has been to elevate the authority of experience (valorized in much feminist and pop writing) over the authority of the intellect, and subtly to change what is meant by knowledge. This shift occurred in the last couple of years of the weekly *New Society*, long the home of the most interesting commentary on popular culture and a site where, uniquely, journalists and academics met on equal terms. A reportorial tradition of outsiders like Angela Carter and Colin MacInnes trying to make sense of social phenomena collapsed into first-hand reports from people presumed by insecure editors to *be* the phenomena – Julie Burchill was *there*, puking in the Roxy.

The problems of such reporting are twofold: experience quickly ceases to be first hand as the reporters distance themselves from it in the very act of reporting; what is reported is not, in the end, 'raw' experience, but its interpretation – an interpretation that convinces by feeding editorial (and readers') expectations. Again, popular culture is taken to describe not the startling, but the familiar.

Reporting from experience, in other words, comes to involve exactly the same sort of nostalgia and celebration of the ordinary as any other sort of English anti-intellectualism. To put it another way, the kind of 'experience' validated in this writing is defined, as we have already noted, in remarkably narrow terms. The implied 'we' of the English press (the Scottish press still works differently) is a we which excludes not just African and Asian British, not just snobs and intellectuals, but in fact anyone who disagrees – this is not a kind of writing that encourages argument; you can't *challenge* experience.

As McGuigan illustrates, there is a strong connection between the media version of popular culture and pop's academic status as the object of 'cultural studies' (and, indeed, cultural studies courses were a spawning ground for eighties style-journalism). In both cases the popular is defined in sales terms; in both cases the focus is on the consumer (cultural production is, it seems, an uncomplicated industrial process); in both cases critical authority is claimed via a particular kind of identification with 'the people': these commentators, whether in print or in the lecture room, are fans, but with special consuming skills; they can read the codes, place the labels, identify the quotes.

If, conventionally, cynicism is a way of masking sentimentality, in the sentimentality of popular culture commentary the romance of the fan conceals both cynicism and bad faith. In the academy, after all, cultural studies, for all its ingenuousness, does seek to rescue 'ordinary' lives from academic condescension, to *complicate* the daily experience of pop music and clothes and magazines by making them the object of high theory. For the new generation of cultural commentators in the press, by contrast, the goal seems to be to render even the most extraordinary icons of popular culture (Madonna or Michael Jackson) into the banal terms of everyday experience: everything odd about popular culture, it turns out, can be *explained*.

This is partly a matter of context. The very act of taking a pop icon – an advertisement, a pop song, a sitcom – into the classroom and examining it in the light of semiotics or psychoanalysis or feminism is to make it strange. The journalist, by contrast, inevitably places the same icons on a familiar shelf, next to all the other consumer goods. As any pop critic knows, for all our good intentions our prime task is as consumer guides – hence the cynicism, hence the problem of critical language.

On the BBC's *Late Show*, where the new cultural 'openness' is most self-consciously celebrated, popular artists are either treated, quite inappropriately, with all the awed attention of high art appreciation, or else they become the object of the quick quip, tricksy treatments which seem designed to show that the form of the programme matters more than the content, that the art of low culture lies in what a clever consumer (or clever director) can make of it. The problem here lies in the packaging – the packages in which items are boxed before they reach the *Late Show*, and the packages in which the *Late Show* feels obliged to wrap them in order to meet its own perceived, overmediated needs.

In other words, the problem of the *Late Show* (which the BBC approaches in more interesting ways in other arts strands like *Arena*) is that it hasn't thought through the implications of its new eclectic account of culture – its assumptions about the high are as limited as its assumptions about the low. In the end, whichever way you look at it, everything has to be *wrapped up*. And what escapes the programme is what can't be so wrapped – the non-commercial that also lacks art status; the culture that doesn't have a niche in the TV market place. The programme does not really challenge high/low distinctions between aesthetic transcendence (real art) and social function (the popular). Rave culture, for example, is inevitably treated as a matter of sociology (not form); literary culture remains a matter of form (not sociology).

The same effect is clear in newspaper and magazine arts sections. Editors still take it for granted that low arts coverage – whether film, TV or music reviews – is best written from the experience of the ordinary listener/reviewer (who has a way with words) rather than by the sort of 'expert' who is employed to cover fine art or classical music. For all the populist tone of, say, the *Guardian*'s art pages, popular culture is actually treated with a distinct lack of seriousness – at least on its own terms. It becomes, rather, a source of populist credibility ('I loved *Batman*'), of self-serving nostalgia (most obvious in television's treatment of its own history), and of intellectual idleness (to treat pop culture *theoretically* is, it seems, to deprive it of its 'fun').

Such arguments beg all the interesting questions about popularity, confusing formal and generic issues with sales figures, displacing questions of creativity on to questions of taste, making ideas and sensations mutually exclusive. More importantly, the populist line fails to recognize that one important function of popular culture, even in its most commodified form, is as an expressive tool for people otherwise excluded from the public voice. Popular culture, that is, becomes one of the most potent challenges to the populist 'we' of the journalist as intellectual. The 'accessibility' of popular culture, in other words, describes the fact not that 'everyone' can understand it, but that everyone can use it, has a chance to be heard, to develop their own language, however difficult or *unpopular* what they say may be.

The 'culturescape' – that pattern of aesthetic symbols and rituals through which people determine their individual identity and social place – is no longer being mapped by day-to-day cultural critics, for all their populist claims. Take the way in which cultural journalism continues to operate 'disciplinary' boundaries and hierarchies. It seems clear to us that performers like the Pet Shop Boys or The Smiths have, using 'trashy' pop forms, come up with much more effective ways of dealing with sex and love, pain and ambition – ways more in tune with the feeling of contemporary culture – than have, say, Ian McEwan and Martin Amis using literary devices. In the same way, dance acts like Orbital or Derrick May draw a more accurate map of the 1992 body – its formation in and by the contemporary experience of desire and space – than any 'fine' artist we can think of. The issue is not whether our judgements here are right, but that such comparisons, now a normal part of cultural adolescence, are excluded from the terms of most cultural coverage.

The problem for arts editors seems to be twofold. First, the popular audience is not an undifferentiated audience, and some sectors of it are seen as more significant than others – 'minority' tastes thus tend not just to be marginalized, but also to be treated as peculiar, as lacking the 'universal' appeal of proper art. (The same argument can be seen in the populist defence of the literary canon – white male authors represent the universal; blacks and women can speak only partially.) But on top of this is an ambiguous attitude to the mass media themselves (this is also apparent in John Carey's book). Even as 'high' culture is enmeshed in the sales process, even as newspapers for their own sales purposes respond unthinkingly to media campaigns, so 'old' art forms – paintings, writing, composing – become the measure against which the new media output is judged.

The second problem for contemporary arts coverage is that we are just as likely, perhaps more likely, to find the unpopular voice, the voice of 'un-English' desires, in the interstices of mass culture – in clubs and comic books, in fanzines and anonymous dance records – as in the subsidized art world. In other words, the opposition set up between the intellectuals and the masses makes no sense culturally. There are 'intellectuals' using pop cultural forms (just as 'high culture' describes, among other things, a marketing mechanism). And the 'masses' are no more likely to be in agreement about their cultural opinions than about their political or religious beliefs. One measure of popular success is, after all, great unpopularity: Madonna is a phenomenon as much for the loathing as for the love she inspires.

Current arguments about popular culture rely on a series of dichotomies: the ordinary versus the élite, the journalist/media worker versus the academic, the conservative versus the progressive. We would summarize all such dichotomies under a more general heading: the culture of self-satisfaction versus the culture of the dissatisfied. From the dissatisfied position, the argument always has to be that life could be different, could be better, could be changed. Both art and education rest on such premises; they are meant to make us see things differently. They are designed to show us through the imagination, through reason, the limitations of our perspectives, to doubt our common sense.

Against this, all versions of populism, left and right, are organized less to reflect what people do think (most people are muddled) than to enable them to think *without thought*. What John Carey forgets (or, rather, pretends to forget for the sake of his polemic) is that his despised intellectuals have had a more profound effect on 'ordinary' people than popular novelists like Arnold Bennett. Whatever her failings as a snob, as a writer Virginia Woolf has inspired generations of 'ordinary' adolescent women, just as Eliot and Lawrence, David Bowie and the Sex Pistols have inspired generations of 'ordinary' adolescent boys. One of the defining qualities of being ordinary, after all, is wanting to be extraordinary, just as the long-term effect of suburbia has been to produce generations of anti-suburban pop artists. What should equally be stressed is that the identification of the 'good' and the 'popular' is a matter of quality not quantity. For cultural judgement, sales figures are an irrelevance: the truly popular describes something remarkable, that work or event or performance that transforms people's ways of sensing and being. This is not a view currently given much house-room. The great failing of our age is the idea, received wisdom from right to left, upmarket and downmarket, that to be popular you have to be populist, which means an uncritical acceptance of an agenda set by market forces. There is no sadder sight than the fortysomething ex-leftist, the thirtysomething ex-punk, the twentysomething ex-stylist, burying their disappointments in their search across the surface of popular culture for pure sensation.

The question, to put this another way, is what is at stake in the argument about popular culture, and the *Modern Review* is symptomatic in its failure to articulate a cultural theory except negatively. It is not a sociological journal (it contains no primary material or research); it is not explicitly a political journal; it is not a literary journal (beyond the assertion of its authors' tastes, there is little personal testimony). If its review format suggests a consumer guide, its reviewing style offers little clue as to who its readers might be, the magazine's basic purpose being to bash received opinion. This is populism as resentment; the dominant tone of the *Modern Review* is petulance: *they* (the left, the academy, the educated) took *our* toys away.

What is interesting about the *Modern Review*'s prominence (within Fleet Street at least, where it provides pop culture criticism for editors who dislike pop culture but don't dare say so) is the end of a particular kind of language. This language is well laid out in McGuigan's *Cultural Populism*: developed from cultural studies, subcultures, deconstruction, filtered through the style and music press, it has dominated the discussion of pop music and pop culture since the early eighties, and now provides the rump of PR, ego and spite which still fills up pages of newsprint.

This language is irrelevant to pop culture producers (except when they need some publicity), to pop culture consumers (failing as it does to reflect most people's experience), and to those of us who would like to see a new language of pop culture: one derived from anthropology, archetypal psychology, musicology, one which has a grasp of pop both as an industrial and as an aesthetic form. It is time to reclaim pop from the populists: they have said much of nothing, but their chit-chat still poisons the air.

References

Carey, John (1992) *The Intellectuals and the Masses*, London: Faber and Faber.
McGuigan, Jim (1992) *Cultural Populism*, London: Routledge.

2 Over-the-counter-culture:
Retheorizing Resistance in Popular Culture

Beverly Best

There is a gap in popular culture theory where 'the text' used to be. In the case of popular music, for example, the politics of production and reception of music have been endlessly theorized with many good results, while investigations of musical texts – uses of sounds and instruments, rhythm, phrasing, time signature, sampling, structure, lyrical content – have often been left to the aesthetic formalism of musicology or the equally ahistorical formalism of some anthropological and semiotic approaches (Lipsitz, 1990). Popular culture commentators must be familiar with popular cultural texts before they can understand what musicians and artists already know: that the difference between, for example, the music of My Bloody Valentine and the music of Whitney Houston can be articulated not just in aesthetic, but also in political terms. The following discussion is inspired by the perhaps naive faith that, despite identical production politics and aside from the myriad ways that audiences interpolate cultural products, there is something about the character of the popular cultural text itself which either limits or enables its functioning on behalf of oppositional cultural and political practice.

This chapter is concerned with ways of theorizing popular culture as a site of oppositional practice. In light of the ambiguity that surrounds much of the language of popular culture theory, I will briefly articulate some presuppositions from which my discussion moves forward: popular culture is neither some pure folk expression, generated 'from the ground up', nor an expression of the corporate powers which govern the culture industries. Here, popular culture is conceived as always *in some way* a negotiation between the culture industries, mainstream or micro media, and the individuals or collectivities within the general populace who provide the content, inspiration, talent or imagination needed for the creation of popular cultural texts. The political and theoretical consequences of distinguishing popular culture from both 'high' culture and 'folk' culture will be addressed later on.

The ground for this discussion is the debate between two different readings of popular culture (to oversimplify): first, the 'pessimistic' legacy of the Frankfurt School theorists, for whom the subjection of popular cultural production to the methods of standardization which govern all industrial production entails that the only social function of popular cultural texts is to reconcile consumers to the status quo, thus reinforcing the domination of capitalism (Modleski, 1986); and second, the 'optimistic' reading associated with some brands of cultural studies, and particularly the work of John Fiske, wherein audiences actively and creatively read and appropriate cultural products (Modleski, 1986) in such a way as to resist ideological domination (Giroux and McLaren, 1994). A great deal has been written on this debate (see, for example, Clarke, 1990 and Modleski, 1986) and these positions are, by now, very familiar. My argument, here, is that contemporary theorists of popular culture must take on the very difficult task of charting a path between the Scylla of optimism and the Charybdis of pessimism in popular culture theory. In other words, contemporary theorizing of popular culture must allow spaces for possible resistance, as well as being able to take issues of domination, exploitation and cultural imperialism into consideration. It must recognize the contradictory nature of popular cultural products, in that they can be the site of both hegemonic *and* counterhegemonic ideological production depending on the context of their reception or production. And while oppositional force exercised through popular cultural production may be ephemeral, it can still be the motor which drives permanent historical change. As Simon Frith reminded us in *Media, Culture and Society* a decade ago, '[t]o assume that what happens to stars and movements in the long term – co-option – discredits their disruptive impact in the short term is to misunderstand the politics of culture'.

In what follows I will look specifically at what the work of Michel Foucault can bring to a theory of popular culture. While I believe that some of Foucault's ideas can be useful in this area, his theory of power can potentially leave one in a theoretical cul-de-sac reminiscent of the hermetic pessimism of many social commentators for whom popular cultural texts are inextricably enmeshed in the hegemonic ideology of the market place and could never be considered as sites of counterhegemonic practice or oppositional cultural identity. In my analysis of this situation, I will take initiatives from some important feminist critiques of Foucault, made by Nancy Fraser, Seyla Benhabib, Elspeth Probyn and Gayatri Spivak. While the arena of popular culture is vast, when specific examples of popular cultural production and reception are required in the following discussion, I have focused on that of popular music.

I

There is a similarity between Foucault's theory of the nature of power and how it functions in modern society and the description put forward by many analysts of popular culture of the mechanism of commercialization characterizing contemporary consumer culture. For Foucault, power is exercised through a vast network of 'micro-mechanisms' which have successfully incorporated the entire social sphere (Foucault, 1980). As subjects are constituted within, and as part of, this network, they internalize the mechanisms of their own control (mechanisms which have many social forms, not the least of which are the notions of truth and knowledge). Therefore, power functions not only on a conscious level, but, perhaps more subsumingly, on an unconscious level through 'continuous and uninterrupted processes which subject our bodies, govern our gestures, [and] dictate our behaviours'. Foucault argues that it is no longer appropriate to characterize power merely as a relationship of domination and subjugation, wherein one party 'has' power and another does not. Instead, *all* individuals simultaneously undergo and exercise this power, which gains its strength by 'produc[ing] effects at the level of desire' and knowledge as opposed to functioning in a 'negative' way through censorship, exclusion or repression.

While the recognition that power works not only in overt but also in discreet and microsocial ways is an important insight, it is possible to conclude that it is virtually impossible to elude or escape the network of control. Any attempt to induce change within the system will only represent a shift in the power/knowledge network, and could not be considered 'progressive' in terms of getting outside the network. Foucault states: 'power [is] "always already there" . . . one is never "outside" it . . . there are no "margins" for those who break with the system to gamble in'. Similarly, for cultural theorists like John Street or Jacques Attali, the intimate three-way relationship between cultural production, the technology of mechanical reproduction and capitalism has resulted in the subsuming of the first two entities in the latter, wherein cultural production and technological innovation are always already underwritten by the interests of capital. For Street, the political sentiments of musicians and music consumers, as well as the character of the musical text, are absolutely irrelevant in terms of how that text functions within the encompassing network of profits and market shares (Street, 1986). Also resonating with Foucault's argument, Attali describes power in the paradigm of repetition (by which he means the ensuing ideological precipitation of the marriage between capitalism and the means of mechanical reproduction) as 'no longer localized in institutions', but 'slip[ping] into homes, threatening each individual wherever he [*sic*] may be' including in front of her or his CD player (Attali, 1985). Finally, with a pessimism so hermetic as to be almost comical, Attali argues that even 'anticonformism creates a norm for replication, and in repetition music is no longer anything more than a detour on the road to ideological normalization'. These types of conclusion are particularly problematic for those theorizing popular culture as a site for oppositional practice.

Nonetheless, the analogy between Foucault's configuration of power and a system of commercial mechanisms can produce useful readings. For example, it can be useful to recognize that, currently, as subjects are materially and psychically constituted within the ever-spreading network of consumer culture, they come to internalize the commercial standards of the culture industry to such an extent that alternative standards of usefulness, pleasure, value or aesthetics become inconceivable. Steve Redhead points out that the concept of the 'incitement to discourse', which Foucault argues facilitated sexuality's historical development as a mechanism of power and control, can be applied to popular culture (Redhead, 1990). Like sexuality, the discourses surrounding popular culture have exploded. While some discourses speak the language of repression and censorship, and others the language of freedom and artistic expression, I believe the most shaping of these discourses in terms of popular culture production is that of consumerism and commodification. In terms of popular music, it is not uncommon for musicians to internalize the standards of commodification for musical texts. For example, the value of a particular musical text is judged according to whether it is a 'sellable' product, where the perimeters of its 'sellability' are a predetermined set of criteria, such as a certain length, structure, rhythm, number of beats per minute, or non-controversial (or in some cases, perhaps, controversial) lyrical content. Similarly. Foucault's description of the mechanisms of power as being so diverse and as operating at so many social levels that even moments of resistance are not outside its network of control, can be likened to the culture industry's ability not only quickly and efficiently to diffuse forms of resistance by incorporating and commodifying the objects, styles or mannerisms of that resistance, but to capture no more than an isolated or fleeting stylistic moment (of music, fashion, etc.), package it, market it, and sell it back to the public as a complete and coherent lifestyle or youth movement. In other words, like Foucault's network of power, the culture industry operates both negatively (in terms of diffusion and censorship) and positively (in terms of generating discourses of control).

While the preceding readings of popular culture may be useful, following the Foucauldean initiative is problematic in terms of theorizing the potential resistance of popular cultural expression to the co-opting forces of commercialization. Foucault does not articulate a way of resisting power's mechanisms; there are no margins outside the network. It would be a hopeless and overly pessimistic view of popular culture to see every instance of resistance to the standardization of commercial industry, or to the unequal distribution of power and resources which characterizes the relationship between commercial industry and the innovators of cultural expression, as irrelevant to – or, worse, reinforcing of – a larger structure of domination such as consumer capitalism. This view of contemporary consumer culture leaves one at a theoretical dead end. Looking to feminist theory for both a critique of this position and alternatives to it, Seyla Benhabib reminds us that, for Foucault, 'there is no history of the victims or subjects of oppression, just a history of the construction of victimization' (Benhabib, 1992). Therefore, in this paradigm, subjects who negotiate and resist power in any way (from demonstrating to boycotting certain products or corporations to defining and living by one's own standards of 'truth' or 'success') do not exist. A more strategically useful conception of the potential agency of subjects in relation to a structure of domination is that of historian Linda Gordon. Even though Gordon is speaking specifically of women in relation to the 'technology' of gender, I believe her characterization of women's subjectivity is also advantageous for those theorizing the resistance of producers and receivers of cultural texts in the context of contemporary consumer culture.

> I use gender to describe a power system in which women are subordinated through relations that are contradictory, ambiguous, and conflictual – a subordination maintained against resistance, in which women have by no means always defined themselves as other, in which women face and take choices and action despite contradiction. (Benhabib, 1992)

The idea that as culturally constituted subjects we embody the contradiction of the social relations that shape us, and that contradiction, as opposed to coherency, guides our actions and reactions, is important here. Contradiction in theoretical discussions has generally been perceived as a signal of error or weakness of argument. Gayatri Spivak, on the other hand, points out that not only is the contradiction entailed in engaged subjectivity irreducible, it can be enabling as well (Spivak, 1990b). For example, recognizing that contradiction is irreducible, and that one can therefore abandon the quest for 'pure', coherent positions in both theory and practice, transgresses the boundaries of Foucault's argument that opposition cannot be effective if it is posed within the same discursive formation of oppression (Spivak, 1990a). Therefore, when a musician composes a musical text where she or he has creatively deviated from the conventionally 'sellable' structure mentioned earlier, or in the lyrical content of which she or he has parodied the conventional subject matter of (more commercial) popular music or challenged certain sexual, ethnic, class or gendered stereotypes, or when a text resonates with the history of subjugated groups in struggle (Lipsitz, 1990, ch. 5), this form of popular cultural production can have oppositional effects on audiences and other musicians. It may, indeed, be a contradiction that the way this text acquires an audience is through circulation in the form of a commodity (i.e., record, cassette tape, compact disc, or concert), and yet this contradiction need not undermine its oppositional potential on other levels. Paul Smith articulates not only the contradiction which characterizes popular cultural texts, but how this contradiction can be used as a pedagogical tool:

> The [Popular Culture Commodity Text] displays internal contradictions, offers particular interpretive choices, alludes to given histories and circumstances. These need to be put into play in all their contradictions, not necessarily as contradictions which need to be resolved, but as contradictions which the students should be encouraged to puzzle. Similarly, the conflict among different students' receptions of the PCCT can be encouraged, further undermining the text's previously silent, unanalysed passage through their lives and marking it as the site of disagreement, not to say struggle. (Giroux and McLaren, 1994)

The concept of 'negotiation' is useful for characterizing many contemporary relationships of domination. Configurations of power can exist in the form of overt force (i.e. wife battering, child abuse, gay bashing, racial violence, military offensives) or what I will call 'negotiated' relations. The feminist in relation to the history of patriarchy, the gay activist in relation to the system of heterosexual norms, or the oppositional musician in relation to consumer culture are examples of negotiated positions. I mean, here, that these subject positions are often enabled by the very structures of domination which they are criticizing and against which they struggle, And instead of weakening the force of opposition, Spivak reminds us that 'learn[ing] to negotiate with the structures of violence' (Spivak, 1990b) allows those oppositional forces to give up the fictional quest for pure positions and use the tools available to them to fight against the other side, even if it means getting their hands dirty. As Steve Redhead argues throughout *The End-of-the-Century Party*, what have traditionally been called 'youth subcultures' or countercultures and theorized as 'authentic', 'folk' or 'grass roots' youth expression existing in clear-cut contradistinction from the dominant culture, are no longer relevant (if they ever were). Here, Redhead describes the complex negotiated relationship that exists between youth cultural expression, the culture industry and mass media representation.

[T]he media identification of various new bohemian lifestyles in the decade since punk is more than a move from dole-queue to art school and back. It represents a complex shaping and reshaping of subject positions within a variety of discourses. The fallout from the 'death of youth culture' is, in part, to be found in the multi-faceted, locally based, bohemian 'undergrounds', which are themselves heavily influenced and shaped by the global leisure industry of which pop is now structurally so much an integral part. (Redhead, 1990)

I am not saying that individuals are *unconsciously* bound to discourses that oppress them, such as patriarchy or consumerism. Subjects *choose* negotiated positions, strategically, just as they choose to grant or withhold allegiance to particular discourses (Modleski, 1991). Furthermore, I use the ambiguous and, admittedly, problematic notion of 'choice' because cultural negotiation is always ambiguous and rarely cut and dried. It is true that, in the context of the production and reception of cultural texts within consumer capitalism, one's 'choice' is limited, for the most part, in the interests of capital. However, it is both misleading and a simplification to call this limitation strictly a function of domination when the existing options, far from anathema to the interests of some subordinated groups, can, in some instances, serve their interests.

Given the negotiated and contextually specific nature of many opposi-tional relationships, it follows that a theory of resistance can be developed not through 'epistemological arguments extraneous to the task at hand' (Benhabib, 1992), but in relation to a particular historical context of domi-nation. Thus, theories of oppositional practice within popular culture need to be constructed situationally. The specific dimensions of either a form or theory of resistance will depend on the nature of the particular struggle in question. And because theorizing popular culture cannot be done 'once and for all' and requires a persistent effort, resistance must be theorized *strategi-cally*; as something which might be effective in one instance and not in another. And, unlike Foucault, for whom the concept of resistance was theo-retically defeating because it entailed *essentializing* both one's own position as the 'unified oppressed' and one's targeted adversary as the sovereign power, Spivak points out that positioning oneself *strategically* in order to achieve the theoretical or practical advantage for the moment does not neces-sarily entail pledging allegiance to that position: 'So once you begin selectively to use idealisation, empiricism, transcendentalism, essentialism, as positions promised within an awareness of the limits of (self) positioning – individual – collective – then you can see them to be strategically effective' (Spivak in McRobbie, 1985).

Nancy Fraser's critique of Foucault's formulation of power is also relevant to a theory of resistance and popular culture. In *Unruly Practices* (Fraser, 1989),

Fraser focuses on what she calls Foucault's 'bracketing' of the normative criteria which are traditionally involved in political theory or practice. In Foucault's theory, because power exists on microsocial levels and because it works through – as opposed to over – virtually every living subject regardless of class, status or situation, power cannot be considered as either good or bad, right or wrong, liberating or oppressive, progressive or conservative. As Colin Gordon explains in his 'afterword' to *Power/Knowledge* (Foucault, 1980), for Foucault, 'the instruments and techniques [of power] are always liable to forms of re-appropriation, reversibility and re-utilisation not only in tactical realignments from "above" but in counter-offensives from "below"'. Therefore, no technology of power can be good or bad because it is constantly being – or has the potential to be – 'turned around'. Furthermore, Gordon argues that the reason why Foucault does not formulate a strategy of resistance is that, in order to determine whether a particular strategy were 'successful', it would mean subordinating 'the category of resistance to the normative criteria of a political programme'. However, questioning Foucault's scepticism towards the idea of normative justification, one wonders how the very notion of resistance, itself, is imaginable outside of a particular context of domination. On the contrary, every form of resistance, to be anything other than meaningless, must be founded on normative criteria, even if those criteria are only temporary, situational or strategic. Any type of engaged social criticism or political practice is conceivable *only* in terms of the normative criteria according to which one discerns whether or not a relation is characterized by domination, exploitation, subjugation, etc. As Fraser argues, by abandoning the notion of normative justification, Foucault can neither distinguish which instances of power involve domination and which do not, nor explain why, in a given circumstance, it may be preferable to resist domination than to submit to it.

A process of normative justification is equally imperative to understand how popular culture functions in a larger social context, because it is through normative criteria that we judge the 'value' (social, political, oppositional, anti-sexist, etc.) of a particular cultural text. For example, theorists of popular culture must be able to distinguish between texts which are misogynist, racist, homophobic, etc. and those which are not. Some critics of popular culture may argue for a type of pluralistic, value relativism which seeks to discern only the 'differences' among cultural texts, as opposed to designating some texts as better than others, for fear of 'essentializing' one definition of cultural value to the exclusion of others. Instead, I would argue that critics must take the risk of developing an evaluative paradigm for cultural texts, even if only temporary and for strategic purposes. As Gayatri Spivak has said, '[u]nless one is aware that one cannot avoid taking a stand, unwitting stands get taken' (Spivak, 1987). Furthermore, acknowledging that we cannot *not* take an evaluative stand is not only the responsibility of social critics, as Paul Smith explains: 'evaluation is not merely an aspect of formal academic criticism but a complex set of social and cultural activities central to the very nature of artistic cultural products and production' (Giroux and McLaren, 1994).

Finally, I want to take a closer look at Foucault's own articulation of the power/resistance situation. It may be that Foucault's position on the possibility of resistance may not be as one-dimensional or pessimistic as I have indicated. For example, Foucault's conception of 'theory as a toolkit' sounds strikingly similar to my version of the *strategic* use of theory:

> The notion of theory as a toolkit [*sic*] means: (i) The theory to be constructed is not a system but an instrument, a *logic* of the specificity of power relations and the struggles around them; (ii) That this investigation can only be carried out step by step on the basis of reflection (which will necessarily be historical in some of its aspects) on given situations. (Foucault, 1980)

While it is true that Foucault did not actually formulate a *strategy* of resistance, nor even 'offer an image of subjects resisting' as Elspeth Probyn has put it (Probyn, 1993), it is not true that he ignored resistance altogether. Even though Foucault's network of power mechanisms appears to be virtually comprehensive, Foucault maintains that it is not necessarily inescapable and that one is not 'condemned to defeat no matter what' (Foucault, 1980). On the contrary, Foucault argues that there cannot be power relations *without* resistances, and that the latter are real and effective because they are formed at the point where power relations are exercised. On the one hand, the preceding formulation would seem to contradict Foucault's earlier argument that both 'oppression' and 'resistance to oppression' are part of the same discursive formation which is itself constituted by the regime of power. On the other hand, the notion that, like power, resistance takes place on many social levels and in many forms can be useful. For example, Nancy Fraser argues that Foucault's 'politics of everyday life' help to open up the previously ignored private or domestic sphere to discussions of the power relations involved there: 'if power is instantiated in mundane social practices and relations', then resistance must also focus on these areas, therefore 'widen[ing] the arena within which people . . . confront, understand, and seek to change the character of their lives' (Fraser, 1989).

II

By insisting on seeing the 'everyday' as an equally significant site of confrontation between power and resistance as other more 'traditionally political' spaces, Foucault also demonstrates that how we define social spaces determines how we are able to envisage the practices that take place there. For example, the way that popular culture has been defined as oppositional to both 'high' or 'serious' culture on the one hand, and 'folk' culture on the other, has been detrimental for a theory of resistance through popular culture. In both popular and academic literature, popular cultural texts have been labelled 'not authentic', commercially contaminated, ephemeral, superficial, fake. In comparison, both high culture and folk culture are often cited as examples of 'authentic' culture. However, it is folk culture on which I will focus here. Folk ideology, which continues to pervade discussions of cultural production (Redhead, 1990) is associated with 'grass roots' or 'street' expression – produced by and for 'the people' – characterized by notions of originality, integrity and truth. Steve Redhead discusses one music magazine editor's telling distinction between what he conceives as 'authentic folk' and 'commercial pop': 'Folk for [Ian A. Anderson] is "non-commercial musics", consumed by "people who aren't willing to be spoon-fed something that the music biz has concocted as a commodity".'

Not only is the distinction between authentic folk music and commercial popular music inconsistent, but it also negates a theory of resistance through popular culture because, according to its logic, 'true and effective' resistance can be expressed only by the 'authentic' text. Opposed to the authentic/commercial distinction, I want to argue that *all* cultural texts, including those labelled 'folk' or 'high culture', to reach an audience must negotiate in some way with the mass or micro media or the culture industry (i.e. with commerce). Dave Haslam, renowned DJ and owner of the now defunct independent Play Hard record company in Britain, has articulated the contradictory position of independents in the music industry in similar terms. Here, the 'independent' company cannot remain pure and uncontaminated by commercial industry, but must negotiate its survival:

> [H]ow independent do I want to be if the cost of being pure independent is to be marginalised . . . And if the only way I can intervene is to be assimilated, perhaps I should allow myself to be assimilated, if that's the only way to work. Because you've got to deal with them, and that's the line that the Underground has to take – that you stake your claim, artistically, which you try to do with as great a degree of independence as possible. But once you move out of the office, then you have got to deal with Thatcher's real world, because otherwise no one's going to hear your records, no one's going to buy your fanzine, and your dream is to be like a little blip and you don't want that to happen. (Haslam quoted in Redhead, 1990)

Even an artist such as Bruce Springsteen, who for many represents integral, authentic expression as well as the essence of the working class in America, has a mediated image and sound, and is as much an evocative industry construction (Redhead, 1990) as are other musicians and bands, such as Deee–lite or Primal Scream, who self-consciously play with imaging and the self-referentiality of popular music history.

Iain Chambers, in a paper titled 'Contamination, coincidence, and collusion: pop music, urban culture, and the avant-garde' (Nelson and Grossberg, 1988), confronting overly pessimistic and defeating readings of popular music and popular cultural expression, draws analogies between the latter and the strategies and effects of avant-garde art in the early decades of the twentieth century. Chambers points out that, similar to the effect that popular culture can have on contemporary paradigms of evaluation, 'Futurism's frantic embrace of . . . the "machine epoch", Dada's direct refusal of "art" and its proclamation of the victory of daily life over aesthetics, and the surrealist project of giving free rein to the unconscious . . . profoundly undermined the traditional demand for artistic "authenticity".' As far back, then, as the turn of the twentieth century, mechanical reproduction was transforming the perception of cultural production so that the concept of authenticity became more and more irrelevant. Furthermore, Chambers argues that the criticisms of commentators who attempted to discredit the expression of the avant-garde are similar to those made against contemporary popular music. The mechanization of popular music (or the complaint that contemporary musicians rarely use 'real' instruments) is pointed to as evidence of popular music's 'non-authenticity'. This criticism is, of course, unconvincing. To say that popular music production cannot be authentic artistic production because of its mechanization (i.e. because of its use of 'programmed synthesizers, drum machines, samplers and electric guitars') would be to discredit the production of film and photography in a similar way; as expressions 'designed for reproducibility' and, therefore, inherently illegitimate and aesthetically impoverished. Few commentators today would judge the medium of film or photography in such a way, and yet many continue to criticize popular music in these terms.

Another criticism of popular cultural production concerns the practice of *bricolage* – yet another common characteristic of contemporary popular culture and the avant-garde – and is articulated in a comment at the end of Chambers' discussion: 'From [one] point of view, the constant appropriation and *bricolage* [taking place in popular cultural production] . . . appear less as a liberatory space and more as a symptom of the immense "tedium of ownership" in a highly developed society and of its need to incorporate and then obliterate difference.' Once again, this criticism makes the mistake of neglecting the complex relationship of negotiation which exists between those individual producers of cultural expression, and the culture industry. To say that 'appropriation, or *bricolage*, is a symptom of the tedium of ownership in a highly developed society' is to imply that the practice of *bricolage* is only a corporate activity; that it is the culture industry's way of homogenizing and incorporating the cultural, ethnic, gendered, sexual differences that exist in 'true' folk expression. While it is true that the culture industry appropriates cultural expression to its advantage, *bricolage* is, of course, just as much a practice of the individual musician, artist, fashion designer, playwright or film-maker. It is used as a way of undermining old meanings or stereotypes, or personalizing and manipulating one's iconic or sonic environment. To need to distinguish, once and for all, whether *bricolage* is a practice of domination or the creation of liberatory spaces is both acontextually impossible and unproductive. Further, to denounce *bricolage* as acontextually a practice of domination betrays a similar tendency to 'romanticize the origins' (Redhead, 1990) of cultural texts, which Gayatri Spivak argues is, itself, a type of 'cultural imperialism'.

In a paper titled 'Can the subaltern speak?', Spivak is concerned with whether it is possible for the subaltern subject to 'have a voice' that is independent of the First World intellectual in the context of First World social theory, or whether it is the responsibility of First World intellectuals to *represent* the subaltern subject in western theory. Spivak approaches this question by looking at a conversation between Michel Foucault and Gilles Deleuze, wherein the latter suggest that it is *beyond representation* (e.g. the practice of First World intellectuals) 'where oppressed subjects speak, act, and know *for themselves*' (Spivak in Nelson and Grossberg, 1988). Within this configuration, Foucault and Deleuze continue throughout the conversation to 'represent' the subaltern subject as the 'unrepresentable subject of struggle and concrete experience' – 'real', 'true', and 'unified' experience – while implicitly opposing this experience to the 'constructed' and 'heterogeneous' experience of the western theorist. The unspoken dichotomy is that of the *essential* identity of the subaltern and the *socially constructed* identify of the western philosopher.

However benevolent this gesture might appear, Spivak argues that it ultimately 'leads to an essentialist and utopian politics' because the intellectual who proclaims not to speak on behalf of the subaltern, 'the Other', the oppressed, must necessarily characterize his or her own role (as philosopher) as 'transparent'; as in no way colouring or constructing the representation of the subaltern, but merely reflecting it. The problem is, the philosopher is never transparent; one cannot refuse the role of 'referee'. And, as Spivak warns, until the intellectual is vigilant about recognizing that such a refusal is impossible, his or her supposed (self) transparency marks the place of interest and power: in other words, it is an 'imperialistic' gesture. Furthermore, the intellectual's 'refusal to represent the subaltern subject', despite benevolent intentions, is an avoidance of institutional responsibility; it is the desire to both *use and deny* institutional privileges of power. As Elspeth Probyn (paraphrasing Spivak) has articulated this point, 'access to

autobiography, for whole groups of people, has only been possible through
the dominant mediation of an investigator or fieldworker' (Probyn, 1993).
The above situation can be described in a scenario: sometimes it is the case
that First World intellectuals interested in the 'voice of the Other' ('benev-
olently' seeking to undo their privilege or, at least, ease their conscience) will
fill this unrepresentable absence with what Spivak calls the 'native informant'
– for example, the élite Third World subject who has institutional privilege
and representative capacity. The problem with this gesture is that the native
informant is *not*, and cannot stand for, the subaltern subject; it neglects the
fact that the subaltern subject is 'irretrievably heterogeneous'. *The* subaltern
subject is a 'catechresis' (another Spivakian usage), or 'a metaphor without
an adequate literal referent' (Spivak, 1990b). The nostalgia, therefore, for the
origins of the subaltern as 'true, concrete, and unified experience' is suspect
on imperialistic grounds (Nelson and Grossberg, 1988).

Now we are able to place our earlier criticism of popular culture as the
practice of 'obliterating difference' in a particular context, in order to discern
its potential implications. Therefore, in terms of this critique, let us say that
the cultural production involved is that of popular music, and that the 'difference' at issue is ethnic difference. This choice of context is not arbitrary:
aside from the fact that it ties in well with Spivak's argument in 'Can the
subaltern speak?', for a while now, there has been much discussion about
the growing popularity and listenership of what has been called 'global',
'roots' or 'world beat' music. This music has been characterized as 'original
and authentic as opposed to popular music'. The ethnic difference viewed
as being subsumed within popular culture is, of course, not the 'ethnic difference' of white, First World, European descendants, but that of Third World
people of colour – our subaltern subject in this scenario – as well as minority
populations within the First World, such as Hispanics in New York, African-
Americans in LA or First Nations people in Vancouver. Roots music, on the
other hand, is theorized as preserving the authentic, original experience of
the Third World or the First World minority populations; it is seen as an
instance of letting these 'subaltern' subjects speak for themselves. In this case,
roots and global music 'come to represent a ready-made, intact "other" voice
which forms a resistance to the total commodification of the First World'
(Redhead, 1990).

I want to argue that theoretically opposing popular music and roots music
in this way is suspect on imperialistic grounds similar to those articulated by
Spivak in 'Can the subaltern speak?' First, the above conception of roots and
global music neglects the fact that the 'global' distribution and reception of
this musical expression, or the reason why it 'gets heard' outside the immediate vicinity of its production, is most often the result of the mediation of
First World commercial industry. To ignore this fact is to perceive First
World corporate mediation as transparent; as merely reflecting Third World

or minority experience and expression, as opposed to facilitating its construction for First World audiences. Second, the perception of roots music as the pure and authentic expression of subaltern subjects ignores the negotiated positions of those subjects. First World mediation of Third World music is one example of this negotiation. Similarly, it is difficult to imagine a more negotiated position than those occupied by minority populations existing, surviving, struggling and succeeding within the 'violent structures' of First World racism. Third, roots music cannot 'represent' the Third World because the Third World is 'irretrievably heterogeneous'; it is a catechresis. This last point is particularly vexing for those commentators who would use roots music as a type of 'native informant' – as the (homogenous) voice of the Other. Such a gesture serves only to ease the conscience of the First World theorist who has not learned to 'unlearn' her or his institutional privilege. Fourth, and finally, in a call for the preservation of ethnic difference (i.e. the difference between the white European descendant and his or her 'Other'), the First World commentator subsumes the differences *within* Third World culture under one category. In other words, by configuring 'fake, constructed first world popular music' in opposition to 'original, authentic music from the third world', the 'irretrievable heterogeneity' of Third World culture and experience is, through an imperialistic gesture, construed as true, concrete and unified – it is, in other words, 'incorporated and obliterated'. These are the more dangerous implications of the benevolent impulses of the 'first world intellectual masquerading as the absent non-representer who lets the oppressed speak for themselves' (Nelson and Grossberg, 1988).

III

The above discussion is an attempt to confront the discrediting of (western) popular culture embodied in such labels as 'commercial', 'manufactured' and 'not authentic', which, in turn, discredit the possibility of seeing popular culture as a potential site of resistance to the dominant (consumer/commercial) culture. In this concluding segment, I will look at some alternative ways that popular culture can be theorized, which leave some hopeful *and* realistic spaces for potential resistance.

In 'Intellectuals, power, and quality television', Ava Collins takes popular culture out of a commercial context and discusses the role it can play in pedagogical situations. She argues that the 'technological revolution' has made it impossible to ignore mass forms of communication and the products they carry in terms of pedagogy (Collins in Giroux and McLaren, 1994). When students step into a classroom, they do not immediately shed their social and cultural skins; most often they are versed in popular culture. Therefore, it would make practical sense to 'retheorize the importance of popular culture

as a central category for developing a theory and practice of critical pedagogy'. Including popular cultural texts in course curricula would have two
desirable effects: first, it would legitimize popular cultural texts as material
worthy of critical reflection and debate (and if these texts are considered
culturally legitimate, resistant practices associated with them could also be
taken seriously); and second, it would affirm to students the relevance of their
experience as producers and receivers of popular culture. As Henry Giroux
and Roger Simon argue, '[e]ducators who refuse to acknowledge popular
culture as a significant basis of knowledge often devalue students by refusing
to work with the knowledge that students have' (Giroux and McLaren,
1994). The social commentator cannot risk negating youth, for example, by
deauthorizing the cultural or social forms through which they make and
transfer meaning. Traditionally, the 'classical' literary form has been the only
form of text to be canonized in course curricula (outside of the fine arts
department). Therefore, the addition of popular music texts in course
curricula can be considered a gesture of resistance to the dominant, exclu-
sionist and often élitist ideology of canon formation. As Spivak notes in 'The
making of Americans, the teaching of English, and the future of culture
studies', 'the debate surrounding the canon and curriculum formation is a
political matter; it involves the securing of authority' (Spivak, 1990a).

Finally, I want to look at how the destabilizing of the authority of
commercial ideology can and is being carried out on the level of the popular
cultural text itself. Earlier I made the point that the 'aesthetic' criteria by
which commercial industry judges the 'value' of a cultural text are those of
the 'sellable' product: that is, whether or not the text can be homogenized,
categorized, standardized, reproduced on a large scale and mass consumed.
The logic that assumes 'the more people buy a record the better it must be'
betrays the criteria of sellability and profit, and is demonstrated in the music
industry's honouring of musicians who have achieved gold or platinum
record status. The implication of this situation for popular cultural theory is
that the struggle between cultural production and the commodity form takes
place not only at the points of production and reception, but also at the level
of the cultural text. Fredric Jameson points out that an important legacy of
Adorno's work on music is the understanding that capitalism doesn't just
work on musical texts from the outside, but that capitalism is 'at work *within*
the musical material, as the intrinsic distortion of it by the commodity form,
which draws the various musical elements, theme, instrumentation,
harmony, indeed the length of development and the overall form itself, into
its orbit' (Jameson, 1971). The relevance of the above for a theory of cultural
resistance is that if the logic of the commodity form wields its authority on
the level of the text, then this authority can also be confronted, challenged
and undermined on this level. The 'profound vocation' of a work of art in
commodity society, Jameson points out, is 'not to be a commodity, not to

be consumed' – at least not in terms of the logic of the market place. A small, but significant, step towards a theory of resistance would be for critics to recognize, first, that cultural texts are, themselves, sites of political confrontation and, second, that artists and musicians are engaged in this confrontational activity all around us, all the time. If 'non-categorizable' music that challenges standardized, 'Top 40' criteria does not seem to exist in quantities that could constitute an oppositional force, it is not necessarily the case that this music isn't being produced. As musician Gary Numan explains in an interview, on being asked 'what is the future of music?':

> At the moment, I think a better question would be 'what is the point of music?' If the radio stations would be slightly more courageous and play something 25 times a week rather than 50, think of how many other acts they could fit in. Sometimes, just a single play could make a big difference. Think of the variety the public could begin to enjoy. Perhaps we would begin to see a chart based on what people actually wanted rather than songs selected from a tiny list presented by the radio stations. People simply don't know about 95% of the music released each week. (Numan, 1995)

I would argue that those musicians and cultural producers who challenge the logic of profitability, and the audiences of their work, can and in some cases have taken on the role of organic intellectuals, to use Gramsci's term; whether it be those musicians who have chosen to produce music independently (which is now a financial possibility) and distribute it directly to dance club disc jockeys, gaining access to audiences directly and bypassing corporate involvement in producing, pressing, marketing and distribution, or bands like Pearl Jam who, having achieved commercial success, have used this leverage to critique the music industry, first, by declining to produce videos as a way of 'advertising' their 'product' and, second, by refusing to do business with Ticketmaster, a company that has monopolized concert ticket vending in the United States and Canada. And as Jameson points out in *The Political Unconscious*, in the fragmented and decontextualized environment of postindustrial society, the proliferation of 'small-scale' political confrontations is the precondition of revolutionary social change: 'overt revolution is no punctual event . . . but brings to the surface the innumerable daily struggles and forms of class polarization which are at work in the whole course of social life that proceeds it, and which are therefore latent and implicit in "prerevolutionary" social experience' (Jameson, 1981).

The relationship between popular cultural *theory* and popular cultural *production* has been, to say the least, less than intimate. One reason for this distance is the orientation on the part of scholars and popular culture producers, alike, to a strict theory/practice dichotomy which has hindered the productive interbreeding of the work of both parties. The notion, for example, that the production of music is a 'real', 'concrete' activity that is opposed to the 'abstract', 'idealized' and 'parasitic' activity of cultural analysis must be disassembled. First, the theory/practice dichotomy in this situation is not benign. *It is directly in the commercial interests of the culture industry* that musicians believe that theoretical discussions of popular music and cultural politics are a threat to 'actual' music production. After all, one can't have musicians – the very bread and butter of the music industry – running around critiquing and challenging the logic of the commodity form. Second, the theory/practice dichotomy obscures a more subtle understanding of the relationship between the two activities. For example, while critics who proceed without the knowledge of actual texts and practices of musicians may, indeed, be guilty of abstracting and idealizing popular music, equally guilty of the latter are musicians and artists who fail to recognize that their work is intimately and inextricably involved in a larger field of cultural politics. The intermingling of theory and production can result in popular cultural texts that are 'self-conscious' of their material environments – a necessary precondition, I would argue, for potential sites of cultural resistance.

References

Attali, Jacques (1985) *Noise: The Political Economy of Music*, Minneapolis, MN: University of Minnesota Press.

Benhabib, Seyla (1992) *Situating the Self: Gender, Community and Postmodernism in Contemporary Ethics*, London and New York: Routledge.

Clarke, John (1990) 'Pessimism versus populism: the problematic politics of popular culture', in Richard Butsch (ed.), *For Fun ad Profit: The Transformation of Leisure into Consumption*, Philadelphia, PA: Temple University Press.

Foucault, Michel (1980) *Power/Knowledge*, ed. Colin Gordon, New York: Pantheon.

Fraser, Nancy (1989) *Unruly Practices: Power, Discourse and Gender in Contemporary Social Theory*, Minneapolis, MN: University of Minnesota Press.

Giroux, Henry and Peter McLaren (eds) (1994) *Between Borders: Pedagogy and the Politics of Cultural Studies*, London and New York: Routledge.

Jameson, Fredric (1971) *Marxism and Form*, Princeton, NJ: Princeton University Press.
(1981) *The Political Unconscious*, Ithaca, NY: Cornell University Press.

Lipsitz, George (1990) *Time Passages: Collective Memory and American Popular Culture*, Minneapolis, MN: University of Minnesota Press.

McRobbie, Angela (1985) 'Strategies of vigilance: an interview with Gayatri Chakravorti [*sic*] Spivak' *Block*, 10.

Modleski, Tania (ed.) (1986). *Studies in Entertainment: Critical Approaches to Mass Culture*, Indianapolis, IN: Indiana University Press.
(1991). *Feminism Without Women: Culture and Criticism in a 'Postfeminist' Age*, London and New York: Routledge.

Nelson, Cary and Lawrence Grossberg (eds) (1988) *Marxism and the Interpretation of Culture*, Urbana, IL: University of Illinois Press.

Numan, Gary (1995) 'Downtime with Gary Numan', *Future Music*, 31.

Probyn, Elspeth (1993) *Sexing the Self: Gendered Positions in Cultural Studies*, London and New York: Routledge.

Redhead, Steve (1990) *The End-of-the-Century Party: Youth and Pop Towards 2000*, New York St. Martin's Press, and Manchester: Manchester University Press.

Spivak, Gayatri (1987) *In Other Worlds: Essays in Cultural Politics*, London and New York: Routledge.

(1990a) 'The making of Americans, the teaching of English, and the future of culture studies', *New Literary History*, 21.

(1990b) *The Post-Colonial Critic: Interviews, Strategies, Dialogues*, ed. Sarah Harasym, London and New York: Routledge.

Street, John (1986) *Rebel Rock: The Politics of Popular Music*, Oxford: Blackwell.

Commentaries

3 'Organized Disorder':
The Changing Space
of the Record Shop

Will Straw

In 1872, just before opening le Bon Marché, his newly-acquired Parisian department store, Aristide Boucicault hurriedly rearranged its layout. In Boucicault's reasons for this reordering, Rachel Bowlby (1985) has suggested, we may glimpse the birth of a distinctly modern conception of commerce and shopping. What is necessary, Boucicault wrote, speaking of his customers:

> is that they walk around for hours, that they get lost. First of all, they will seem more numerous. Secondly . . . the store will seem larger to them. And lastly, it would really be too much if, as they wander around in organized disorder, lost, driven crazy, they don't set foot in some departments where they had no intention of going, and if they don't succumb at the sight of things which grab them on the way.

Part of the original appeal of the department store, Rachel Bowlby has argued, rested on the fact that in entering it one did not directly encounter the proprietor or salesperson. There was no sense of obligation to buy something, little risk that one would be asked what one was looking for. The moral equation between entering a shop and making a purchase, typical of earlier forms of commerce, had been broken. The customer's relationship to goods on offer was now marked by an individual, touristic compulsion to explore, rather than an obligation rooted in interpersonal contact.

This sense of wandering around in 'organized disorder' may be said to mark the present-day experience of stores specializing in recorded music. The small or mid-sized chain stores of a decade ago are gradually disappearing within North America and elsewhere, giving way to sprawling superstores with their segregated sections, multiple floors and careful construction of architectural confusion. This combination of confusion and enticing promise reaches almost caricatural levels in the HMV Superstore on Yonge Street in Toronto. Here, on entering, one immediately confronts two sets of stairs, each leading to another floor whose precise function is not obvious to the first-time visitor. At the downtown Sam The Record Man outlet in Montreal, the upper levels are organized as a set of interconnected garrets, through which even experienced customers are likely to stumble, confused, in their search for a way out. On my last visit there, I noticed a new sign inviting customers to seek directions if they were lost.

In 1995, in what seemed a frenzied rush to gargantuan monumentality, global retain chains specializing in home entertainment software leapfrogged over each other in their efforts to construct the world's largest store. In May, the US-based Tower Record chain claimed that its Tokyo store, at 52,000 square feet, was the world's biggest. It encompassed, the trade press reported, 'seven floors of merchandise, another floor for events, and three basements, one of which contains a cafe' (Jeffrey, 1995). The HMV outlet on Oxford Street in London, which the *Guinness Book of Records* had designated as the world's largest record store (at 36,000 square feet) was itself dwarfed on 1 June by the new Virgin Megastore, only 200 yards away, which (at 67,718 square feet) claimed the title of 'world's largest home entertainment store' (Clark-Meads, 1995). In Las Vegas, in August, a merging of the Tower record outlet and a store belonging to the Good Guys! electronics chain produced Wow! The Multimedia Superstore, which sprawled over some 60,000 square feet (Fitzpatrick, 1995).

Few spatial environments crystallize so perfectly an emergent set of cultural and commercial relations as does the contemporary record super-store. As the most visible piece of the material culture in which popular music is embedded, the superstore has emerged concurrently with two ideas whose validity it appears to undermine. One of these is the claim that commerce in a post-Fordist age will find its expression in the boutique rather than the democratically expansive stores of the past, in narrowly specialized and niche-targeted retail outlets whose inventories are regularly remade in response to rapidly shifting tastes. The abundance and pluralism of the record superstore, in which may be found much of the accumulated history of recorded sound, would seem the symmetrical opposite of the post-Fordist boutique. Another set of ideas has turned on the prediction that the sound recording as physical object – as embodied in the vinyl album, compact disc or cassette – is on the verge of disappearance, to be replaced by bits of data downloaded into the home via the Internet or other channels. For this scenario to be convincing, we must believe that, like the dinosaur, the record store has grown to its greatest size just before the moment of its extinction.

The record superstore is the product of several observable socioeconomic trends. One such trend is the ascendant popularity of mammoth, warehouse retail outlets across a number of industries (most notably, in North America, in the office supply and pharmaceutical products industries). Another is the move towards concentration within the recorded music industries (in particular, within distribution). As the number of distribution entities has shrunk, the ability of any one of these to deal with major retail chains and reach store shelves has grown, expanding the range of titles offered by such chains. More broadly, the replication of monumental superstore structures has come with the revitalization of city core economies, in which both museums and those shopping sites which seem museum-like have come to play a prominent role.

At the same time, the record superstore is an architectural expression of the broader reordering which has gone on within the culture of popular music – one through which musical tastes and consumption habits have come to be fragmented, distributed across an expanding array of niches. Once oriented towards producing a limited number of blockbuster successes, record companies are more and more the exploiters of accumulated back catalogues or infinitely differentiated niche markets. For the most optimistic of industry observers, their market has come to be characterized by a new, stable predictability: jazz reissues, classical compilations and alternative rock albums now sell in numbers which lend themselves more easily to procedures of rational calculation. For other analysts, however, the sprawling pluralism of the contemporary record store threatens a dispersion of the market into anarchic confusion. As tastes fragment and few records attain the sales levels of a *Thriller* or a *Purple Rain*, consumer choices no longer manifest themselves as broad, collective swings towards this album or that. Instead, they are spread among thousands of choices from repertories accumulated over fifty or sixty years. As the sections within superstores proliferate, and with them the number of titles for offer, marketing experts begin to speak of 'selection stress': the 'anxiety [of] a music buyer faced with the enormous selection in most stores', as Josh Kaplan, founder of the marketing firm Intouch, argues (Rothman, 1993). A whole range of technologies, subsidiary media and marketing strategies are now marshalled to reduce this stress, to direct the buyer comfortably and confidently to specified titles.

The Swing Vote and the Comfort Level

Over the last twenty years, a prominent theme of record industry discourse has been the need to reduce the intimidation seen as endemic to the environment of the record store. This intimidation is itself traced to two features of popular musical culture: the existence of sounds which are oppressive and knowledges which are unevenly distributed. Paul du Gay has written of the retail revolution which, since the 1960s, has appeared to empower customers by making them, rather than salespeople, the bearer of knowledges about goods on offer. '[S]elf-service', he suggests, 'has functioned as a "technique of individuation" for consumers, constituting them as self-regulating, autonomous individual subjects exercising choice in a world of goods' (du Gay, 1993). In the record retail industry, this same self-regulation had led to large segments of the population viewing the record store as an alien, humbling experience.

In the late 1970s, in the midst of the record industry's economic slump, the trade press was saturated with rhetoric about the need to win back adult record buyers. Demographic studies showed a long-term shrinking of the primary audience for rock recordings (males aged 18–24); wooing back the older, so-called casual buyer was instituted as the challenge of the 1980s. The diagnosis of why North American adults had ceased buying records in significant numbers throughout the 1970s focused, for a time, on the spatial environment of the shopping mall chain store. Narrow and deep, the chain store confronted middle-aged shoppers with young, frighteningly subcultural sales clerks and heavy metal music blasting from an entrance which was itself blocked by displays of unrecognizable (to these shoppers) current recordings. Prominent in the folklore of the record industry during this period were stories of adults entering a record store, asking for records by Perry Como or Bing Crosby, and meeting blank stares of non-recognition from sales clerks.

In the context of declining sales, the industry's salvation, it was believed, required turning away from rock, and toward so-called non-perishable classes of product, such as children's music, easy listening, classical music and reissues from the past. 'Non-perishable' meant that these forms did not rise and fall with the rhythms of fashion; stores could maintain titles in inventory for long periods of time. The ideal purchaser of these non-perishable recordings, industry discourse suggested, was the young adult woman. '[S]he's uncommitted,' industry executive Michael Kapp of Warner Special Products described this kind of consumer: 'She isn't really into music, doesn't read hip music magazines, doesn't go to concerts, but [she] reads shopper guide columns and is about ready to hook up with cable tv or buy a video game.'

One of the most famously effective means of reaching these buyers involved campaigns which encouraged young adult women to buy recordings as gifts (presumably for men.) The 'Give The Gift of Music' campaign of the early 1980s was targeted precisely at so-called casual buyers. These were not to be found in record stores themselves, but, rather, 'walking up and down the aisles of your customers' chain, discount or department store'. Females aged 30–9, whom research found to spend 25 per cent of all gift dollars, were designated the 'swing vote' within industry discourse, those who could make the difference between a record's profitability or failure.

During this period, as well, labels producing so-called Middle of the Road recordings explored what were termed non-traditional sales outlets for recordings – liquor stores, perfume stores and gift shops – bypassing a record retail sector considered inhospitable to their target audiences.

The recording industry's construction of a 'casual buyer' has typically conflated the ageing adult and the female. Both are seen as slow in their response to shifting trends, and much less involved in the circulation of music-related knowledges than is the male consumer in his late teens or early twenties. Each of these consumer groups, according to the industry's understanding, nevertheless possesses specific virtues. The 'casual buyer' has no prior inclination to purchase records; once convinced to do so, however, she is easily swayed by advertising strategies. In this, she is diametrically opposed to the 'core' male buyer, who is always willing to buy records, but notoriously selective in his buying decisions. The wooing of the largely female, 'casual' buyer is regularly painted in the terms of chivalrous guidance. Having defined musical recordings as appropriate gifts, the industry will offer benevolent instruction as to which recordings are suitable for that purpose.

If the compact disc has emerged as one of the most dazzlingly effective of commodity forms, this has little to do with its technical superiority to the vinyl record (which we no longer remember to notice.) Rather, this effectiveness has to do with its status as the perfect crossover consumer object. As a cutting-edge audiophile invention, it seduced the technophilic, connoisseurist males who typically buy new sound equipment and quickly build collections of recordings. (Indeed, by the late 1980s, and because of the CD, the proportion of males within the US record-buying audience had reached peak levels.) At the same time, its visual refinement and high price rapidly rendered it legitimate as a gift. In this, the CD has found a wide audience among the population of casual record buyers.

These audiences, distinct and opposed in a variety of ways, find a partial convergence within the reissue strategies of record companies. The jazz or classic rock connoisseur seeks and now finds the range of titles which archiving impulses require. The casual buyer, establishing a collection which is likely to remain limited, finds titles catering to an implicit demand for canonical representativity. For the record companies and the retail sector, the significant challenge of the near future is that of delivering information. Means must be developed to inform connoisseurs of ongoing reissue programmes; at the same time, the anxiety of casual buyers about their lack of expertise must be overcome.

In this context, there is a preponderance of moralizing exhortations, directed at those within the record retail industry, to increase the level of comfort of those browsing in their stores. Classical, jazz and alternative rock music are regularly characterized as 'intimidating', in that they present the would-be buyer with the horrifying possibility of making a wrong choice.

In the marketing of jazz, a principal means of anxiety reduction is the release of recordings in series marked with prestigious trademarks and guaranteeing a continuity between titles. (An overinvestment in the trademarks of defunct companies and other signs of originary authenticity characterizes CD reissues overall.)

The strains within this moralizing are most visible in discussions of the popularizing of classical music. Guided by the conviction that 'ageing baby-boomers are looking for something new and mellow to listen to', labels have sought to render classical music friendly and populist, promoting it on television during basketball games, through movie soundtracks or via tie-ins to Martha Stewart cookbooks (Cox, 1992). In the experience of one distributor of classical music, 'racks that highlight chart successes and include recommendations of titles made the consumer "more comfortable"', as *Billboard* put it in 1991. For traditional classical labels, such as Deutsche Grammophon, this is frequently seen as shameless pandering, a squandering of the prestige capital accumulated by these labels or by the orchestras and composers they have presented.

If record stores have become larger, it is in part to accommodate all customers: the casual *and* the legendary 'core' buyer of records. The latter, obviously, can wallow in the archival inclusiveness of the superstore. For the casual buyer, the sprawling abundance of the superstore – its mixing of historical times and endless subdivision of tastes and genres – although likely to intimidate, is just as likely to comfort. Just as it suggests an endless set of knowledges not yet mastered, its flattened sense of equivalency means that none stands more privileged than another.

Space and Stasis

The effects of the CD on the layout of the record store are easily traceable, but they must be seen against the background of a larger audience fragmentation of which they are both a cause and an effect. The predominance of the CD has grown during a period when radio has come to play a much less significant role in stimulating record sales than in the past. In North America, this has come as the majority of radio stations have moved away from playing current music. The declining promotional role of radio has encouraged the turn towards reissues, just as this turn itself has weakened the link between the records put on sale and what is heard on radio. Record companies, to remain profitable, have come to depend on the tighter but more predictable profits which accrue from the sales of thousands of back catalogue titles. While current recordings obviously continue to be released, they do so within a context of increased audience fragmentation. (One can own two albums on today's *Billboard* Top 10 without ever having heard most of the others.) In this context, the processes by which consumers come to know about and seek out records are increasingly differentiated, grounded in the everyday minutiae of word-of-mouth or highly specialized magazines. Seeking to influence sales, record companies have extended the hand of chivalrous and polite guidance to all buyers.

To benefit from massive reissue programmes and from the pluralism of current product, record stores themselves have had to enlarge their physical space so as to offer an enormous range of titles. (They can no longer sacrifice the revenues from marginal forms, such as alternative rock, to speciality stores.) This requires extensive capitalization, both to expand and subdivide the physical space of the retail store, and to maintain large, slow-moving inventories over long periods of time. This requirement, more than any broader economic trend, may serve to explain the recent disappearance within Canada of the A&A and Discus chains, both of which lacked the resources necessary to maintain and expand inventories.

The important tension within the record retail sector presently is that between the offering of a potentially chaotic abundance and the marshalling of a variety of means for focusing consumer choice and producing order from amidst this chaos. The changing architecture of the record store over the last half decade reveals the new importance of consumer information and its delivery. The rise of in-store listening booths, give-away magazines and label display racks is a direct result of the declining role of radio as a force in stimulating record sales. These forms and technologies all presume a redefinition of record buying as an activity stimulated by discovery, previewing and experimentation, rather than repeated exposure or peer group reinforcement. They are meant, in other words, to contain the epidemic of 'selection stress'.

In this context, the industry's conceptualization of buyer behaviour has shifted considerably. This is no longer imagined in causal terms, as the effect of particular promotional media on collective buying decisions. Rather, it is perceived as a set of coherences which link the observed purchase of one title to the possible or probable purchase of another, along a calculated series. Here, the acquisition of information on individual buying habits has become embedded within new technologies which create buyer profiles and guide their choices. The most discussed of these, offered by Intouch of San Francisco, involves listening stations in record stores, for the use of which identification cards are required. A customer who samples any pop/dance record is offered a sneak preview of the new album by another pop/dance artist; later, he or she is mailed information on upcoming albums of similar style. Record companies, in turn, receive data on which cuts the customer listened to while using the machine. This is combined with demographic information supplied when the customer applied for a card.

The emergence of these information systems and technologies has been embedded within an ongoing campaign against waste, against the failure to use the most trivial sorts of information. One effect of this preoccupation with data has been the diminished presence, within North American record stores, of deletes or 'cut-outs'. As cash registers are linked to inventory control systems, and these to record companies and their pressing plants, the risks of overpressing and ordering have been reduced. Slow-selling stock is reallocated to other branches; best-selling titles are printed as they are needed. The effect, for long-time browsers like myself, is a redefinition of the record store's promise of discovery. Once, a decade ago, it was based on the enticing likelihood of stumbling across bins of cheap, failed albums or overruns. Now, the pleasure of discovery has been directed towards taste-fully packaged reissues selling at catalogue prices.

These changes, like so many others reshaping our cultural landscape, may leave us with a paralysing ambivalence. In an age when in-store giveaway magazines build credibility by running negative reviews, or when listening posts invite us to test the latest alternative rock obscurity, traditional critiques of record industry hype or shrinking choice seem quaintly inappropriate. Longstanding concerns about the neglect of once-marginal forms or performers are disarmed as major firms rush to reissue their back catalogues in lovingly designed collections. Complaints about the élitism implicit in CD pricing policies wither when attractive soul reissues on compact disc sell for less than a current 12" vinyl dance single.

What has withered as well, amidst the new fragmentation of musical tastes, is music's role in producing and registering disruptive shifts of popular atten-tion. As musical tastes divide, they appear to be more purist: industrial rock, rap or country albums now reach the Top 10 without the obvious signs of compromise or hybridization. The rationalization of distribution, sales and promotion has helped to transform the market for records into segregated blocks of loyal core buyers rather than a site for crossover or collective re-direction. In this context, successful records seem more authentic, more faithful to their generic traditions, than at any point in recent history. 'There is an increasing proliferation of street-edge music,' record label executive Barry Weiss of Jive Records said recently, and 'the old rules don't apply as much'. Under the new rules, a Nine Inch Nails album makes the *Billboard* Top 10 in its first week of release.

With so much that seems positive in these changes, we may overlook the new segregations of taste and audience which have resulted. Few collective gatherings are as racially and socially homogeneous as a Green Day concert, for example, and a mid-1990s Pink Floyd show in New York was, by all accounts, one of the most exclusively white events in that city's recent history. As record superstores beckon with their pluralist abundance, maga-zines, radio formats and the broader logics of social differentiation have circumscribed tastes and buying patterns within predictable clusters. What has been lost, arguably, are those (politically ambiguous) moments of crossover or convergence which regularly undermined music's usual tendency to reinforce social and racial insularity. Stumbling around the record superstore, 'lost, driven crazy', the paths we follow are likely, nevertheless, to map the stubborn lines of social division.

References

Bowlby, Rachel (1985) *Just Looking: Consumer Culture in Dreiser, Gissing and Zola*, London: Methuen.

Clark-Meads, Jeff (1995) 'London stores set world standards: with HMV, revamped Megastore enters record book', *Billboard*, 17 June.

Cox, Meg (1992) 'Classical labels tune in new listeners', *Wall Street Journal*, 9 April.

Du Gay, Paul (1993) '"Number and souls": retailing and the de-differentiation of economy and culture', *British Journal of Sociology*, vol. 44, no. 4.

Fitzpatrick, Eileen (1995) 'Vegas is 1st to be Wow!ed by Superstore', *Billboard*, 19 August.

Jeffrey, Don (1995) 'Tower's Solomon weight expansion, stock offering', *Billboard* 27 May.

Rothman, Mark (1993) 'A new music retailing technology says "Listen here"', *Billboard*, 19 August.

4 Spatial Politics:
A Gendered Sense of Place

Cressida Miles

Social space this remains the space of society, of social life. [One] does not live by words alone; all 'subjects' are situated in a space in which they must either recognise themselves or lose themselves, a space which they may both enjoy and modify. (Lefebvre, 1991)

This analysis seeks to identify the question of a gendered sense of space in the 'youth subcultural place of punk'.[1] I do not intend to advocate the idea that punk began in London during 1976 and simply ended with the death of the Sex Pistols. Rather, I am providing an account that honours the multiple subjectivities and localities and temporalities that make up the punk subculture. To view punk as a chronology in terms of the genesis of the 'Bromley' contingent and punks' subsequent fragmentation in terms of the death of key icons would be to place emphasis on authenticity (I was there in '76, where were you?). Therefore, I am suggesting that there were many people who held an affinity with punk outside of a fixed three-year time span in many localities. There are even those who still identify with punk, although they have dropped their 'spikey hair' and 'dog collars'.[2] This particular version of punk takes a look at gender relations within the context of sexuality. The intention is to pluck women out of subcultural time, because in this space they break their silence. Here subcultural research has to hear their voice and take note: as in this instance women refused to ride pillion in subordination to their male subcultural fellow travellers.

My analysis involves an integral application of the theories of Lefebvre (1991) as a means of understanding and redefining subculture in terms of spatiality. This approach makes it possible to take into consideration gender issues which had been excluded in subcultural accounts. Therefore it is necessary to locate this account in relation to the development of feminist critiques concerned with masculine bias in subcultural accounts (McRobbie, 1975, 1981, 1994; Roman *et al.*, 1988). In my own analysis I consider how resistance takes on a contextual emphasis within a specific subcultural place, in which the reference points are constantly transforming and opening new youth subcultural options and possibilities for meaning and representation.

Second, I shall consider how identity is negotiated through movements in a subcultural life biography, which implies a self-reverential and active negotiation within this space. Third, representational spaces are sites of complex symbolisms that are polysomic and transformative, whereby female punks played a part in the consumption and production of space and contributed to the creation of 'representational spaces'. While these spaces provide sites of autonomy, they still interact with discourses of femininity in late modernity.

In conclusion, I wish to argue that, while my emphasis relates to punk, subcultures are places that constantly modify and transform themselves through time and space. This specific 'place' is one where women are able to find pleasure and dismay in the possibilities and restrictions that their experience of femininity offers them.

Identity is The Great Big Part You See (Polystyrene, 1978)

> Subcultures are . . . central to the construction of identity outside class ascriptions . . . if subcultures are solutions to collectively experienced problems, then traditionally these have been the problems experienced with young men . . . These subcultures in some form or another explore and celebrate masculinity, and as such eventually relegate girls to a subordinate place within them. (Brake, 1985)

While Brake recognizes the poverty of a feminine emphasis in subcultural theory, it appears he is reluctant to tease out the construction of female identity. His treatment continues to give subcultural space to men, who are available to do their 'resolving'. However, Brake (1980, 1985) does recognize that a subcultural identity is negotiated with reference to institutionalized social relations, such as family members, workers or pupils. Retaining a theory of contradiction, he argues that women experience subordination in both the dominant culture and the space of subculture. While this type of approach views femininity as being constructed and defined through discourse in both public and private spheres, it does not look at the experience of women in subcultural space.

Brake's (1980) analysis of hippie women drew attention to the contradictions manifested in a culture that advocated a variety of freedoms. In this subculture, woman was represented as childlike and innocent, as holy Madonnas, pre-Raphaelite, yet sexually available. Sexual freedom was viewed as integral to this 'Aquarian revolution'. Sexual freedom came with a price, as egalitarian values had a double-edged currency, where women had to take responsibility for their sexual freedom within the parameters of patriarchy in respect of birth control and child care. Here subcultures do not provide means of escape or time to resolve problems faced in everyday life. Yet it would also be limiting to view the place of women in subculture as fixed. McRobbie has continued to note the absence of such issues during the past two decades. However, few ethnographies are available to begin to excavate the position of female experience, especially in relation to that of men. This type of approach would yield an analysis that identified contradictions and undermined the view that subculture itself is the raw material of revolution. McRobbie (1981) provided a critique of subcultural accounts that privileged the position of the working-class male who inhabited the public space of the street. McRobbie (1991) concluded that Willis did have something analytical to say about masculinity, and furthermore that subculture itself might not be a place for feminine pleasure: 'What's more, women are so obviously inscribed (marginalized and abused) within subculture as static objects (girlfriend, whores or 'fag heads') that access to its thrills . . . would hardly be compensation even for the most adventurous teenage girl' (McRobbie, 1980).

This explanation still fails to account for the place of women in subculture, and even implies that women prefer to do other things (maybe sit in their bedrooms and listen to records). Yet by the early eighties, female punks were highly visible on the street and gave emphasis to the role of women as actively playing with subcultural identities.

Hebdige (1979) argued that scraping away the meanings behind the signs was a useful means of interpreting youth subcultures. In his analysis of punk, women were viewed as playing defiantly with signifiers; their use of iconography played with the illicit and the darker side of sexuality. 'If following Eco's dictum . . . we speak through our clothes, we do so in accents of our sex' (McRobbie, 1981). However, this semiotic reading never exacted how and where they did this, and did not question how the style of these women varied according to time, locality and subject positioning as a result of the production of various subgenres within punk itself. Hebdige (1979) recognized himself that his semiotic reading provided an account of punk in which the subculturalists would probably not recognize themselves. He conceded that an approach that reads style for meaning must take account of the everyday life of subcultural participation.

Hiding in the Light (Hebdige, 1988) provided Hebdige with a means of discussing subculture in terms of a postmodern and more spatially oriented focus on representation. He argued that women in punk 'interrupt the image flow . . . They play back images of women as icons . . . They skirt round the voyeurism issue.' Here the female body was viewed as a site of empowerment, a place where power can be appropriated within sexual discourse. Perhaps the piercing practices of some punks provided a symbolic means of reinscribing the body. Such practices can be interpreted as playing within the 'darker side of narcissism', and if the body is the bottom line, then piercing becomes an act of refusal – a tactical block, a place to regain control. Here an interplay exists between the representation of the subcultural body and sexual discourse, as Michel Foucault argues, where sexuality is the end product of any and all the discourses that define it, analyse it, propose to control it and emancipate it. For Foucault, sexuality has no reality, no subterranean core outside of these discourses.

The point I am making is that subcultural space, especially where it provides objections to ideologies and ways of being, is never outside of discourse. Identity is mediated in relation to something else. Any analysis of female sexuality must view it within the context of discursive regimes that attempt both to construct and to modify the female body.

Roman (1988) provides a critique of subculture that embraces an understanding of discourse thorough materialism, semiotics, feminist epistemology and ethnographic methods. This relational analysis of gender uses the 'slam dance' as a means of understanding feminine space at gigs and within wider subcultural context. Roman positions these women in terms of their class, employment status and family relations. She argues that the young women understand and negotiate their subcultural position in terms of femininity and sexuality – the self is viewed as a site of contestation. This methodology does not treat discourses of social relations as necessarily bounded by stable or unchanging codes and subcodes. Rather, it recognizes that the relations among and between them are conjectural and contextual.

The ritual of slam dance involves physical contact and risk of damage, and happens during gigs that play hardcore music. The body is used to situate one's self within space and time, a space and time that is inscribed with gendered boundaries. Roman observed the women withdrawing their presence from the dance floor when men began to slam. The women were in fact creating safe pockets where the men could not bait them, yet even in this avoidance they were called 'lezzies'. When the men left the floor, the women returned and danced together, thus reclaiming the space. Roman suggests that this is a means for the women to identify both territory and mental space.

These women use the language of a *down there* space, away from the presence of the masculine touch and gaze, which characterize the *up there* space. This assertion of difference is not confined to a critique of masculinity, but also relates to class differences between the women. This conflict occurs because of social relations outside of the gigs. The working-class women see their lives as different from those of the middle-class women, the defining

features being the latter's economic independence and ability to set up their
own homes. It is interesting that these working-class women felt that, in the
private space of their own homes, they were more equal to the male punks
– they articulate a sense of regaining control. Control also worked within
the confines of the gaze. One woman told Roman that this was significant:
she felt empowered by gazing from a distance at the men, since this did not
involve relations of intimacy, which she viewed through her personal experience in terms of power and domination.[3]

This account of subculture attempts to rewrite the 'missing women' back
into subculture with a more subtle notion of resistance: by analysing the
social relations of the slam dance and comparing by class the young women's
discourses concerning their mode of participation in it. I refine the concept
of resistance first by specifying the conditions under which the young
women's intentions may not be romanticized as radically transformative, and
second by showing how their subjectivity is heterogeneous and contradictory (Roman, 1988).

The analysis is localized and says something about the experience of
American punks in the eighties. Its significance is that it indicates that subcultural space is neither static nor homogeneous, and it also considers the
relationship between femininity and masculinity as a process of negotiation.

Looking Beyond the Mirror

It is beyond doubt that the relations of inclusion and exclusion, and of expli-
cation, obtain a practical space as in spatial practice. 'Human Beings' do not
stand before, or amidst, social space, they do not relate to the space of society
as they might a picture, a show or a mirror. They know that they have a
space as active participants. They do not merely enjoy a vision, a contempla-
tion, a spectacle – for they act and situate themselves as active participants.
They are accordingly situated in the enveloping levels each of which implies
the other, and the sequence of which accounts for social practice. (Lefebvre,
1991)

Inherent in Lefebvre's work is a notation of the dialectic and how space itself
is produced in social terms. Using the concept of identity in terms of femininity, a spatial analysis like the one above would question how women in
punk negotiate their place and identity politics in a more 'subterranean'
culture. A subcultural identity could imply a new way of looking at the self,
as it involves a shift in the space of social positioning and provides new modes
of understanding. This becomes a place to rethink the self actively, even by
virtue of embracing Otherness.

Femininity is an experience of Otherness, and is embedded within discourse and ideology. Femininity is so naturalized that difference is subtly asserted, making it difficult to notice contradictions in everyday life. Historically, the separation of private and public has positioned women in less public spaces, belonging to the home and within the tight rein of an ideological corset of feminine attributes. Sexuality has also been a site for power play, through reproductive technologies and moral censorship.[4] Censorship feeds its way into everyday life, its subtle contradictions are glossed over and young women are constructed along lines of good or bad – drag or slag. Young women are measured for their likeness or rather their positioning to mothers, whores, mistresses, spinsters and lesbians. Subcultures are not magically protected from these constructs, yet for some women in punk there was a place to be angry and to celebrate the illicit and clandestine – for some a means of seeing critically into the mirror and of challenging the reflection.

Subverting Sexuality

The punk culture was never homologically coherent. There were different aesthetics in punk style which spoke different versions of reality. The subculture itself was located in a broader spectrum of musical associations and recycled subcultural forms: psychobillies (half punk, half rockabilly), scooter boys, vampiresque gothics and new romantics. The last two groupings had some affinity with punk, in that they accentuated the pleasure of dressing, albeit much smarter in the case of the latter, and in the case of the gothics, sexuality, decay and bodily fluids became the point of connection.

Punks played with the darker side of sexual symbols: transsexuality, asexuality, S/M, piercing of the flesh and the restraint of bondage. The illicit and illegal were celebrated defiantly, and signs were rescripted, displaced and used as semiotic warfare. Not all women in punk bought into the illicit sexuality residing in punk; some preferred an indeterminate look as a refusal of femininity – the army boots and combat pants – while others flirted defiantly with sex as a public weapon, wearing bondage pants, studded wristbands and torn-up stockings. These tactics were part of a broader subcultural picture where a space was won and ideologies were repositioned. Women could play in bands, and it was common during the early days for all-female bands to express their anger.

> Punk didn't do much to challenge male sexuality or image . . . but it still gave women a lot of confidence. Boy bands were getting up on stage who couldn't play a note . . . so it was easy for girls who couldn't play to get up on stage as well. By the time they developed, women were singing about their own experience in a way they hadn't done before. (Viv Albertine of The Slits)[5]

Sexuality in fact, though, was challenged and questioned, and the body was used as an avant-garde aesthetic. Attention was drawn to body parts, zips exposed flesh and the body was used as a swear word. Fetish icons were worn aggressively for shock value and contrasted with the popularity of the Laura Ashley floral dress. Purity had no place in punk aesthetics, as illustrated by the representations of gender and sexuality that became polarized within punk. Siouxsie Sioux, Wendy O Williams, The Slits, Lydia Lunch and Nina Hagen among others represented the illicit and perverse. These angry yet highly sexualized women soon became representations of a subcultural space, and while they presented their punkish perversity on stage, other women were also exploring their identity in similar ways. Ironically, for every value that these women challenged, there were still punk men out there who took these images and used them as pin-ups. But in this case such action was not offensive, since the bringing out of sexuality in quite aggressive and confrontational ways was intended not only for the punk gaze, but also for the public. Here the pornographic and sadomasochistic sign system had been rewritten in subcultural space: this is the translation of perversity within punk and perversity as parody, where a critical and confident edge was retained.

Female sexuality was certainly an issue within punk. Many women I conversed with spoke of their enjoyment in flaunting an overt sexual persona without fear. Some women I talked to also had associations with the light sex industry through hostess work, or jobs as assistants in fetish clothing shops. One woman saw her work in a Soho rubber shop as a means to an end – in this shop she could obtain rubber clothing and S/M equipment at a low cost. The rubber clothes were part of her punk image, her interest in which later led her into the fetish scene in London. At this point in the early eighties, many punks slipped into the fetish scene because it provided an alternative atmosphere to the 'pub scene'.

Fetish clubs are in fact sites of sexual diversity which operate on an aesthetic and stylistic level and also in terms of rejecting sexual values inherent in the dominant culture. They appealed to many female punks who played with perversity. One women spoke of how being involved with punk provided her with a chance to explore her sexuality through body piercing and latex.[6] Piercing as a practice gained visibility with the shock tactics of punk, and became a symbol of it. However, the broader practice of body piercing became accessible to this woman through an awareness of other subcultural worlds. Being in this subcultural space created the possibility of crossing over into other modes of self-expression. Here a subcultural auto-biography develops in a reflexive manner, where the body becomes the interface between sexuality and the self.

A number of women I spoke to viewed punk as giving them a place to express their sexuality through style. In some cases this expression was a means of celebrating the youthfulness of the body. One woman who had spent her punk years in Brighton and Yorkshire felt that she was able to escape the domination of labels enforced upon young women who did not conform to 'sexual standards'. As a punk she felt she was able to have sex freely. She said that punk didn't make her a feminist, but through her attraction to the anarchic spirit of punk she felt free to act as she pleased. Other women I have conversed with felt that promiscuity was part of the playground of punk. Many women also took 'speed' in this context, which heightened their confidence and enabled a sexually confrontational attitude to men. Ironically, during the sixties, girlfriends of mods who used this drug complained that it ruined their partners' sexual drive.

While some women felt a sense of sexual freedom through the appropriate of whips, chains, PVC and latex, for others this look was not appealing because it drew far too much attention to the body. Many young women opted for a 'safer' and more asexual identity. In Yorkshire during the early eighties there was a mix of styles; however, the more sexually overt style was often accorded a night-time existence. A group of women I conversed with chose the comfort of monkey boots, combat pants and overcoats. One of these women spoke of her awareness of patriarchal attitudes that lingered in the area where she lived, and of how her image conflicted with feminine expectations:

> The girls I went to school with expected to become machinists. My mum wanted me to work in a building society – to better myself. When I started to dye my hair and became aware of politics – you know, the news and stuff – she freaked out. My dad was a local lad, he was hard, he hated my look. He reckoned that no decent man would want me – I didn't want a decent man, they just want you in one place, at home with a baby . . . The town lads were bastards. They used you for one night and that was it, you were a slag. I didn't give a shit, I liked sex anyway.[7]

This account recognizes the contradictions of femininity that some young women still face. The freedom of this female was constrained by the symbolic residues of a working-class culture, and also conflicted with the experience of women from the south, who came from a more middle-class background. Obviously, for some women punk did not provide an open space free from constraints in the dominant culture, and in this instance the relations between male and female punks were in no way egalitarian. Subcultural space as such does not guarantee freedom from constraint, but for some it provides a site of reflection and negotiation. Where a punk identity intersected with other sexual subcultures, there appeared to be a greater sense of tolerance and awareness of sexuality within the context of the Other. For example, in Torquay many punks went to the gay bar because their appearance was not considered smart enough for straight pubs. It could be the case that the gays recognized these punks as subcultural Others and accepted their liminal positioning within the town.

In terms of temporality, the identity of being a punk had a profound influence on the lives of some women. Many women viewed punk as a place of sexual freedom because of the style and the attitude it cloaked them with. Others saw punk as a place to explore micro politics, in that they were able to engage in the political issues raised by lyrics in punk rock. A female from Middlesbrough said that she heard the word 'anarchy' and decided to find out what it was about because it was a popular currency in the language of punk. She felt that being a punk opened her eyes to a subversive way of seeing the world, and influenced her development and life biography. Many ex-punks I spoke to believed that aspects of the fragmentary ethos of punk never left them as they outgrew their subcultural affinities. Viv Albertine (of the female band The Slits) felt that her involvement in punk was all about going against the grain, especially in terms of sexuality: 'The whole thing was about looking at things with a fresh eye, and sexuality had to be looked at, there were so many problems that had to be solved' (Savage, 1991).

On a more conceptual level, the punk space can be interpreted in terms of prohibition. The subtle workings of sexual prohibition are mediated through time and space. These feed into the social relations of space through ideas and representations. However, this does not imply that social space is fixed through this process: certainly in the case of women in punk, sexuality was renegotiated in terms of punks' own use of symbolic representation. The women in punk bands became symbols of prohibitions that had encoded sex within designated urban spaces – in this case, sexuality was used as a tactical block. However, it would be overdeterministic to argue that it was the direct appeal of such images that seduced women into the space of punk. For many women their subcultural affiliation grew out of friendship networks. It is therefore possible to suggest that, until people are embroiled within a specific space, implications are unknown; in this context, entering into a subcultural space opens up 'unknown pleasures' and conflicts. In this sense social space involves the recognition of a 'subjective space' which is wrought with contradictions and can be 'qualified in various ways because it is essentially qualitative, fluid and dynamic' (Lefebvre, 1991).

From the Street to the Shop and Back Again

Space is divided up into designated (specified, specialised) areas that are prohibited (to one group or another). It is further subdivided into spaces for work and spaces for leisure, and into daytime and night time spaces. The body, sex and pleasure are often accorded no existence, either mental or social, until after dark, when the prohibitions that obtain during the day, during 'normal' activity are lifted. (Lefebvre, 1991)

The punk shop played with illicit signifiers. Here in this space there no prohibitions. The shop 'Sex', established by Westwood and McClaren, was not only a play on signs, but also a plotting point for the shock tactics involved in the early expressions that punks conveyed to the public. 'Sex' could embody everything that was not accorded a respectable existence in everyday life. The shop transformed day into night and was intended to make people feel uncomfortable. Its ethos was animated through the interests of the punk performance artist who translated the ideas into practice. Savage describes Jordan, the manager of this shop, as 'a living advertisement of the new shop, having turned her body into an art object . . . she had an appearance so stunning that every time she stepped out of the door she put herself on the line. Her life was pas de deux with outrage . . . Jordan's own appearance began to reflect the shop's wares' (Savage, 1991).

The creation of the punk shop became a feature in many localities. The image each shop created appealed to those who enjoyed hanging out in such an environment, and those who enjoyed the pleasures of subcultural consumption.[8] Here clothing provided a meeting ground for social interaction, a place to find out what was going on, what gigs were on the horizon. In Torquay the shop 'Individual Fashions' became a meeting ground for local punks; it was a place for the younger punks to truant off school or to meet up with a boyfriend. The owners of the shop had a vehicle that transported stock and local punks to various gigs and events. The van was sprayed with the logo 'We are all prostitutes, only some are more expensive than others.' If the street was the testing ground for style, then the shop was a forum creating an image that was a representation of the space the punks inhabited. The space of the punk shop, however, was not always safe from outside censure. The company 'Artificial Eye' deliberately used prohibited signs as part of its overall design concept. The shop in Kensington market had a torso of Jesus displayed at the entrance to the shop which was lit with fairy lights and wrapped in barbed wire. The rest of the shop transformed day into night. The Jesus feature created an uproar among the Jewish community in that area, who demanded that the object be removed. In this instance the sphere of consumption was as offensive off the street as on it. Consumption in this context bears a relation to a system of subcultural values that laughs in the face of dominant morality. In the punk shop, nothing was safe. Sexuality was fetishized and recoded to suit a punk identity, and signification was used as a weapon to offend and annoy. For many young women, shopping took on a range of illicit connotations which matched their refusal of a conventional feminine identity.

Conclusion

From the social standpoint, space has a 'dual nature'. On the one hand (in any given society), there is a dual general existence. On the other hand, one (each member of a society under consideration) realities oneself to space, situates oneself in space . . . One places oneself at the centre, designates oneself, measures oneself, and uses oneself as a measure. One is in short a 'subject'. It also implies a location, a place in society, a position. On the other hand, space serves as an intermediary or mediating role: beyond each place or surface, beyond each opaque form, 'one' seeks to apprehend something else. (Lefebvre, 1991)

While ideologies of femininity shape the very experience of women in everyday life, the space of punk as a subcultural alternative provided a place to comprehend the self and to refashion the self in relation to illicit values and codes. The activities that female punks were involved in, such as making and selling punk, bore in some way upon their identity negotiations in the temporal biographies of the females I conversed with. Some of these negotiations extended into other subcultural identities which went far beyond the pure adornment of a punk style.

Punk clothing did not mirror everything it appeared to signify; at times the symbols were meant only to signify chaos and confusion. For some women the flirtation with the sexual codes in the punk wardrobe was not viewed as liberating in any sense of the word. For these women, punk style was modified to suit a less sexually overt set of symbols and signs. As a subculture, punk provided a place to experiment with, a space of open possibility, movement, experimentation, pleasure and dismay.

Later versions of punk, such as the Riot Grrrl movement in the USA and UK, provided direct fora for the challenging of feminine ideologies and a feminine subject positioning. Taking the DIY ethos of punk that had inspired early female bands like The Slits, the Riot Grrrls made music, but beyond that gave a subcultural network of emotional support to young women. Home (1995) argues that this movement is in fact a transformation of punk. The difference between this subculture and punk in the early days is that the women in this space recognize themselves as being firmly situated within patriarchal discourse and problems of 'race' and class. Their very being challenges this subject position and seeks to comprehend something beyond this set of relations.

Punk as a subculture had many means of expression that cannot be equated with a cohesive movement belonging to any one moment in time or space. Likewise the subject nature of experience within any given subculture changes according to the input and actions of those who participate. For many of the women I conversed with as a punk, and as an ex-punk gathering a retrospective account of the subculture, I found that the significance spoke through the way in which many of these women viewed punk as a subtle means of identity negotiation. Punk was therefore viewed as a space to comprehend the self and to experience Otherness. In the life biography of one young woman, the subculture provided a text of pleasure, in which she viewed being a punk as a 'learning experience', belonging to 'a happy family of weirdos'.

Notes

1 There are a number of problems involved in using the terminology of youth subculture. These arise partially from theoretical traditions that have come to be associated with the term. Youth subculture has come to denote 'resistance' in a micro political sense, in terms of a class relation. The analysis I am using retains a notion of resistance, but one that is located within the politics of everyday life. Furthermore, while subculture implies a limited space, the word 'youth' is at times overtly limiting, as it refers to a specific state of temporal development, between childhood and adulthood. In actual terms there is no real age limit on subcultural participation. However, in this analysis most of the women I conversed with were aged between their teens and late twenties. Some accounts were articulated as 'memories' of being punk, while others were gathered from the present at different moments in the temporality of the punk subculture.

2 There are more recent variants of punk that have surfaced in other subcultures, which indicate that the form has been rewritten and the spirit lives on in other movements (e.g. Neo Tribal punks in the USA and the Riot Grrrl movement).

3 In this woman's personal biography, she had encountered familial sexual abuse and as a result viewed male intimacy with caution. In her quiet space she could enjoy the male body from a distance.

4 The legal discourses surrounding the Contagious Diseases Act confined the spread of venereal disease to the responsibility of women, who were viewed as vampires of the nation's health. Women were positioned as moral gatekeepers, and their sexuality was accordingly measured, observed and controlled.

5 Cited in Savage (1991).

6 In this case the punk identity was refashioned to accommodate the practice of body piercing, which was more associated with the fetish scene. The subcultural identity of one place can therefore lead into another.

7 The name of the woman has not been cited for reasons of privacy. This interview was conducted as an oral history, a recollection of being a punk. The woman later associated herself with the thrash metal scene, which was a logical subcultural progression for some punks in this area. Also it was the only place for punks to move into when the momentum of punk was on the decline.

8 The role of consumption has been given attention in McRobbie (1988). A particular feature of punk shops is that second-hand clothes were often on sale. Such clothes gained a new currency despite the fact that they no longer had the value of new clothing. In relation to punk and associated subcultural identities, the second-hand clothing that was considered glamorous was also purchased by gothics and new romantics during the early eighties.

References

Brake, Mike (1980) *The Sociology of Youth and Youth Subcultures*, London: Routledge.
    (1985) *Comparative Youth Cultures*, London: Routledge.
Hebdige, Dick (1979) *Subculture: The Meaning of Style*, London: Routledge.
    (1988) *Hiding in the Light*, London: Comedia.
Home, Stewart (1995) *Cranked Up Really High*, Hove: Codex.
Lefebvre, Henry (1991) *The Production of Space*, Oxford: Blackwell.
McRobbie, Angela (1981) 'Settling accounts with subculture', in Tony Bennett, Colin
    Mercer and Martin Woollacott (eds), *Culture, Ideology and Social Process*, Milton
    Keynes: Open University Press.
    (1988) *Zoot Suits and Second Hand Dresses*, London: Macmillan.
    (ed.) (1991) *Feminism and Youth Culture*, London: Macmillan.
Roman, Christian (ed.) (1988) *Becoming Feminine*, New York: Falmer Press.
Savage, Jon (1991) *England's Dreaming*, London: Faber and Faber.

5 Let's All Have a Disco?
Football, Popular Music and Democratization

Adam Brown

FIFA, however, makes the people who run England's clubs seem the models of modest and sensible ambition . . . FIFA President Havelange's suggestion that football should be played in four quarters, so the telly can run more ads, is grim evidence that money matters more to him than the game. But if that's the direction we're heading in, me and millions like me will stop going. Because this is our game, this beautiful game – it doesn't belong to Coca-Cola or JVC, or to Mars or Gillette . . . So keep your hands off, greedheads. It's a game of two halves – and we like it that way. (Davies, 1991)

. . . they're going towards the realisation of all the hopes we ever had about rock-'n'roll as truly the democratic art form, the democracy has got to begin at home; that is, the everlasting, and totally disgusting walls between artist and audience must come down, élitism must perish, the 'stars' have got to be humanised, de-mythologised, and the audience has got to be treated with more respect. Otherwise it's all a schuck, a rip-off and the music is as dead as the Stones and Led Zep's has become. (Bangs, 1990)

This chapter will consider ways in which it is possible to look at contemporary aspects of popular culture – and in particular the pop music and football industries – in relation to concepts of democratization. It will be focusing on participants in both popular music and football who have, in different ways, challenged the control of their industry, their popular culture. In the first part I will consider some of the difficulties of such an approach, and in the second I will be looking at a football fan organization and aspects of dance music.

In some ways, perhaps, it may seem a strange notion: what should two highly commercial, hierarchical industries have to do with democracy? After all, both to traditional Marxist accounts of popular culture (especially those in the tradition of Theodore Adorno) and to some readings of the negation of meaning in culture (especially the flat hyperreality of Jean Baudrillard), the idea is anathema. Even within the perhaps more sympathetic subcultural approaches, the 'power' (or 'resistance') assigned to subcultural members is more often in terms of a cultural positioning against dominant cultures, rather than in terms of democratization.

I will argue that the answer lies somewhere in the perceived possibilities for change in these industries as exhibited over recent years, as well as in the ever-changing production and consumption of popular culture in general, and pop and football in particular. Perhaps most importantly, I will argue that the concept of democratization is visible in the overt regulation and control of popular culture, and in demands from some participants for a greater control of, and access to, their particular cultural industries.

I will also argue that a combination of positions established within cultural studies and beyond may be needed to appreciate the democratization contained in contemporary popular culture. Thus, at times it is necessary to refer to the ideas of hegemony associated with Gramscian approaches (particularly with reference to the establishment and regeneration of power and consent); notions of postmodernity (particularly with reference to the breaking of established hierarchies and symbolic resistance); and approaches which raise the importance of political economy (for instance, Street's or Frith's work on popular music, and Williams' or Taylor's studies of the football industry).

In this respect, it is possible to use the notion of 'democracy' in three interlinked ways: as a way of looking at the relations of power in the production and consumption of popular culture; at times as a way to describe the content or character of popular culture; and as a way of describing both *institutional* and *non-institutional* aspects of control.

I will first give a characterization of each industry under consideration, which, on the face of it, would suggest that any pretension to democratization is difficult.

The Popular Music Industry

The popular music industry in the 1990s is a voraciously commercial beast. It has been estimated at being worth £19.5 billion worldwide, and is Britain's fourth largest export earner. The phonogram industry is dominated by six huge transnational conglomerates – Sony, Time Warner, EMI-Virgin, Polygram, MCA (owned by the Japanese electronics giant Matsushita) and the BMG Group – which effectively control the industry. Between them they account for over 90 per cent of US sales and between 70 and 80 per cent of worldwide sales. The industry is organized in a particularly hierarchical way: from the aforementioned transnationals, to (subsidiary) major recording companies, to small-scale and independent record labels, to musicians (on various levels) and fans.

Those at the 'top' of the hierarchy use this structure to control those lower down – a fact displayed most spectacularly in George Michael's prolonged attempt to break free from his draconian recording contract with Sony. They also use their position of power to further their own interests over pop's consumers: the controversy over the introduction of CDs, and the phasing out of vinyl, being just one example.

What is also true is that it is increasingly difficult to separate the music from other aspects of the entertainment industry. As Burnett writes:

> The vertical and horizontal integration of the music, film and television production and publishing industries, and alignment of technology development and ownership that is coupled to production and distribution control, has never been more closely linked to the power centres of the media and electronics industries in America, Europe and Japan. (Burnett, 1995)

Certainly, the concentration of these transnational corporations has increased dramatically in the last ten years, with Sony's takeover of the CBS group being only the most spectacular example. This has heightened the debate over the control of media and cultural industries, raising questions over the 'defence' of culture from such irresistible market forces.

The Football Industry

The football industry provides something of a different character. Direct control on a global scale is here exercised not by transnationals, but through a rigid structure of the game's ruling bodies – FIFA, UEFA and the national associations (in England, the FA). These determine the rules of the game, control the major tournaments at all levels, and can legislate against and punish individuals, clubs and national teams involved. While being controlled by very different sorts of bodies to the phonographic industry, football has in the last ten years, however, become increasingly dominated by commercial concerns.

The 1990 World Cup in Italy has been cited as a watershed in football's realization of its money-making potential, raising £33.6 million from rights to televise 66 hours of football, among TV companies which were anxious to maximize ratings figures and therefore advertising revenue. In England this has resulted in a restructuring of the game, with the formation of a breakaway FA Premier League (from the previously four-division Football League) in 1992. The Premier League then negotiated a five-year,

£305 million television deal with Rupert Murdoch's Sky satellite channel. At the time of writing, negotiations are under way at all levels of the game for new television contracts which are likely to break all previous records, and further restructuring seems likely.

On the face of it, then, football is governed by official bodies which have at least some semblance of democracy (clubs, nations and continental organizations have varying degrees of voting rights at their respective levels of football). Increasingly, however, those who determine the development of the game are transnational media empires (such as Murdoch's) and the major advertisers (such as Coca-Cola), who see televised football as an important way of selling their products.

Indeed, FIFA has in recent years been accused of 'selling the soul of the game' purely in the interests of attracting more money from television and advertisers. For example, under the draconian leadership of Joao Havelange, numerous changes in the rules of football have been implemented and proposed by FIFA. The most recent of these has been the attempt – against much opposition – to widen and heighten the size of the goals to increase the numbers of goals scored, and therefore (it is presumed) the attractiveness of the game to television audiences, not least in the previously unbroken market of the USA.

At a more local level, football authorities and football clubs are able to exercise an equally draconian control over their 'consumers', football supporters. Changes in the consumption of football have been imposed often against the wishes of the vast majority of fans. In England, for instance, the introduction of all-seater stadia, and a dramatic increase in prices of admission imposed by clubs eager to maximize incomes, have angered many fans. This has been followed by similar moves, for example, in Germany.[1] Both football authorities and individual clubs are able to impose all kinds of restrictions on the consumption of the game (and therefore on the character and meaning of the popular culture) against the wishes of fans, and indeed are able to change the very nature of football fandom.

Problems for Democratization

The development and power of the integrated, concentrated, global media industries which increasingly dominate both pop and football would seem to suggest – rather than a democratization of popular culture – intersect on an ever more regular basis, as Redhead (1995) among others has argued. This has been visible with the increasing use of censorship against different forms of popular music (mostly the recorded form); and in football with the introduction of legislation in the UK to control the activities of football supporters.

Also on a general note, both cultural industries illustrate a degree of control over their product which takes little account of other participants lower down their hierarchies – footballers, musicians and fans. Increasingly, the ability of individuals and organizations to determine the production and consumption of cultural products is determined by those organizations' and individuals' economic power, although this is neither complete nor overriding. Further, it is not now necessary for those individuals and organizations to be connected directly to the cultural product (as is the case with advertisers).

What makes the democratization of popular culture (in this case, football and music) even more unlikely, it would seem, is that in both cases those at the very bottom of the hierarchies are huge, fairly disparate masses of people. The sheer number of people involved in football and popular music differentiates them from other cultural industries, as amateur participants and as consumers. It has been estimated that aggregate attendances at football matches in England for the 1993–4 season topped 15 million. Worldwide sales of LPs in all formats in 1990 have been estimated at 2,555 million units. While both these figures inevitably include people who watch two or more football matches, or who buy more than one LP, they do indicate huge numbers of people. What is more, these are the people who actually *buy* the cultural product on sale, and do not include those who merely listen to music on the radio, at nightclubs, etc., or those who watch football on television, listen to commentaries on the radio, or read the press coverage.

Participants, then, are not an easily identified or quantifiable group, and their sheer breadth and depth would make any notion of representation difficult, even if that representation had any potential against the might of controlling interest described above. In fact, in terms of representation, we are considering almost everybody.

Combined with this is the fact that various interests seem to desire an ever more passive audience in both cultural industries. Through commercial initiatives, as well as legislative actions, there appear to be processes of pacifying audiences more than ever. Again, and perhaps ironically, it could be argued that the passive nature of audiences of the cultural industries (or culture industry) which Adorno so famously described ('to be carried away by anything at all . . . compensates for their barren and impoverished existence') is more appropriate than ever. Certainly, the process in English football over the last five years (changes in consumption at the stadium, for instance) and legislative actions against participants in popular music (particularly with reference to rave or house culture) could support such a thesis.

Legislation

How, then, can we consider democratization in relation to football and
popular music? To begin with, the process by which law and policy intersect with popular culture is something of a double-edged sword. On one
hand, for example, in terms of the infringement of civil liberties of football
and popular music fans contained in the Criminal Justice and Public Order
Act 1994, this can hardly be said to be aiding democratization. However, it
does represent a reduction in the autonomy of bodies within those industries to act, as they have largely done in the post-war years, as they want.

Most recently, the European Court has ruled that both the transfer system
which operates in European football and the restrictions on the number of
foreigners who can play in a club team are illegal. The 'Bosman Case' as it
has become known (after the Belgian player, Jean-Marc Bosman, who took
UEFA to the court), has illustrated the limits of the power of a football
authority across a continent. Also, the Labour Party in Britain has recently
issued a Charter for Football which promises that a Labour government will
take a much more proactive role in the running of the game. Legally, too,
football has found that an increasing number of violent incidents on the pitch
are being dealt with by courts of law, rather than by the disciplinary procedures of the Football Association concerned.[2]

The music industry, too, has come under increasing public scrutiny. In
1993 the UK's Monopolies and Mergers Commission investigated the
pricing of compact discs. Although it found in favour of the record companies, the investigation was a serious cause for concern to an industry anxious
to preserve its independence.[3] The raised profile of popular music censorship – the high profile of the censorship lobby in the United States, and its
concomitant rise in the UK – also points to an increase in public interven-
tion in the industry. Finally, the policies of some national governments –
particularly in France, Canada and Australia – which have sought to protect
their 'natural cultures' by creating quotas of 'foreign' music (mostly of
Anglo-American origin) allowed to be broadcast, have been another restric-
tion on the power of the transnational music industry.

While one would not necessarily want to claim some of these actions as
indicators of democratic progress – certainly not in the case of pop censorship – they have illustrated a limit on the powers of the cultural industries
under consideration. It could also be argued that at least the actions of nation
states, law courts and the European Union are under some kind of democratic control through the election process (not that these issues are likely to
make or break governments), whereas football authorities and record
companies are under no such control.

Furthermore, even though media conglomerates seem to be increasing
their influence in both music and football (while not necessarily connected

directly to the cultural product), this has raised concern, certainly in European nations, about their power. This concern has, for example, manifested itself in action by the European Union to limit the opening of its markets to American media corporations in the 1993 General Agreement on Tariffs and Trade (GATT). 'The Europeans', says Burnett, 'rejected a complete opening of their movie, music and other entertainment sectors' and insisted 'that the entertainment sector in its member countries be at least 50% of European origin whenever practicable.' While the Americans lamented that 'people can be controlled in what they want to see and hear', from another standpoint, this could be seen as an important brake on the further concentration and homogenization of an already dangerously monopolistic sector.

I now turn to some other aspects of the football and music industries. I will first consider some general themes in democratization and popular culture, before looking at specific examples.

'Popular' therefore 'Democratic'?

In general terms, popular culture – and this is certainly true of the two cultures under consideration here – seems to display what Stauth and Turner have called an 'egalitarian ethic'. This contrasts with the approaches of those such as Adorno, who argues that mass culture should be regarded as an element within an incorporationist ideology or institution which has the effect of pacifying the masses through the stimulation of false needs via the 'culture industry'. In contrast Stauth and Turner argue that:

> Firstly, we need a dialectic view of the contradictory features of all culture (both high and low), since mass culture contains the potentials of an egalitarian ethic in sharp contrast to the rigid hierarchical divisions embodied in traditional culture. Secondly we need a more positive view of consumption . . . which would avoid the implicit puritanism of the critique of mass culture. (Stauth and Turner, 1988)

The contention that popular culture contains contradictory elements within it – progressive and reactionary, liberating and oppressive, democratic and anti-democratic – is something which has been argued by numerous commentators and seems clear. The impact of Gramscian ideas on cultural studies allowed for the adoption of more flexible approaches to the study of the organization of power and representation in popular culture; indeed, the Gramscian-derived framework of hegemony-ideology-common sense remains the most productive approach to be constructed within cultural studies.

Further, the impact of the 'politics of pleasure' – as an analysis of the enjoyment that participants get from both popular music and football – also needs consideration. De Certeau's and later Fiske's success is to emphasize how subordinate elements may attempt and achieve victories over dominant elements, even within mass, commercial cultural industries such as popular music and football. De Certeau (1984) argues that, while members of popular culture cannot gain control of the production of culture, they do control its consumption – the ways in which it is used. If popular culture has to 'make do' with what is offered to it, it still has the potential to 'make over' these offerings to its own ends. The fandoms and subcultures associated with the football and music industries certainly seem to fit with this model.

The degree to which pleasure is free from ideological constraint is borne out in many accounts of participation in football and music. In this, I would argue, the industries of football and popular music have a democracy almost inherent in their content and operation: celebration, enjoyment, the mass at play are all central to both football and music. Ideas concerning the 'carnivalesque' have been important in establishing Stauth and Turner's more positive view of consumption, as with, for instance, Richard Giulianotti's study of Scottish football fans (see Giulianotti, 1993).

While accepting this, it does not seem possible to extend it as far as Fiske does in his celebratory account of consumption. I would agree with the argument that Fiske's view of the popular becomes so optimistic, so celebratory, that there seems little need to worry about the function of representation in reproducing the status quo. Though we must retain a sense of the transgressive or tactical possibilities of popular culture, it is also essential to retain a sense of the frame within which they are produced, within which even the carnivalesque must be licensed. To rephrase the old Marxist maxim, popular culture produces its own pleasures, but not in circumstances of its own choosing.

However, football and music are usually consumed in mass audiences, where the importance of the shared, collective pleasure is central. The notion of 'the crowd' is important in that it both heightens the pleasure of the consumption of popular music and football and plays a crucial role in its production – indeed, it is difficult to imagine either existing at all without that mass audience (although both can be, and often are, consumed in various ways 'individually'). Here, the consumer in football culture and popular music culture is also very much the producer.

It seems correct to argue, as Stauth and Turner do, that 'modest defence of mass culture through a consideration of the egalitarian feature of mass consumption is associated historically with the democratization of the mass'. Further:

At the very least, we should see a tension or conflict between mass cultural systems, the cultural industry and the cultural élite, since this relationship of conflict in culture simply expresses underlying tensions which are political and economic in character. The existence of mass culture does not necessarily lead to mass incorporation in a dominant culture, since many aspects of mass culture are oppositional.

This is certainly borne out when one considers, for example, the development of the football industry: the imposition of price increases as part of a general modernization programme is an economic policy to alter participation in the industry, and, given the responses of the 'mass' in their opposition to exclusion, it illustrates cultural conflict.

However, more specifically, recent years have shown a politicization of elements of both football and popular music which, in different ways, have been framed around discourses which are either overtly or more subtly debates about the democratization of popular culture. I wish to focus on two examples: the growth of campaigning support organizations in football – illustrated by the Football Supporters' Association – and the politics of some recent movements in popular music, most notably dance or house music. Both examples illustrate, I believe, a concern with the control of the industry *and* the meaning of their culture in a way which challenges the assumptions of contrasting approaches to popular music.

The Football Supporters' Association

As Arthur Hopcraft argued in *The Football Man*:

> The point about football in Britain is that it is not just a sport people take to, like cricket or tennis or running long distances. It is inherent in the people. It is built into the urban psyche, as much a common experience to our children as are uncles and school. It is not a phenomenon: it is an everyday matter. There is more eccentricity in deliberately disregarding it than in devoting a life to it. It has more significance in the national character than theatre has. Its sudden withdrawal from the people would bring deeper disconsolation than to deprive them of television. The way we play the game, organise it and reward it reflect the kind of community we are. (Hopcraft, 1968)

Let us consider ways in which participants in the football industry have organized and campaigned, and attempted to democratize the industry. I will focus upon one organization, the Football Supporters' Association (FSA), as a representative body of football fans. The FSA represents a politicization of English football's fandom and an economic and ideological challenge to the hegemony of the industry. It should be noted, although there is not space to consider this in any detail, that this politicization has occurred alongside the rise of independent fanzines and other club-based supporter organizations which have been particularly prominent in recent years.

The development of the culture of football support has been marked by a concern over the direction of the game's modernization. As we have seen above, the role of FIFA – particularly its desire to make football ever more attractive to advertisers through television – has had a dramatic effect on the global scene. The staging of the 1994 World Cup in the USA is only the most obvious example of this obsession. In England such concerns have manifested themselves through a number of developments.

First is the frustration felt by fans since the early 1980s over their lack of input into the game, and concerns with the perceived demise of football at the time (financial crises, maladministration on a chaotic level, and the real and perceived problems of hooliganism being the most obvious). Second is the commercialization of football – the introduction of advertising, battles over television rights, and the desire of bigger clubs to earn a bigger share of money available, resulting in 1992 in the formation of the FA Premier League. Third is the mistreatment of the fans: government obsessed by law and order implementing more draconian control of fans, the state of many of the nation's grounds and the threats to safety that these posed, as well as the continuing refusal to pay attention to the warnings and wishes of supporters.

The FSA was founded in 1985, perhaps professional English football's worst ever year.[4] Its aim has always been to influence the development of the game in the interests of football supporters. As such, it is something of a unique organization in cultural industries: there is, for instance, no equivalent grouping in the music industry. The FSA thus represents an essential factor in any assessment of the democratization of popular culture – its ability to influence and resist the changes in a modernizing football industry will be crucial to the development of the game. The FSA has been cited as one element in a successful cultural contestation in football, and as such it is important in its role as challenging the football hierarchy's hegemony.

Before 1985 only the National Federation of Football Supporter Clubs represented the general interests of football supporters. However, without a national individual membership, it represented only a somewhat official aspect of football fandom. Many of the supporters' clubs were in one way or another tied to their clubs, and were involved in raising money for the club, facilitating relations between supporters and clubs, but rarely influencing the direction or decisions of the football industry.

The FSA was formed following the Heysel disaster in Belgium where thirty-nine Juventus fans died. It was felt that there was a need for a national organization that would represent and campaign on behalf of football supporters, in view of the hostile attitude of the Thatcher government and the hysteria that accompanied these events in much of the media. In 1985 the FSA correctly realized not only that there was a crying need for an organization without the Federation's historical baggage, but that the organization should represent *all* fans, whether members of a supporters' club or not.[5]

The key to the FSA's success has always been its ability to gain media attention and achieve a profile far above that which its membership would suggest. This has been true from the early post-Heysel days, to the tragedy after Hillsborough and into the current era, where FSA National Committee members regularly meet with the FA and Premier League, and where they are instrumentally involved in the establishment of the Premier League's Supporter Panels (club-based arenas for discussing issues important to football fans). As Rogan Taylor argues, the 'current representation of supporters to Government, football authorities and various other bodies – though hardly satisfactory – is more frequent and serious than ever before' (Taylor, 1992).

Through the chairmanship of Rogan Taylor, the media were skilfully handled and the organization was able to sound both credible to ordinary supporters and acceptable to the (often highly suspicious) media. The FSA, argues Taylor, kept up a series of high profile, public campaigns which kept it in the media spotlight and, inevitably, drew a stark contrast to the Federation's historic failure to grab the media's attention. It was a deliberate tactic by the FSA, recognizing the central role that the media plays in cultural industries. The strategies employed by the FSA, argues Taylor:

> led the national media – probably for the first time – into the habit of consulting supporters' representatives over a period of great public and Government concern about the future of football and its fans. In the end, the FSA's efforts raised the public awareness of supporters (as opposed to 'hooligans') to a level that also raised the Federation's profile.[6]

Of course, the FSA also had a good deal to complain about. The 1980s proved to be a time of increasing legislation aimed at controlling football supporters, spurred on by a prime minister who rarely hid her dislike of the game and its people.

The FSA was and is a vital protesting element in football fandom in a wide variety of areas: the post-Heysel trial of Liverpool supporters; the blame heaped on ordinary fans by the banning of English teams from European football; the draconian and increasingly military surveillance and control of fans inside football grounds; the blanket assumptions (in Britain and abroad) that *any* violence involving English gangs (especially at the 1988 European Championships) was necessarily the English fans' fault; the identity card scheme entailed in the 1989 Football Spectators Act; the (mis)management of English fans at the World Cup in Italy in 1990, where the FSA ran successful 'fan embassies' to provide information and an information channel to authorities; the Taylor Report, and in particular the all-seater stipulation; the formation of the Premier League and the deal with BSkyB; huge increases in the cost of admission to football; and the problem of racism in the game.

At every turn and in every major development of the regulation and control of football in England since 1985, the FSA has been there to offer criticism, campaigns and alternatives. If nothing else, and this is in no sense an uncritical assessment, its mere presence has been one of the (only) constant factors pulling the balance of power within football, however negligibly, toward the supporters. Jary *et al.* have argued that:

> The organisation operates as a 'pressure group' seeking to represent the grass roots opinion of football supporters. It has established a regional structure, and it has opened up contacts with the police and especially with the media that have made it today a prominent participant in football politics. In brief the aims of the organisation are: (1) to improve the image of the game, (2) to improve the standard of the services provided for fans, and (3) to achieve representation for fans at every level of the game's hierarchies. (Jary *et al.*, 1991)

Further, in line with an assessment of participants who are low in the hierarchy of cultural industries, a bottom-up analysis is appropriate:

> It is the maintenance wherever possible of a subservience of commercialism and private interest . . . which is the *central* aspect of what fanzines and the FSA as a social movement have set out to preserve. It is in this *above all*, and also in their participatory, grass roots, spontaneous, collegial modes of organisation, that we would most wish to present fanzines [and the FSA] as constituting a highly significant instance of the existence of cultural contestation over the central orientation and values of modern sport. Moreover it has been to date, at least in part, a *successful* contestation with the increasingly insistent commercial tendencies in modern spectator sport, which threaten to incorporate it fully as part of a centrally managed commercial – and commodified – leisure *provision* often presented by its advocates as mere 'modernisation' when the reality in fact is that choices between competing forms of leisure organisation remain.

Indeed, it has been argued that, certainly in the early years of the FSA, the organization formed part of an alternative football network with the fanzines, especially in that the FSA is an organization whose fortunes appear in some ways coterminous with the flowering of football fanzine culture, whose membership includes many producers and readers of fanzines. What can now be added to this in the years since 1990 are the independent supporters' organizations, which have a more focused, club-based approach. This places the FSA as part of a 'successful cultural contestation' in the field of football; there is a refusal, argue Jary *et al.*, of the position of being mere 'recipients' of [football] culture, very much in opposition to Adorno's arguments on mass cultures.

The FSA, in conjunction with the fanzine explosion and more recently the club-based independent supporters' associations, has built up a 'culture of opposition' in the game. This is reflected in developments in football fandom in several positive ways: a change in atmosphere occurred at football grounds as hooliganism declined and became less fashionable; football fanzines became a national phenomenon as numbers of titles increased from around 35 in 1988–9 to over 1000 at present; a cultural crossover with music became discernible on the terraces of England; and fans began to demonstrate actively against what they saw as wrong in the game, and what they wished to change.

The FSA was claiming in 1990 that: 'We are backed by a network of independently produced supporters' publications that have grown from nothing in 1985 to projected sales of 1.5 million in 1990. Last year we presented a 400,000 signature petition to parliament against compulsory ID cards.' In anticipation of the World Cup in 1990, the FSA claimed that:

> The World Cup provides us with an opportunity to spread news of our organisation further afield and play a vital role for improving the tainted perception of England's football followers. Our aims centre round providing an information and advice service for law-abiding fans, marginalising the troublemakers by providing positive activities for true football fans.[7]

Despite such evidence, however, the FSA is still a relatively weak organization, certainly in the terms of the football industry hierarchy: the enormous power of commercial interests, of the football organizations and, even at a club level, of the football clubs' boards of directors always outweighs the power of the FSA. The democracy that the FSA strives for is rarely realized. In this sense, it is possible to criticize some of the more optimistic interpretations of the FSA's position.

The organization faces some serious problems. First, in the most general terms it is trying to represent an impossible-to-define group of citizens in opposition to very easily identified persons and interests at the top of the industry's hierarchy. It is trying to gain representation where, as Taylor illustrates, little has existed in the industry's 100-year history. The FSA is trying to have its opinions listened to when most clubs know that they can rely on the brand loyalty of supporters to carry on providing the clubs' revenue.[8]

Despite these structural weaknesses, the organization has faced problems of its own. Its actual membership strength has been hard to define due to dual membership categories of local and national status (Jary *et al.* say that it is variously stated as between 5,000 and 40,000; the latter figure seems ludicrously overoptimistic). What is certain is that its membership reflects no more than a vocal, articulate minority of football supporters, nor does it reflect the high media profile that the organization has been able to maintain.

This discrepancy with the media has been a result of the organization's short history and the tactics adopted in actively seeking a media profile, a strategy which perhaps reflects the organization's top-heavy nature. Compounding problems has been the lack of a high-profile, unifying campaign to win supporters' imaginations in the years since the ID card campaign. Although the all-seater proposals were opposed by most football fans, this opposition failed to manifest itself as, or the FSA failed to make it, an effective national campaign. The more recent opposition to admission increases may, however, prove to be the mass campaign that the organization needs.

The current chair, Tim Crabbe, outlined a key weakness of the FSA in 1994:

> The FSA made itself heard during the eighties, but we have never been a mass organization. The club-based nature of football support in Britain meant that those fans who did get motivated drifted off into fanzines and club-based Independent Supporters' Associations (ISAs). Whilst these developments have been important, issues still remain which require responses at the national level.

However, given the structural and inevitable weaknesses, there are signs that the organization is addressing these problems. In line with the contention of Jary *et al.* that the FSA and fanzines should form some kind of alliance capable of 'successful cultural contestation', the development of links between fanzines, ISAs and the FSA is now a high priority for the FSA.[9] Further, there are moves to create one national supporter organization which accommodates such club-based concerns.

The FSA has proved itself to be an effective and articulate campaigner on behalf of football supporters. It has had some considerable successes – notably, the opposition to the ID card scheme, the England fan embassies abroad and its campaign against racism. However, beyond these single issues, the FSA has played a crucial role in altering the perceptions of football supporters held by the media, public, football authorities and government. Admittedly, this has been in conjunction with the emergence of fanzines and changes in football fan culture, but the FSA has played a crucial role. As such, it has managed to counter a hegemony by creating an alternative and redefining the meaning of its culture: it has, to use Gramsci's words, gone some way to creating a different common sense with regard to football supporters. This may well be its greatest achievement.

In terms of differing notions of democratization, then, the FSA has been able to challenge the meanings of a culture, as well as influencing (to a degree) the control of the industry. Certainly, given the overwhelming power of the commercial and football interests against the FSA, and given the lack of an alternative representative of supporters' interests, an increase in fans' influence is essential for any serious democratization of the game.

Popular Music and the Democratization of Popular Culture

But the capacity to face the world, to create yourself, your own clothes, your own music, to be independent, all these are lessons. In this sense the recent acid-house movement has realised this 'do-it-yourself' project: home-based electronic equipment and sampling allow the production of your own music using the most heterogeneous musical sources . . . Popular music has been for several decades the channel whereby those preoccupations which belong to avant-garde art are democratised. (Mignon, in Redhead, 1993)

As with the previous discussion of democratization and the football industry, this section will look at the ways in which developments in popular music have raised questions of democratization. In this I will look at both the production and the consumption of music in relation to issues of control and democratization.

Through a number of front-cover articles in the music press and style magazines, it could be argued that a 'new' politicized pop emerged in Britain in the early 1990s. Yet for many, pop music developments in the years at the end of the 1980s and the early 1990s have been ones of 'hedonism in hard times' – the pursuit of pleasure as an escape from the effects of a recession-hit economy. It has been argued that this has been most graphically illustrated in the house music scene, where a drug culture of enjoyment and dance seemed far removed from previous analysis of punk (and other music, and youth) subcultures. Richard Jobson, ex-lead singer of 1970s new wave band The Skids, lamented the lack of overt rebellion in pop in the late 1980s and 1990s:

A tidal wave of hedonism spread through the eighties culminating in a new youth movement – acid house. It was a dance and drug culture that, like punk, panicked the authorities into reacting as though the country was in revolt, but they needn't have bothered . . . rave was about as potent as a cup of cocoa.[10]

This approach has been echoed by others, such as ex-punk and *New Musical Express* (*NME*) journalist Tony Parsons.[11]

However, a number of different examples of what can loosely be termed 'musical movements' have pointed to a politicization of popular music; a radicalism which owes much to discourses of empowerment and even democratization. This is true of Riot Grrrl,[12] of determinedly 'anti-racist' elements in contemporary pop, and of the emergency of 'new punks' – the New Wave of New Wave, as the *NME* tagged them. All of these seemed to illustrate a concern in emerging new music with issues of access, control and, either overtly or by implication, democratization.

However, it is some aspects of house music on which I wish to concentrate here.

House music and democratization

The dance music explosion which began in the UK at the end of the 1980s has illustrated some important developments in the democratization of the music industry. I will briefly consider three areas in which I think dance music has impacted on the issues of politicization and democratization in the music industry. These are the democratization of the sound and musical experience; the challenge to the music industry's hegemony; and the politicization of dance music.

I will not attempt any comprehensive analysis of the impact of the latest phase in dance music's development, given space restrictions (house music has received a more adequate appraisal elsewhere). I shall not seek, either, to explore the myriad of distinctions evident in house music, and may interchange house with rave and techno, no doubt much to the consternation of purists.

Democratization of the musical experience

Derived from a collection of 1970s disco, early 1980s synth-pop, Euro pop, Hi-NRG and the black electronic house/techno of Detroit and Chicago, the British house scene has had an important impact upon the ways in which music is produced, understood and consumed. Central to its production has been the use of the sampler: the ability to lift sounds (bass, keyboards, vocals) electronically from other sources, and combine them with an electronic drum pattern (sometimes also sampled) and also sometimes original vocals or instrumentation.

Simon Reynolds has argued that sampling has both democratic and undemocratic aspects. He says that it takes the fictitious nature of recording even further, creating events that 'could never have happened' and he argues that house has 'a kind of democracy of sounds'. Certainly, sampling and house have been able to open up all kinds of musical possibilities – an ability to mix and match previously created sounds, to develop new ones and to break barriers between artist and consumer. Reynolds again:

> Hip hop and house are the latest phases is an unwritten (because unwriteable) history of black pop: a history determined not by sacred cow artists but by producers and backroom technicians, a history conditioned not by individuals and their notions of the meaning of music (as with rock) but by changes in technology, in what it is possible to do with sound.

In such a sense, house provides a challenge to traditional (rock) notions of music making and authenticity, posing a challenge (aesthetically and organizationally) to assumptions about popular music. House does not value what Frith has termed 'rock authenticity', ideas of originality (in the strict sense of the term), or production (where the artist is seen as having some kind of primary physical contact with an instrument). Sampling does produce original music, but it does so partly by copying, appropriating, changing and recontextualizing previously recorded sounds. In this sense it marks a departure from previous forms of pop music.

Sheffield techno artists LFO have highlighted the departure that has been made with the development of electronic and digital music.

> It must be hard to make music with guitars . . . Or hard to do something new. A guitar can only make a few notes really . . . On the other hand a synth has got hundreds of sounds on it and there are hundreds of different synths that all sound different from each other. If people say it must be easy to do what we do, well, it is in that it's easy to get a new sound out of a keyboard and it's hard to get a new sound out of a guitar.

Of course, such an attitude has provoked reactions from the 'rock orthodoxy', claiming that house is not 'real' or 'authentic' music, and that, rather than democratizing music, it has just allowed talentless people to make records. However, the *opportunities* illustrate a democratic potential in the ability to produce sound, a cultural terrrain over which such battles of access and quality (an unavoidably subjective term) can be fought.

Bearing in mind the arguments that a sense of the social and economic conditions in which such popular culture occurs must be maintained, Reynolds (1990) is absolutely correct to argue:

> Sampling may well produce a groundswell of bands making their own music (as with punk) but those individuals will still be buying music-making technology from companies that are vertically linked to the major record companies (as with punk). Also, although sampling makes certain effects more

attainable to the impatient, it can't democratize the unequal distribution of brilliance.

Linked to these ideas about the democratization of the music is the democ-ratization of the musical experience; a consumption- rather than a production-based development. House music's consumptive 'spiritual home' is the rave, a phenomenon which generated a large-scale media moral panic in the late 1980s along with legislation to regulate it. This echoes arguments outlined about above the democracy of the mass, of the popular, especially in an otherwise increasingly privatized musical consumption.

In some senses this experience recalls de Certeau's *jouissance* (yet here a collective one), an ability to escape, through intense pleasure, the confines of society's rules. Reynolds recognizes this when he argues that:

> House is a kind of pleasure factory (an organisation, in fact) . . . If house, acid, new beat etc., are radical, it's a radicalism that's inseparable from their simple effectiveness, pure pleasure immediacy . . . No delay, no mediation, but a direct interface between the music's pleasure circuitry and the listener's nervous system.

Furthermore, I would say, raves support the argument that the audience, the consumer, can also be the producer. Here the similarity with football is striking: the crowd is not just a collection of passive individuals who have little or no impact upon the 'event' which is being consumed; they are inte-gral to it. Raves without 'consumers' as with football without crowds, lose their social (and democratic) meaning: they are 'living cultures' made possible only by those who attend them. This very much recalls Lester Bangs' notion of 'the disgusting walls' between producer and consumer coming down (Bangs, 1991).

This was certainly a feature of house music in its early years, yet some would argue it is now visible *only* in what have been termed 'true under-ground clubs', and although DJs have to some extent replaced the role of the band or the performer, there is a strong sense in which nobody even cares who made the music, that there is a deconstruction of stardom.

It would, however, be difficult to maintain that this has seriously threat-ened the music industry's hierarchy, or that it has been expressed in economic terms in relation to developments discussed at the start of this chapter. The creation of star DJs, for instance, supports the argument that, if the scene is 'democratic', it is democratic with a capitalist inflection; the music is pure product, consumer-tested on the dance floor, with an in-built obsolescence factor. This raises questions of organization and of politiciza-tion in house music, to which I now turn.

Rave organization and democratization

Funhouse Promotions in Manchester provides an example of the house experience in organizational terms. For much of 1990–2, Funhouse, or Freedom To Party (as it was originally titled as a students' society) set up raves, many 'illegal' or certainly on the edge of legality. As Andy Stratford of Funhouse argues, it was a response to the difficulties faced by both consumers and producers of house music: the restrictions imposed upon 'pay-parties' by government legislation and licensing, as well as the existing obstacles (distribution, retail, public 'performance') to house music producers playing that music in public. Stratford says:

> The established business can't deal with either white labels or the type of events which we want to go to. Freedom To Party was organized because it became illegal to organize paying raves, and the business couldn't deal with the hundreds of self-financed, self-produced white labels. The aim for us is the music, the feeling, the energy, not the promotion of the artist or creation of profit. What is developing is a split between the underground and the business.

This declaration of intent is, it should be noted, in sharp contrast to the strongly entrepreneurial spirit of many initial promoters of house music, such as chair of the Association of Dance Party Promoters, Tony Colston-Hayter. What the Funhouse organization did was to organize raves in disused warehouses, where publicity was necessarily word-of-mouth to avoid legal action, and where there was no charge for admission (although collections were made to help with costs). DJs would play music mostly available only on very limited edition 12-inch, white label releases, with no record company involvement, which used a completely separate distribution system from established ones. It was, in effect, a complete by-pass of the music 'industry'.

What is particularly interesting about this type of organization is that it is both a product of, and a challenge to, existing hierarchies. As Stratford has argued, restrictions and controls from government and industry have forced house music's producers and consumers to establish their own networks of production, distribution and consumption. In a sense the creation of a 'new underground' at the turn of the decade challenged both the record industry hierarchy (the underground is an alternative network) and the state (through rave's illegality). It is these challenges which prompted sections of the Criminal Justice and Public Order Act 1994.

Although Funhouse's example offers a plausible alternative to the industry's hegemony, more recent discourses have suggested that the situation is now more complicated than a straight oppositional one, recalling

Reynold's assertion that house has an in-built 'capitalist inflection'. For instance, house has in many ways become mainstream, and major labels have learned to incorporate it into their rosters. Debates on house music and the music industry at the 1994 'In the City' convention illustrated the antagonisms and conflicts that exist, with some maintaining that house should remain underground and that the operation of the major labels was 'stifling creativity'.

This indicates alternative views concerning the position of house music in relation to the music industry's hierarchy (and the state): one an incorporationist stance and the other a separatist one. It not only complicates the simple 'house music versus the music business' opposition, but also raises questions of incorporation and emasculation, similar to debates about punk in the 1970s. What does seem to be different with house music, however, is that it has maintained an element of independence; it has remained on the edge of incorporation, for a considerable time, unlike previous genres. Certainly, the house scene seems to offer a greater democratic potential, and house music's historical location – given the advances in reproductive electronic media and the ease of independent production – has had an important effect in developing this potential.

Politics in house

One further area needs to be discussed briefly, and that is the impact of law on popular culture, an impact which has seen the politicizing of house music and the rave scene. The Entertainments (Increased Penalties) Act 1990 (also known as the 'Bright Bill') and the introduction of new police powers in the Criminal Justice and Public Order Act have given a greater political dimension to house music. This dimension was certainly less evident in the early, hedonistic years of acid house, as well as in commentaries about house, such as Simon Reynolds' description of it as a 'pure pleasure immediacy'.

The crossovers between ravers and New Age Travellers produced a second moral panic in relation to house music, largely due to the media attention given to one outdoor festival at Castlemorton, in the summer of 1992. The legislative reaction was the Criminal Justice and Public Order Act 1994. This piece of legislation, as with the Bright Bill earlier, has forced house music's consumers and producers into confrontation with the state.

In the weeks before the introduction of the Bright Bill, flyers were distributed in Manchester about a demonstration against it. The flyer read:

THE PARTY'S OVER! New Laws, March 9th. Without your support we will have to return to the ancient 2am licensing laws and have the government decide our form of entertainment. We have come this far together so do not be defeated at the last hurdle. The new laws mean that you can be imprisoned for attending a party as well as organising one. It is up to every one of us to continue the stance against the oppression of dance. THIS REVOLUTION WILL BE TELEVISED. Hard Core Uproar.

Similarly, following the announcement of the Criminal Justice Bill hippy-house act, Eat Static issued a statement saying that: 'The government is frightened of the sheer popularity of something they don't understand and have no control over. The new bill won't stop partying, but it will create extra tension and more hassle.' The hedonistic pursuit of Reynolds (pure pleasure) had turned into a conflict with the state. It forced politicization on a musical scene which, in its hedonism, was almost completely removed from established politics.

This is perhaps illustrated most graphically by the specificity of the Criminal Justice and Public Order Act 1994. Clauses 58 to 64 of the Act were specifically designed to give the police extensive powers to prevent outdoor raves and festivals taking place, and mean that those attending as well as those organizing raves or festivals now risk prison sentences. Perhaps most significantly, the Act unprecedentedly targets house music. Clause 58 defines 'music' as wholly or predominantly characterized by the emission of a succession of repetitive beats. This is thought to be the only time that legislation has attempted to define a specific popular music genre and to criminalize it, and recalls the cultural specificity of the targeting of football supporters' civil liberties.

What is very clear from the responses of many participants in the music industry, and those involved in house music in particular, is that the new legislation is an attack on *their* music. The specificity of the legislation seems to support such an assessment, but it has certainly also forced politicization on a particular musical genre and its participants.

While it is not yet possible to assess the impact of the new legislation on ravers and travellers, it seems certain that it will increase the conflict between popular youth cultures and the state. Clearly the fear is that civil liberties issues in house music will become central: yet it has also confirmed that the law has had a considerable influence on certain developments in the musical and cultural form of house music.

The democratization of sound and experience, as well as the challenge of alternative organizational networks which house has presented, has been complemented in recent years by a politicization of the house and rave cultures. Although it has not been possible to discuss all of these developments fully, it is important to recognize the democratizing elements which have accompanied this biggest of recent youth/music cultures.

Participation and Conflict

What is central in both football and music is that they confront the problem of democracy and popular culture on a number of levels. On one level, issues are taken up where participation itself is threatened. This is true whether one considers the 'global' power blocs outlined above or, more locally, the threats expressed on the ground: the restrictions on participation and the meaning of 'football support' in England through the introduction of all-seater stadia, price increases and the restructuring of the game to the dictates of television; and the ability to make music, the means of enjoying that music and legislative control aimed at one particular genre of music.

On another level, questions are raised about the ownership of culture, its regeneration and threats to that regeneration. Important here are the meaning of being a footballer supporter in the 1990s, the creation of a house music scene outside the established music industry, and the conflict which exists between these and the 'establishment' outlined at the beginning of the chapter.

Third, both examples illustrate concerns with control, where control is about the exercise of power, and democracy is the check on that power. In this there seems to be a determination in some sections of popular culture overtly to challenge attempts at control – whether that is a restructuring of the football industry, or legislative clamps on participation in house music. This is because, above all, such attempts at control or restructuring are really attempts to define the meaning of, and participation in, these popular cultures.

Notes

1   German 'Fanprojekts' organized several demonstrations in 1994–5 against the intro-
    duction of all-seater stadia, protests which were backed by the Football Supporters'
    Association in England, which had already suffered by their introduction.
2   The Scottish Football Association recently lost its right to impose a twelve-match ban
    on Everton striker Duncan Ferguson, as the law courts ruled that because Ferguson
    had already served a prison sentence for head-butting an opponent, any further
    punishment represented the SFA acting beyond its powers. Radio 5 Live, 2 February
    1996.
3   'In the City', international music convention, Manchester, September 1994.
4   1985 was probably the worst year for the image of professional football (and espe-
    cially its fans) in its (by then) 100-year history. The trouble and tragedies at Bradford
    City's Valley Parade stadium, Birmingham City and Luton, and most infamously the
    deaths of 39 Juventus fans at the Heysel Stadium, made for a disastrous year for foot-
    ball and its fans. Only the tragedy of Hillsborough, where 95 (now 96) Liverpool
    supporters died on 9 April 1989, matched these events in terms of genuine horror
    and its attendant media moral panic.
5   Another organization did appear briefly on the scene. Launched at Reading and called
    Supporters United, it failed to sustain itself.

6 *No More Heroes*, BBC TV Scotland, 1993: video in Manchester Institute for Popular Culture archive, Manchester Metropolitan University.
7 At Italia 90 the FSA ran an 'embassy' for fans.
8 Bill Borrows, former editor of Manchester City Fanzine, *Blueprint*, has argued, 'Football isn't a business in the normal sense for one very important reason, and that is brand loyalty to the club. That's why it's not the same as marketing chocolate bars or washing machines.' Interview with the author.
9 A national network of independents has been established recently, with the full encouragement of FSA. Several of these are not affiliates of the FSA.
10 In a 1993 TV programme looking at youth culture in the 1990s.
11 Parsons has argued that this lack of 'rebellion' is mirrored in the lack of new talent, saying: 'Where is the new stuff? Simply, there isn't much. There's a souped-up disco called techno and a bit of unreconstituted heavy metal, but that's about it. Pop music, like the culture that spawned it, is suddenly barren.'
12 Lucy McKenzie, a Scottish Riot Grrrl: 'The main point about Riot Grrrl is realizing that you can do anything for yourself, though when I got into it I didn't really do anything. I thought I couldn't because I was just a fifteen-year-old girl – there's no way that I could ever put on a gig, be in a band or write a magazine, nobody would be interested in it. And I just found out that you can, that your ideas are just as important as a man in a suit.' *No More Heroes*, BBC TV Scotland, 1993.

References

Bangs, Lester (1991) *Psychotic Reactions and Carburrettor Dung*, London: Serpent's Tail.
Burnett, R. (1995) *The Global Jukebox*, London: Routledge.
Davies, Pete (1991) *All Played Out*, London: Mandarin.
De Certeau, Michel (1984) *The Practice of Everyday Life*, Berkeley, CA: University of California Press.
Giulianotti, Richard (1993) *A Model of the Carnivalesque?*, Working Papers in Popular Cultural Studies No. 6.
Hopcraft, Arthur (1968) *The Football Man: People and Passions in Soccer*, Harmondsworth: Penguin.
Jary, David, John Horne and Tony Bucke (1991) 'Football fanzines and football culture', *Sociological Review*, vol. 39, no. 3.
Redhead, Steve (ed.) (1993) *Rave Off*, Aldershot: Avebury.
—— (1995) *Unpopular Cultures*, Manchester: Manchester University Press.
Reynolds, Simon (1990) *Blissed Out*, London: Serpent's Tail.
Stauth, S. and B. Turner (1988) 'Nostalgia, postmodernism and the critique of mass culture', *Theory, Culture and Society*, vol. 5, no. 2/3.
Taylor, Rogan (1992) *Football and its Fans: Supporters and their Relations with the Game 1885–1985*, Leicester: Leicester University Press.

6 Rave Culture:
Living Dream or
Living Death?

Simon Reynolds

'Rave is dead', or so the pundits say. Yet there's a sense in which it's bigger than ever. Not only is the spectrum of nineties youth culture dominated by the ever-widening delta of post-rave scenes – trance, ambient, handbag house, garage, jungle, happy hardcore, gabba, Scottish bouncy techno, Megadog-style crusty-rave, *ad infinitum* – but it also seems obvious that more people are involved in the weekender/ecstasy lifestyle than ever, as veteran ravers hang on in there, while each year produces a wave of new recruits. But as for the rave myth, the ideal of love, peace, unity, positivity – well, that's been smelling funny for quite a while.

Alive, but dead; more popular than ever, but a cultural cul-de-sac – this is, of course, how people have felt about rock music for decades. When Johnny Rotten sneered 'Ever felt like you've been cheated?' on stage at Winterlands in 1978, it was meant to be the death-knell of rock 'n' roll. Thirteen years later, with 'Smells like teen spirit', Nirvana could still find exhilarating musical life in the reiteration of Rotten's message (rebellion is a con, a sales pitch, mere grease for the wheels of commerce). Talk of the death of rock or the death of rave refers not the exhaustion of the music's formal possibilities, then, but to the seeping away of meaning, the loss of a collective sense of going somewhere. This chapter looks at the ways in which rave culture – in so far as it has proved incapable of delivering on its utopian promise – has turned from living dream to living death. And it suggests that the very notion of 'rave culture' may in fact be a contradiction in terms.

Disunity

Just as the Woodstock convergence gave way to the fragmentation of seventies rock, just as punk split into factions based on disagreements about what punk was about and what was the way forward, so too has rave's E-sponsored unity inevitably refractured along class, race and regional lines. Each post-rave fragment seems to have preserved one aspect of rave culture at the expense of the others. House music, in its more song-full, hands-in-the-air, handbag form, has reverted to mere disco, the soundtrack to trad Saturday Nite fever. Progressive house and garage is just your pre-rave metropolitan clubland coked-out élitism back in full effect.

Techno, ambient and electronica strip rave of its, well, raveyness, to fit a white studenty sensibility; it's the new progressive rock, not just because of its denegrified Tangerine Dream textures, but because of the boys' own aura of anal-retentive connoisseurship that surrounds it, the contempt for pop (i.e. handbag, any dance record that makes concessions to a 'girly' sensibility), and the vague, ill-defined conviction that something radical is at stake in this music.

Jungle also incites a similar sense of urgency and zeal, and for my money, musically substantiates it; at the same time, it's the post-rave offshoot that has most thoroughly severed itself from rave's premises. You could call it 'gangsta rave', in so far as jungle has taken on hip-hop and ragga's ethos of masked self-containment and controlled dance moves, and shed rave's abandonment and demonstrativeness (ultimately derived from gay disco). Ecstasy has been largely displaced within the jungle scene in favour of cocaine and marijuana; the latter, with its increasingly high THC content, creates a sensory intensification without euphoria, tinged with nerve-jangling paranoia. This drug-state fits perfectly jungle's ultra-vivid synaesthetic textures, hyperspatialized mix-scapes and tension-but-no-release rhythms.

Music designed expressly for the E experience is still big: the old skool rave spirit endures in Scotland, and through the popularity of happy hardcore pretty much everywhere in Britain apart from London. Scottish bouncy techno and happy-core (aka 4-beat) have preserved in miniature form the lost euphoria and togetherness of 1988–92, but on an aesthetic level they've arrested the music's development, expunging all post-1992 developments and focusing on cheesy piano riffs, Joey Beltram-style 'Mentasm' synth-stabs, shrieking diva-vocals and above all the stomping 4-to-the-floor beat (i.e. all the whiter-than-white elements that activate and accentuate the E-rush and encourage dancers to 'go mental'). Even as it resurges, happy hardcore is itself splitting up and hybridizing – one element looks set to merge with Dutch gabba to form a new, breakbeat-free sound that some call 'funcore', while there's even talk of 'intelligent' or 'futuristic' happy hardcore as opposed to mere crowd-pleasing fare.

Jungle, happy-core's estranged cousin, has of course already split up into at least three increasingly antagonistic subgenres. It seems that, once broken, the 'we' that each post-rave subgenre addresses can only get smaller and smaller; schisms and sectarianism proliferate *ad absurdum*.

Going Nowhere Fast

So the rave myth of transracial, cross-class unity lies in tatters. Still, there are various attributes shared by all the post-rave subscenes. And the two elements of rave culture that are most radical and 'subversive' are also what make it nihilistic and anti-humanist: namely, the intransitive nature of the rave experience, and the music's asexuality.

By 'intransitive', I mean the music and the culture's lack of objective or object ('to rave' is literally an intransitive verb); the cult of acceleration without destination, the creation of sensations without pretext or context. Rave culture has no goal beyond its own propagation. I first noticed this in 1992, when hardcore was in supernova, just before its disintegration into jungle, drum & bass, happy, etc. Rapt by the pirate radio stations, by the listeners' paged-in shouts and MCs' invocations, I was struck by both the crusading zeal and the intransitive nature of their utterances: 'rushing!', 'buzzin' hard!', 'get busy!', 'come alive!', 'let's go!', 'time to get hyper, helter-skelter', 'hardcore's firing!', even simply 'belief!!'. During the pirates' phone-in sessions, it was like there was this feedback loop of ever-escalating exultation, switching back and forth between the station and the junglist 'massive' at home; the whole subculture resembled a giant mechanism designed to generate fervour without aim, a shared hallucination of being in-the-place-to-be. Massification, amplification and excitation: this alone was the pirates' *raison d'être*. At the heart of rave lies a kernel of tautology: raving is about the celebration of celebration. Tautology is bliss, someone said; when rave culture's 'desiring machine' (Deleuze and Guattari, 1987) is really crankin', when you're one of its cogs (locked into the pirate signal or plugged into the sound-system's circuitry), well, there's no feeling like it. Trouble is that the machine tends to wear out its human components; drugs are required to bring the nervous system up to speed; the human frame was not built to withstand the attrition of sensations.

There also comes the inevitable point at which rave's 'desiring machine' turns 'fascist' (as Deleuze and Guattari put it): when the single-mindedness turns to tunnel-vision, when getting high becomes getting out of it. Suddenly the clubs are full of dead souls, zombie-eyed and prematurely haggard. Instead of togetherness, sullen moats of personal space reappear; smiley-faces give way to sour expressions, bitter because they've caned it so hard that the old buzz can't be recovered. For some, any old oblivion will do; they become connoisseurs of poisons, mix 'n' matching toxins to approximate the old high.

This moment of burn-out, when the scene crosses over into the 'dark side', seems intrinsic to any drug culture. It happened in Haight Ashbury in the late sixties, when speed and STP killed the luv 'n' peace vibe. It happened in the Los Angeles rave scene a few years ago, when punters shifted allegiance from increasingly unreliable ecstasy to soul-corroding crystal meth (a vaporized form of amphetamine). It's also happened to Scottish rave, with some punters taking five or more pills per session, and the rising use of sleeping pills like Temazepam (either to help the raver come down after a night of excess or just to get even more 'off ma heid').

Above all, it happened to UK hardcore in late 1992, when happy rave tunes gave way to 'dark side' jungle. Stripping away the squeaky voices and melodramatic strings (the fluffy 'feminine' and 'gay' elements that made 'arkdkore ravey, jouissance-y), DJ/producers created minimalist drum & bass, the voodoo sound of compulsion for compulsion's sake. Thematically and texturally, hardcore began to be haunted by a collective apprehension that 'we've gone too far'. At first there were tracks that exuded a vibe of dangerously overwhelming bliss, such as the jouissance-overdose title and languishing langour of 4 Horsemen of the Apocalypse's 'Drowning in her'. Then came 'dark side', a style that appeared to reflect long-term effects of ecstasy and marijuana use: depression, paranoia, dissociation, creepy sensations of the uncanny. Tunes like DJ Hype's 'Weird energy', Origin Unknown's 'Valley of the shadows' (with its 'felt that I was in a long, dark tunnel' soundbite), and an entire mini-genre of panic-attack songs like Remarc's 'Ricky', Johnny Jungle's 'Johnny' and Subnation's 'Scottie' (the latter featuring the cheerful sample-hook – 'we're not gonna die, we're gonna get out of here'!).

The 'dark' trend was driven partly by a desire to take hardcore back underground by removing commercial, uplifting elements, thereby alienating 'lightweights'. But it also reflected the pharmacological reality of the subculture in late 1992 and early 1993: on the one hand, a dip in the quality of ecstasy, with a predominance of pills consisting of speed and LSD, or even a dash of downers or smack; on the other hand, the fact that if you take pure MDMA regularly its blissful effects wear off, leaving only the jittery speed-rush. Both syndromes (fake ecstasy 'cocktails' and tolerance of E's effects) are exacerbated because ravers inevitably take more pills in a futile attempt to recover the fast-fading rapture of the olden, golden days.

But even if you could manage to get consistently reliable high-quality ecstasy, the fact is that E-based lifestyle is a dead(ening) end; weekly use gradually empties the brain of the substances whose release MDMA triggers in a rush and gush of euphoria. My sense is that the intransitive, go-nowhere aspects of rave culture are almost chemically programmed into MDMA itself.

Among all its other effects, E incites a sort of free-floating fervour, a will-to-belief – which is why the most inane oscillator synth-riff can seem so numinously radiant with MEANING. But at the end of even the most tearing night out, there can be a disenchanting sense of futility: all that energy and idealism mobilized to no end (except to line the pockets of the promoter, and Mr Evian).

From another vantage point, rave can be seen as the ultimate postmodern experience (culture without content, without an external referent). Or as a Bataille-like sacrificial cult of expenditure-without-return, a glorious waste of energy and resources into the void. Or even as the quintessence of Zen (the emptying out of meaning, via mantra and koan; the paradox of the full void). But you can have your fill of emptiness; even bliss can get boring.

There's another Zen aspect to rave music – its resemblance to tantra (Zen sex magick), which abolishes traditional sexual narrative (arousal/climax/resolution) in favour of an infinitely sustained pre-orgasmic plateau, during which the adept enters a mystic hallucinatory state. Both ecstasy and amphetamine tend to have an anti-aphrodisiac effect. E may be the 'love drug', but this refers more to *agap e* than to *eros*, cuddles rather than copulation, sentimentality rather than sticky secretions. E is notorious for making erection difficult and male orgasm virtually impossible. A real dick-shriveller, it also gets rid of the thinks-with-his-dick mentality, turning rave into space where girls can feel free to be friendly with strange men, even snog them, without fear of sexual consequences.

Arguably one of the few truly new and 'subversive' aspects of rave is that it's the first youth subculture that's not based around the notion that sex is transgressive. Rejecting all that old-hat sixties apparatus of libidinal libera-tion, and recoiling from our sex-saturated popular culture, rave instead locates *jouissance* in pre-pubescent childhood or pre-Oedipal infancy. This was more explicit in Britain a few years ago, (when ravers sucked dummies, tracks sampled kiddies' TV-themes or nursery rhymes, and vocal samples were whisked up into a delirious babytalk babble), although child-like clothing, accoutrements and hair are still fashionable among American rave-girls (Bjork's space-pixie image is a big influence). It's noticeable that in the UK jungle scene – as timestretching allowed for the return of more 'mature', measured vocal passion as opposed to kartoon squeaky voices, and as coke 'n' spliff supplanted E – so too the lecherous gaze (for men) and sexy, scanty clothing (for girls) has returned.

It's intriguing that amphetamine (of whose pharmacological family E is a member) should be related to this cult of pre-sexual innocence. Speed is the anorexic drug, suppressing appetite along with sex-drive; anorexia has long been diagnosed as a refusal of adult sexual maturity and all its concomitant hassles. Speed/ecstasy doesn't negate the body, it intensifies the pleasure of physical expression while completely emptying out the sexual content of dance; it allows a 'regression' to the polymorphous 'body without organs' of infancy. Particularly for men, the drug/music interface acts to dephallicize the body and open it up to enraptured, abandoned, 'effeminate' gestures. But removing the heterosexist impulse can mean that women are rendered dispensable. As with that earlier speed-freak scene, the mods (who dressed sharp and posed to impress their mates, not to lure a mate), there's a homosocial aura to many post-rave scenes. There's a sense in which E, by feminizing the man, allows him to access *jouissance* independently rather than seek it through women. Hence the self-pleasuring, masturbatory quality to rave dance – closer to the circle jerk than the courtship rituals that most forms of dance dramatize.

Rave is a culture of clitoris envy, a low-brow version of Jacques Lacan's green-eyed feelings about the mystic Saint Teresa. Malcolm Bowie (1991), paraphrasing Lacan, describes women as 'perpetual motion machines programmed to produce their own rapture', and writes of how 'an uncaused, unlocalisable and ineffable pleasure-spasm' incited Teresa's enraptured contortions. Pure rave! Rave's epileptic stimuli-bombardment (convulsive beats and strobes) reflects the subculture's essence: 'nympholepsy' – 'an ecstasy or frenzy caused by desire of the unattainable'.

The samples that feature in rave music – orgasmic whimpers and sighs, soul-diva beseechings like 'the way you make me feel', 'you light my fire', 'loving you' – induce a state of (that word again) intransitive amorousness. The ecstatic female vocals don't signify a desirable/desirous woman, but (as in gay disco) a hypergasmic rapture that the male identifies with, and aspires towards. The 'you' or 'it' in vocal samples refers not to a person, but to a sensation. In truth, these are love-songs to the drug (or rather the synergistic interaction of drug/music/lights), love-hymns in praise of luv'd up-ness, or in the case of Baby D's 'Let me be your fantasy', a love-tribute to the rave scene/dream itself. American cultural studies professor Lawrence Grossberg (1994) cites a poll of young people in Britain which found that, while kids listen to music for three times as much of their leisure-time as kids did in the mid-1970s, they place music way down on the list of things they care about (after education, home, friends, money, sex, appearance, work, going out, sport, hobbies and football). Of their functional attitude to music (as backdrop to other more meaningful activities), Grossberg notes 'rather than dancing to the music you like, you like the music you can dance to'. All that I'd add is: 'you like the music you can drug to', the music that best intensifies the chemical's effects.

With E, the full-on raver lifestyle means literally falling in love every weekend, then (with the inevitable mid-week crash) having your heart broken. Millions of kids across Europe are still riding this emotional rollercoaster. Always looking ahead to their next tryst with E, dying to gush, addicted to love, in love with . . . nothing.

Nowhere People

In her memoir *Nobody Nowhere*, the autistic Donna Williams (1992) describes
how as a child she would withdraw from a threatening reality into a private
pre-verbal dream-space of ultra-vivid colour and rhythmic pulsations; she
could be transfixed for hours by iridescent motes in the air that only she could
perceive. With its dazzling psychotropic lights, its sonic pulses, the
onomatopoeic, nursery-rhyme doggerel of the MCs, rave culture is arguably
a form of *collective autism.*

Rave's relentlessly utopian imagery – events/promoters called Living
Dream, Fantazia, Rezerection, Utopia, even – often seems like the return of
sixties psychedelia. Back then, the counter culture was engaged in an attempt
to reverse, *en masse*, the Oedipus Complex (the trauma that breaks the
infant's paradisical symbiosis with the mother, and teaches it to live with lack,
to settle for less). From the Situationists' 'take your desires for reality' to Jim
Morrison's 'we want the world and we want it NOW', the late sixties anti-
Oedipal impetus was at once poetic and psychotic.

Rave culture has never really been about altering reality, merely
exempting yourself from it for a while. In that sense, rave is really a sort of
dry run or acclimatization phase for virtual reality; it is adapting our nervous
systems, bringing our perceptual and sensorial apparatus up to speed,
evolving us towards the post-human subjectivity that digital technology
requires and engenders.

That old 'erotic Marxist' Herbert Marcuse warned about 'repressive
desublimation', of capitalism's erosion of Christian pleasure-fear in order to
create a consumer culture of high-turnover hedonism. Today, we might talk
of repressive/regressive de-Oedipalization as a prequel to our insertion into
the digital domain, our *virtualization*. Computer games and rave culture
seem, in this dystopian view, to be creating a subjectivity geared towards
fascination rather than meaning, sensation rather than sensibility; creating an
appetite for impossible states of hyperstimulation, they are to virtual reality
what cocaine is to crack.

The spectrum of rave music runs from the psychotic (explosive, a retali-
ation against reality) to the autistic (implosive, a secession from reality). With
its hyperphallic sonic *rigor mortis* and 200 bpm blitzkrieg velocity, its
stormtrooper stomp-beats and death-swarm synths, gabber is psychotic.
Gabber fans grind their teeth, shake their fists in the air and pogo up and
down on the spot. The solipsistic furore of anthems like Sperminator's 'No
woman allowed', Predator's 'Mind of a lunatic' and Comababy's
'Comababy' can be traced back to Human Resource's 1991 ur-gabba classic
'The dominator', with its Lacanian epiphany: 'There is no Other/I wanna
kiss myself'. At the other extreme lies the autistic tendencies of 'electronic
listening music' or 'new complexity techno': the peculiarly use-less, uselessly

peculiar sonic *objets d'art* constructed by the likes of Autechre and Christian Vogel: small boys playing with tekno toys, lost in their own little world of chromatics and texture and contour, molding sound like Play-doh.

It Made You an Oxymoron

Is the notion of 'rave culture' a contradiction in terms anyway? Is it possible to base a culture around sensations rather than truths, fascination rather than meaning, *jouissance* rather than *plaisir*? Without wishing to get too Matthew Arnold about it, we might define culture as something that tells you where you came from and where you're going; a force that nourishes, heals, imparts life-wisdom, enriches one's inner life, sensitizes the human spirit, and generally makes life habitable.

From this humanist vantage point, 'rave culture' is frankly oxymoronic. From the wizz-driven rollercoaster of hardcore to the ganjadelic womb-bath of ambient, rave music is about an affectless intensity. Perhaps the real question is whether any form of recreational drug use is an adequate basis for a culture. In rave's case, the quest for 'altered states' is devoid of the millenarian spirituality of sixties hippies or Rastafarian dub. Most of the 'mystical' implications read into rave culture, by the likes of Fraser Clark or Spiral Tribe, are simply elaborate rationalizations/spiritualizations of 'getting off your face'.

From a post-human/anti-humanist standpoint, of course, the sensationalism of rave music is simply *très* avant-garde. Back in the sixties, Susan Sontag (1969) celebrated cutting-edge modern art as 'a form of discipline of the feelings and a programming of sensations'. She went so far as to suggest that 'the feeling (or sensation) given off by a Rauschenberg painting might be like that of a song by the Supremes'. As a prophetic vision of today's dance track as an engine for programming sensations and triggering motor/muscular reflexes, Sontag's intuition was spot on. The rhythms and textures of jungle, trance, garage, etc., each make you move through the world in a different way, recalibrate and recondition your body.

The avant-garde/postmodern nihilism of rave music is signalled by the metaphors that it seems to demand – all connotative on enTHRALLment, of loss of control to some über-force, but also of utter futility – like the metaphor of the rollercoaster (going round in circles, going nowhere fast), or the metaphor of crack (when you get into jungle, or happy hardcore, or gabba, all other sonic simulants seem boring, too slow). There's a sense in which rave music is only 'about' its own sensations. Instead of the rock notion of 'resonance' (with its psychological/sociological connotations), rave is about frequencies; it's music that's oriented toward impact rather than affect.

Going AWOL

I know of nothing else that bugs me/More than working for the rich
man/Hey, I'll change that scene one day/Today I might be mad/Tomorrow
I'll be glad/Cos I'll have Friday on my mind . . . Tonight!/I'll spend my
bread/Tonight!/I'll lose my head . . . Monday, I've got Friday on my mind.
(The Easybeats, 'Friday on my mind', 1967)

Amazing, isn't it, that nearly thirty years on, the Easybeats' awesome mod
anthem 'Friday on my mind' still describes the working-class weekender life
cycle of drudgery, anticipation and explosive release. What really grabs my
ear is the poignancy of that line, 'Hey, I'll change that scene one day'. Nearly
thirty years on, we're no nearer to overhauling the work/leisure structures
of capitalist existence. 'Today I might be mad': all that rage and frustration
goes into going mental at the weekend, helped along by a capsule or three
of instant unearned 'glad'ness.

Like football fandom, rave is a remnant of working-class consciousness,
the vague sense of collectivity that abides after the death of organized labour
with all its myths of fraternity and shared destiny. (No coincidence that at
soccer matches, fans have taken to dropping Es, heightening the atmosphere
of homosocial passion.) Jungle is the next stage: rave music after the death
of the rave myth, of its ethos of spurious but life-affirming *bonhomie*. Punning
on the Labour history of co-operatives and friendly societies, I'd call jungle
an 'unfriendly society'. Musically, jungle is cyber-dub; politico-spiritually,
jungle is dub reggae secularized, updated in synch with an atomized, increasingly cybernetic reality. Instead of roots reggae's 'I-and-I', jungle is about
'I-against-I'; the music offers dread without Zion.

Jungle insiders always talk of it as 'a way of life'; the famous ardkore club
AWOL is an acronym for that phrase as much as for the idea of truancy,
going 'absent without leave'. On close inspection, that 'way of life' boils
down to little more than music and drugs. If you're right in the thick of it,
the minutiae of the music's evolution, the endless search for the perfect
breakbeat, the to-and-fro dialogue of jungle's collective creativity (what Eno
calls 'scenius' as opposed to 'genius'), well, it's totally enthralling. Step
outside its parameters for a moment, though, and you might think jungle,
or any post-rave scene, is more a case of 'get a life' than 'way of life': a
pseudo-culture, in other words.

Rave music, then, is riddled with Zen-like paradoxes. It's music of resistance and acquiescence, utopian idealism and nihilistic hedonism. It's both
escape route and dead-end, orgasmotron and panopticon, space and cage.
It's still the best thing we've got going in this country. But is it enough?

References

Bowie, Malcom (1991) *Lacan*, Boston: Harvard University Press.

Deleuze, Gilles and Felix Guattari (1987) *A Thousand Plateaus: Capitalism and Schizophrenia*, Minneapolis: University of Minneapolis Press.

Grossberg, Lawrence (1994) 'Is anybody listening? Does anybody care?: On talking about the state of rock', in Andrew Ross and Tricia Rose (eds), *Microphone Fiends: Youth Music and Youth Culture*, London: Routledge.

Sontag, Susan (1969) 'The basic unit of contemporary art is not the idea, but the analysis of and extension of sensations', in Gerald Emmanuel Stern (ed.), *McLuhan: Hot and Cool*, London: Signet.

Williams, Donna (1992) *Nobody Nowhere: The Extraordinary Autobiography of an Autistic*, New York: Doubleday.

7 Fear and Loathing in Wisconsin

Sarah Champion

Out Come the Freaks . . .

For three days and two nights we grabbed Freedom in our mouths and held on tightly. We tasted Freedom on our tongues and it was sweet. We swallowed Freedom in our guts and it was warm. We inhaled the scent of Freedom and it made us high. We achieved Freedom together – it filled our bodies and commanded us to dance. (David Prince, *Even Furthur* rave fanzine, May 1995)

The rhythms are like gunshot, each beat a bullet, blowing away your body bit by bit until it feels like you're completely invisible – lost in the music. It's the middle of the night and it's raining, but this doesn't seem to dampen the ravers' euphoria. The repetitive, stomping beat of a techno sound-system blasts across the valley. Green lasers carve a ceiling across the sky and the raindrops caught in the beams form a shower of green glitter. At the top of the hill, a wicker man burns, and as the DJ spins harder and faster beats, lightning streaks across the sky. Soaked to the skin, 4,000 of us just keep on dancing, grinning – can this really be happening? And *here* of all places . . .

It's early summer 1995 and I am in the heart of the Midwest's Great Lakes: land lumber mills, cider farms, cheese castles and tractor malls. The nearest town is Lakewood, Wisconsin – a town so small its newspaper prints the school dinner menu. The map is peppered with place names like Deadman's Lake, Hell Acre Springs, Mosquito Creek, Chicken Foot Valley and Bear Paw Mountain. The venue is Paul Bunyan's Ski Slope: a snow-mobiling centre in the winter and a site for zydeco festivals in summer. The event? 'Even Furthur', a four-day outdoor party, drawing 4,000 'ravers' from across America.

The town of Lakewood has never seen anything like it. Teenage girls and boys swarm down the road – some look 'cyberpunky' with cropped hair, dyed electric blue; pierced lips, nostrils, eyebrows and tongues; sci-fi make-up and mirrorshades. Others look like young children – sporting Sesame Street T-shirts, teddy bear rucksacks and pig-tails and chewing on baby's dummies (pacifiers). Most wear baggy West Coast hip-hop pants, with bikers' chains swinging between belt and back pocket. Out come the freaks . . .

A sequel to the previous year's 'Furthur' festival, the party is named after the slogan on the front of Ken Kesey and his Merry Pranksters' bus (made legendary by Tom Wolfe's *Electric Kool Aid Test)*. 1994's 'Furthur' was the first of its kind, a three-day outdoor techno party. The sequel, 'Even Furthur', declares itself a celebration of 'the flowering of summer and our culture'. It is a celebration of the Midwest's rave scene and therefore located equidistant from its main hubs – Milwaukee, Madison, Chicago and Minneapolis.

Who would have thought *this* would be the heartland of America's new guerrilla party underground? After all, this is classic rock territory, where the radio stations spin Supertramp, Boston, Van Morrison and The Who round-the-clock. Yet this rock establishment is being challenged, as dance culture begins to infect the Midwest (an area including Illinois, Michigan, Wisconsin, Minnesota, Indiana and Iowa). In a way, it's a homecoming, for it was here in the Midwest that it all began, house music being invented in Chicago and techno in Detroit in the early 1980s. Inevitably, like many American pop cultural trends, its home success has come only after it has been taken up by the British, altered and sold back as a European fashion (just as Liverpool bands in the 1960s picked up on the rhythm and blues records arriving on ships from the States and sold them back in the form of The Beatles).

How did it happen? Well, to rush through a quick history – acid house emerged in 1987–8 in England, via the Spanish island of Ibiza, where an influx of ecstasy (MDMA) pills arrived in the clubs. The new (or rather redis-covered) drug kept clubbers dancing all night. The ideal sound-track was found to be Chicago's urban dance music, house, and the ideal environment either warehouses or huge outdoor events. Over the following years, this has become the basis for the biggest, most universal British youth culture since the 1960s. The music, venues, fashions and drugs may have evolved and diversified, but no one can deny dance music's domination of the charts and youth culture in the 1990s. Not just in Britain, but throughout Europe, and gradually spreading across the world.

As a truly 'underground' and also illegal culture, it was down to a few enthusiastic pioneers to make it happen. English DJs inspired by acid house, but disillusioned by British licensing laws and weather, soon emigrated to the west coast of America and by 1991 had launched huge parties like 'Toon

Town' in Los Angeles and San Francisco. Not long afterwards, a DJ called Frankie Bones launched raves on the east coast with his 'Stormrave' parties.

In Britain, acid house began in the big cities of Manchester and London, then spread outwards – to Stoke, Coventry, Aberdeen and Liverpool. America's rave scene has followed the same pattern. What began in the cool conurbations, Los Angeles, San Francisco, Miami and New York, in the early 1990s, had by 1995 truly reached Hicksville.

Ravin' USA

'I meet people from California and they say, "Oh you're *still* raving – that's such an old thing to do!"' a girl with pig-tails and a Sesame Street backpack told me at 'Even Furthur', as she danced all night in the mud. Not only was raving alive and well outside the big cities, but it was becoming a powerful youth culture, growing from the underground up, the sounds, styles and philosophies continuing to evolve. This is raving, but not as we know it. This is *Raving' USA*.

In Wisconsin, I meet innumerable exuberant kids who've driven for up to twenty-four hours, across several states, to party. They bounce up to me and ask, 'What's your name? Where are you from? What are you "on"?' I have a weird sense of *déjà-vu*. It transports me back to Shelley's Laserdome in Stoke-on-Trent in the north of England in the early 1990s, when the UK's rave scene was in its emergent stages. Kids would gather from all over the country (holding impromptu parties in motorway service stations on the way home).

The American kids still adopt many of that era's crazes – facemasks (as sported by Altern 8 in 1992), baby's dummies and children's TV kitsch. But dance culture is a virus which mutates as it spreads, and in the Midwest they have taken 'rave' and made it their own. In 1995 the Midwest ravers had a distinctive style: remixing the first forty years of youth fashions, from hip-hop and skatewear to rocker and punk kitsch. As well as Converse and Adidas trainers and California's super-baggy, 'Q' hip-hop pants, the kids had a strange obsession with spiky punk 'dog' collars and bikers' chains. One horrified Chicago newspaper described them as 'vampires'.

'My first rave was Reunion, New Year's Eve three years ago,' says Sal Schneider, from a Minnesota town named St Cloud. He wears a mad woolly hat; mirror shades; a bony grin; and the ultimate cyber accessory – 'train track' teeth braces, customised in silver and green to resemble circuit boards.

'My friend had told me about it – I didn't understand what he was talking about. He said, "Picture this . . . you're in a warehouse with speakers 75 feet long, 14 feet high." I'm like, "NO WAY!", and he's like, "You wanna go?" We went . . .'

Where Californian number plates boast 'Land of Sunshine', Wisconsin's are sloganed 'America's Dairyland'. The global party adapts to local environments – in Blackburn (in the industrial north of England) acid house parties happened in warehouses; in Berlin techno took over East German bunkers; in Wisconsin it's ski-slopes and . . . *cow sheds?*

'We drove for four hours out to rave on a farm,' says Sal. 'It was like a barn dance, except they were playing trance, house and hardcore. I just remember walking in, smelling manure and thinking "Oh, no!" We were dancing on hay next to cows in stalls. At 5 a.m. they threw us out because it was milking time.'

In the tiny towns along Lake Michigan – Racine, Mantiwoc, Oshkosh – you will also find 'dayraves' in municipal parks and 'microraves' for fifty to a hundred people. At one 'dayrave', I witnessed sound-systems nestling in glades of trees and in the midst of ecstatic dancers, kids having barbecues . . . only in America!

'I got a Furthur flyer when I was at a microrave in Baltimore. I found out about that on the Net,' says one wide-eyed girl. 'Microraves are great – fifty to seventy people max, soooo neat, sooooo coool.'

In a country so vast, where gas is cheap, flyers have been known to list the driving time (in hours) from major American cities. The immense size of the country makes publicizing parties with flyers difficult, however, so many kids find out about parties on the Internet – after all, every college kid has access to it for free. There are bulletin boards and web pages across the States, with rants on the politics of raving and info on up-coming events. Of all these, mw-raves (@ hypereal.com) is one of the most passionate and has helped unify this unique scene.

At 'Even Furthur', the ski lodge is a café and the slopes around provide camping. Sound-systems have been given an open invitation to set up. On the top of the ski hill, there's a progressive-house posse with disco lights syncopating on the horizon. Marquees in the valley are stacked high with speakers, various Midwest DJs are spinning tunes, and hundreds are dancing in each tent. Around campfires on the hillsides, UFO abduction stories are traded.

Where the yellow 'Smiley' represented acid house's ear-to-ear grins, silliness, celebration and childlike fun in Britain, in America it has been replaced by a luminous flying saucer. On dancefloors across the country, the favoured logo on T-shirts, hats and fender stickers is a Martian spacecraft or a green, wide-eyed alien head. They're produced by fashion companies like Liquid Sky Design (New York), Anarchic Adjustment (San Francisco) and, most prominently, Alien Workshop and Shwa! Accessories include handy 'alien-spotting guides' available on chains to wear round your neck at parties (just in case).

'Most ravers out here seem to believe they've been abducted by aliens,' one American rave promoter told me. On alt.raves and all across America's on-line party discussion network, there are reportings of UFO sightings and kidnappings at raves. In California, ufology is a whole subcult, with 'support groups' for abductees and their resulting psychological problems. Could it be that, continuing the lack of meaning or religion displayed by the 'slackers' or 'Generation X', the only thing left for American kids to put their faith in is beings from other planets?

There's something appealing about the idea of getting abducted. One moment you're driving home from a party, the next being experimented upon in a space craft. It has the same escapist appeal as raving itself – like sometimes when you're dancing and you feel like, if you dance hard enough and fast enough, the music will swallow you up; that you will leave your body, leave all the earthly problems behind and have a better life.

> When I started my record label, I thought the flying saucer was a perfect logo, because it related to psychedelic music. Psychedelics are about escaping the reality we are in and exploring other realities. I believe UFOs are a reflection of our desire to have faith that there are worlds beyond that which we experience. Young people in America are in a state of depression. They're desperate to contemplate that there's something else – something beyond their depressing lives – hence raves and believing in UFOs. (Matt Adell of Organico Records, Chicago, whose logo is a flying saucer)

As well as UFOs, the importance of cars is another American twist on rave culture. Like a scene out of *American Graffiti*, a bunch of ravers cruise the parking lot in a low-riding, white Cadillac with red leather seats – windows down, silver space-shades on, techno pumping. Cool or what? The site is crammed with beat-up Station Waggons, Oldsmobiles and Fords with huge hand-painted signs declaring 'Even Furthur' in Merry Pranksters style and customized number plates with slogans like 'GUNS KILL'. As they have done in the parking lots of sporting events and concerts for years, they 'tail-gate' – open up their car's boot and party out of the back.

For many of these kids, raving is just a natural step on from following The Grateful Dead. Over the last twenty-five years, a festival/party culture grew up in the parking lot of their gigs. Often Deadheads didn't even see the band, but would hang out by their cars, taking drugs, cooking food and playing music. There's even a recipe book, *Cooking With The Dead*, telling of the kids who lived on the road, making enough cash to get to the next gig by selling food. The death of The Grateful Dead's singer, Jerry Garcia, in 1995 was, perhaps, a timely event, opening the way for rave culture to replace it.

Stairway to Heaven

We're pagans: we worship big walls of sound. We believe in decadence and hedonism – staying up from Friday through 'til Sunday morning, doing drugs and listening to really heavy music.
We pride ourselves in *massive*, like super-loud, sound-systems. We like to make it so that no matter where you go the sound is loud and heavy – whether you're right next to the speakers or in the other room! In Canada or New York, you get massive sound-systems, but everyone is 20 feet from them. You come to the Midwest and the kids totally get into being *part of* the speakers. You can't get any more into the music than when it's three inches from your face! (Kurt Eckes of Drop Bass Network)

Deadheads are not the only connection between rave and what went before. Out here, in the Midwest, the ravers actually *head-bang* to techno. They press their bodies against the speakers for hours on end. The scene truly is about going 'Even Furthur'. Part way through the weekend, I clearly remember the DJ playing a techno cover version of Black Sabbath. Four ravers lined up behind the record decks and head-banged like they were in the Queen car scene in *Wayne's World*. In Britain everyone assumed America's rock domination would prevent the spread of dance music. Not so. In fact, the two seem to merge out here in the Midwest.

If metal could cross over with rap, then I suppose it's inevitable it could meet dance music half-way too. And if punk and metal were ever to morph into techno, Milwaukee, Wisconsin had to be the place. Also known as 'Brew City', it is a town renowned for beer, heavy rock, The Violent Femmes, a large German population and an annual Satanic 'Metafest'. Now there's also Drop Bass Network, the promoters behind 'Even Furthur' and many other Midwest raves. Bizarre as it may seem, in the early 1990s Germany and Wisconsin became linked by common pounding beats.

'Milwaukee is the home of German immigrants in America, with lots of German neighbourhoods,' explains one Midwest raver. 'Heritage is a very strong factor in the music that's going to come out of a city. The hugest influence in Milwaukee music are the German bass beats.'

Described as 'techno pagan rituals', Drop Bass Network's raves jumble up biblical references with hedonism; 'peace-'n'-love' with Satanism. Although a pagan, tribal ritual, ecstasy and raves in Europe have always been an uplifting celebration, but here in the Midwest they're into the 'darkside'. They use skull and 'Exorcist' logos on their invitations, and, like the Dutch 'Hellraiser' parties, pictures of hell fires. 'Demons of the darkside taking control of your soul,' promised a flyer for their Grave Reverence party ('Helloween '93'); 'An epic pagan gathering of the tribes of evil.'

Our whole intention was to get the metal kids into the rave scene. Personally the dark side appeals to me more than the good side. We threw a couple of parties that were based on hell. The whole motif of the place was that you were in hell. People really got off on it! What we realized was that there's this core group of kids at our parties who were really into this whole concept of evil. It doesn't go along with the whole happy rave image, I know, but that's what we and our parties are about. It's dark, but not depressing – just sort of unifying. You got this super heavy music and 1,000 people crammed into a small space – it's a really intense experience. (Kurt Eckes of Drop Bass Network)

Drop Bass Network also became a record label – an outlet for the up-coming purveyors of 'gabber, acid, hardcore, hard techno' whom they were booking and inspiring. This posse became collectively known as the Midwest Hardcorps and included Woody McBride, DJ Hyperactive, Freddy Fresh, Astrocat and Delta 9. They also released New York's storm-troopers Adam X, Jimmy Crash and Frankie Bones. Here are a few words that have been used in reviews and press releases to describe this strand of the techno genre: gritty, churning, lashing, grinding, throbbing, enforcing, strong, stomping, undescribably noisy, carnal, terrifyingly mean. Sound familiar? They could easily be describing death metal.

'Musically beat and melody communicate much more immediately than language – lyrics,' one raver enthuses. 'That's why techno is getting massive here – it takes you on an emotional journey: hits you right in the gut and carries you.'

The metal-rave crossover at first seems bizarre. How did dance music evolve from the sexy, funky, black gay club scene of Chicago to this aggressive, sexless (almost exclusively white) rave culture? I suppose there's an historical precedent – after all, wasn't the blues hijacked by the likes of Elvis, while its black originators remained obscure? The same is true of dance music in America. The black DJs, from Frankie Knuckles to Derrick May, who invented it remain obscure, while the new white musicians from England and Germany steal all the glory.

Back in the Day

The first music I was into was heavy metal – Kiss! Then when I got to high-school I was into the punk scene. I liked English punk like Sex Pistols and GBH of course, but mostly I loved Los Angeles bands like Black Flag.
In the fall of 1988, my life was changed. I made my way to a club in Chicago and took ecstasy. It was all by chance. I'd never taken drugs. I didn't even drink. I'd never heard dance music or been to a club. I was into skating and

hanging out with all these skateboarders. One of them had just gotten out of college. He took us to this club called Medusa's in Chicago. It blew me away. I'd never even danced before. It was probably one of the best times of my life. (Kurt Eckes, Drop Bass Network)

It was by chance that many white American college kids stumbled on dance music. Chicago's notorious under-age party club Medusa's was responsible for turning many of the Midwest's white industrial/punk kids on to dance. Until then, house had been an exclusively black (and before that gay) scene. Medusa's mixed it up in every possible way. While Frankie Knuckles and Farley Jackmaster Funk spun upstairs, downstairs you would hear New Order and 'alternative' tracks.

Every influential movement begins with the inspiration of a few maverick individuals. The Midwest is no exception. For the full picture you have got to go much further back – back to London in 1988–9, where New York DJs Frankie Bones and Lenny Dee would fly in to play acid house parties. You could draw a ten-year dance family tree, with pioneers crossing the Atlantic in both directions.

'26 August 1989,' says Frankie Bones, remembering the date that he first experienced an English rave religiously.

> I was told there'd be 5,000 people, but when we started getting to near the party there were cars everywhere. Turned out there were 25,000 people. I just remember getting on stage and not feeling nervous because I realized that at last my big chance had come.
> The best moment was my third big 'rave' – Ipswich. We were stuck in traffic on a country road in the rain, when I heard two of my tracks at the same time: 'Loony tunes' coming out of one, 'Bonesbreaks' out of the other. I was just coming up on an 'E'. I remember feeling like I was melting into the back seat.

He took what he'd seen back home, where he tried to recreate it, opening a record store in Brooklyn and organizing raves. 'It started with giving people "E" in their apartments,' he explains. 'Then we had an out-of-control two-day party at my friend's mansion in Long Island. It was like something out of a movie where people lost their minds.'

Bigger parties evolved near the crazy dead-end street in Flatbush where Frankie Bones grew up. They would wheel their sound-system down the train track, into the tangle of goods warehouses, storage yards and tunnels, on stolen subway-repair carts.

> At the end of my block in Brooklyn were the train tracks where I played as a kid: always getting into trouble for breaking windows, starting little fires,

graffiti, going exploring. It was that knowledge I used for the parties. We'd make people park their cars ten blocks away and walk down the tracks half a mile. No streets ran adjacent to the tracks and so when the cops asked where you going and you said 'a party', they were like 'What party?' There were times when the cops heard the music, but they had no idea where we were, or how to get to us. We didn't even need generators – we just jacked into sockets and stole the electricity . . . Except that one time we plugged into the street-lights, but unfortunately, when it got to daylight at 6.30 a.m., all the power cut out.

Frankie Bones' regular parties became known as 'Stormrave', growing to 5,000 people by November 1992, and booking DJs like Josh Wink, Sven Vath and Ritchie Hawtin (then unknown). Frankie Bones had achieved his mission. He had launched rave culture in New York City. Not only that, but they were a catalyst for a party scene that stretched right up the north-east of America from Washington DC to Baltimore and Philadelphia. They sowed a seed, which would also result in my being at a vast techno festival in Wisconsin some three years later.

These New Yorkers took the rave ethos that they had witnessed on their many trips to spin in the UK and tried to recreate it in tuff ass NY style. In turn, Milwaukee punk Kurt Eckes stumbled upon them, and returned to his hometown on a mission to reinvent rave for rock-weaned Wisconsin kids. And so the cycle continues.

Pills 'n' Thrills

Just like in the UK, it is the combination of music and drugs which has fuelled the passion of America's rave scene. In Wisconsin, the kids enthused about ecstasy (or 'X' as they call it, when they come up to me and ask me if I'm 'X-ing') and how it makes them dance. 'The hundreds of others dancing makes me feel happy,' burbled one of the many free 'ravezines'. 'I gotta dance! Dancing has become an outlet for my soul, a spiritual high. It has become my religion.'

Another teenage raver agreed: 'I used to dance to Madonna, I wonder if she'd come do a rave? It takes a while of raving to get this, but raving is not about being cool like just about every other music has been. It definitely moulded me into someone different. I think everyone should take ecstasy at least twice.'

Says another, 'In a "club", if you bump someone they'd fume – like, "Hey, don't touch me, I'm beautiful". Here it's like, "Touch me, I'm beautiful and so are you."'

This enthusiasm for ecstasy, however, had already begun to backfire by

1995. As in Europe, the American raves experienced a 'honeymoon period' when everything was 'loved up', after which it started to go wrong as impurities appeared in the pills and the kids started to experiment with alternatives. On the west coast (San Francisco, Los Angeles), as well as ecstasy and LSD, crystal meth, an extreme form of speed, took over and the casualties fell thick and fast.

In Brooklyn where it all began, it also took a nightmarish twist: the biggest drugs in 1995 were angel dust (PCP), heroin and special K (ketamine, an animal tranquillizer). Says Frankie Bones, 'The ravers go down to Harlem to buy PCP. What ecstasy does in a positive way, PCP does negatively. It's an intense trip. Believe me, I've done it. Your adrenaline is up and you got loads of energy, but it's Satanic and negative like a horror movie.'

As well as the pure MDMA pills, made out in Arizona labs by the million, 'dirtier' drugs became a part of the party scene in the Midwest too. Then there's nitrous oxide (dental anaesthetic gas is the most popular form here, sold from tanks in $5 balloons). Discovered way back in 1772, in the times when you could still buy opium over the counter, nitrous oxide became known as 'laughing gas'. In the 1840s, side-show entertainers on America's snake-oil circuit would demonstrate its intoxicating properties. The effect on those who inhaled was to make them, 'Laugh, Sing, Dance, Speak or Fight', according to the leading trait of their character. Its body-numbing, unconsciousness-inducing hallucinogenic effects had been forgotten, until it was revived in the late 1960s by the hippies. Sold illegally from tanks at Grateful Dead gigs over the past two decades, it is now the cheapest high at techno parties and by 1996 was inspiring techno music with slow, distorted, warped sound.

I Fought the Law

In England, acid house incurred the wrath of both the tabloid newspapers and the authorities, and now this has happened in America too, as I discovered to my cost on my first visit to a Midwest rave in 1994. I guess it was inevitable. What else could have been expected at a rave in Hixton, Wisconsin, 'population 305'? In the middle of the night, my friends and I had found ourselves looking straight at the badge of a Wisconsin cop. Next thing we were all spreadeagled against the van, guns in our backs, an eerie silence all around as they told us to take out our 'weapons and needles'. I was under arrest for being 'hippie shit'.

'Gee!' exclaimed a female officer back at the station. 'You're English. Do you know Def Leppard?' I was searched and the ridiculous contents of my pockets logged – 'several colour balloons', 'a packet of Trebor mints', 'five party invitations', and an 'orange face mask'. The officer grappled with the concept of a 'rave' and told me she liked old-fashioned music, 'like The Who'. She studied my flyers, for parties all over the Midwest. 'These look very "psych-eee-delik",' she commented accusingly. 'Aren't The Who psychedelic?' I asked. She went quiet. 'What does this mean?' she wondered pointing to graphics depicting a record and a letter E, equalling a smiley. I shrugged.

Raving is America's new outlaw culture. At 'Even Furthur' local motels switched on their neon 'No Vacancies' signs at the sight of approaching ravers. On another legendary occasion, in an echo of our own 'Summer of Love', at Hallowe'en the police raided Milwaukee's 'Grave Rave' and arrested all 950 people. Welcome to America's new 'prohibition'. The laws differ from state to state and from county to county; and at the 'discretion' of the local sheriff.

'The cops are catching up and shutting us down and the media is constantly going on about sex-and-drugs orgies,' said one 22-year-old girl who had been arrested at 'Love Generator' in St Louis for photographing a cop busting the party. As in the UK, the local papers run regular stories on this corrupting new youth culture. In one, it said: 'the "event" seemed to be promoted by a mysterious organization called "RAVE", no one quite knowing who this was or what the letters stood for . . .'.

End-of-the-Millennium Party

> When I was a little kid, my Pop used to take me to Disneyland every six months. There was a ride called Future World where New York met Tokyo, all skyscrapers, trains and cars like weaving in and out Metropolis. Years later I saw Koyannisqatsi, with all those people shooting about, back and forth, back and forth . . . no one ever connecting. The American rave scene is an opposite vision of the future where everyone is rushing together, making connections.
> I don't think that there's one person here I couldn't walk up and say 'hi' to. Once you're past that hurdle, you can communicate with people all over the world. It's not a naive ideal. Globally, there's a generation of people disenfranchised, who feel that they're being left behind. (Kurt B. Reighly, freelance dance journalist, New York)

Hooking into the bleakness of America's disenfranchised youth (as 'slacker' culture did earlier), raves were spreading throughout America by 1995, from Denver and Cleveland and Indianapolis to Memphis and Nashville. In Wisconsin, by a campfire up on the hill, I met a bunch of guys drinking beers. One was a self-confessed hick, 'born in Kentucky; brought up on AC/DC, Malbro', Bud and trucks'. 'Even Furthur' was his first rave and he was 'digging it'. Among the crowd there were frat-boys, cheerleaders and casino dealers, and they were all getting the vibe and talking with an optimism not heard since the hippie sixties.

'Raving is not a new idea,' enthused one 18-year-old girl from Milwaukee. 'It's totally primitive: totally tribal. It gives us hope. After all the shit society gives kids – divorce, alcoholic parents, drugs – we can get together and take care of ourselves. We can pull something positive from this.'

Since the sounds of Chicago's black dance clubs combined with the 'new' drug ecstasy in 1987–8 in England, dance culture has grown and grown, gradually replacing what went before to become the dominant youth culture. It spread through Britain, then throughout Europe and is now a major force in almost every country in the world. A nation born and bred on 'rock 'n' roll', America is the biggest hurdle to its worldwide domination. But consider this – it took 'punk rock' over fifteen years to conquer the USA (finally doing so in the form of Nirvana). Perhaps dance culture is following a similar route, gradually infiltrating the continent's teen culture. It may just make it in time for a mass end-of-the-millennium rave.

8 The House Sound of Chicago

Hillegonda Rietveld

Well, this is the house that Jack built, I can tell you that. (Sherman, 1992)

Introduction

House music is a dance music which gained an increased popularity during the eighties and nineties in clubs and at parties in west European cities such as Amsterdam, Manchester, London, Stockholm and Rome, as well as in North American cities such as New York, Chicago, Los Angeles and Baltimore. The formal aspects of house music include a steady, repetitive beat between 120 and 140 bpm[1] and the use of sequencers,[2] synthesizers[3] and, since the mid-eighties, samplers.[4] Many styles of music can be assimilated within its tight 4/4 pattern. This results in a music which includes various cultural traces, which in turn means that many people from mainly urban western(ized) areas are able to identify with this musical aesthetic form. Its basic effect is to 'pump' a desire into human bodies to move, to dance and 'let go'. To some people consuming house music is a form of escapism; for others it is a way of life comparable to a religion.

Since 1986 the tag 'house' has at times been used as a marketing tool in the mainstream record industry as well as in a more marginalized cultural context. The meaning of the term has changed over time and in specific social and cultural contexts. However, the music it initially referred to has historically developed in an African-American environment, in North American urban centres such as New York and more specifically in Chicago, where the term 'house music' was used to indicate a kind of urban DIY electronic disco music, incorporating a rich African-American cultural tradition which can be traced to jazz, funk, soul music and gospel, mixed with European music styles like electronic trance and electronic pop music. The European market has no tight connections with an African-American history and its politics, so when it became successful in Europe, some of its original sensibilities were subdued.[5] In Europe, house music developed either stylistically into the realm of pop music or structurally in specific dance floor settings.[6] In this way house music has acquired new meanings, whereby a similar range of production technologies have been used for similar spaces and rituals of consumption.

In this chapter, I want to show that the Chicago-produced dance music which acquired the tag 'house music' has come into existence in a space created by an exclusion of certain identities in a racist and homophobic American society. In the face of racial and sexual discrimination, the production and consumption of this music has generated a sense of community,[7] of belonging, thereby creating its own definitions of 'normality'. However, although during the eighties Chicago produced its own identifiable dance sound and party scene with a name tag, 'the house that Jack built' has never been an isolated musical community. As Will Straw has put it:

> A musical scene, in contrast [to a musical community], is that cultural space in which a range of musical practices coexist, interacting with each other within a variety of processes of differentiation, and according to widely varying trajectories of change and cross-fertilisation. (Straw, 1991, p. 373)

This chapter is an inquiry into the way that the concept of 'house', its name and the discourses that surround it, has come into being in a local historical and geographical sense, with a specific focus on Chicago. This will include a description of its 'original' setting and of some of the local power structures that were part of the conception of house music. It will be shown that the specific historical and social context of the cultural tapestry of Chicago has led to a musical scene which has produced a dance music with recognizable local characteristics, while this music is at the same time part of a wider international flow of (musical) communication.

In the House that Jacks

According to Frankie Knuckles, when he arrived in Chicago in 1977 there were mostly drinking places with juke boxes; perhaps the city had about two or three clubs that employed DJs at the time (Knuckles, 1990). Given this situation, and Knuckles' experience in the mushrooming underground 'gay' discos in the 'hip' city of New York, he became resident DJ in the Chicago dance club The Warehouse in 1977, after his New York DJ colleague Larry

Levan did not take the job (Martin, 1992). There he gained a large audience. He had access to a lot of records shipped from New York. He also had a specific style of playing records that set him apart from the few other local DJs. Rather than playing one record after the next, he would mix Philadelphia soul music, New York club music, Euro-disco and sound effects such as a running train in order to create a sound-track for the entire night (Cosgrove, 1988). According to Berry, this is in line with a traditional African-American jazz attitude that plays with past and present forms of sounds in order to create a new form each time, thereby paying homage to a tradition and to a line of cultural ancestors (Berry, 1992). His audience favoured an up-tempo type of disco, at around 124 bpm. He also restricted old and new disco favourites to make it fit his 'dance floor', his audience. He would use his own rhythm makers and drum machines and would totally re-edit a song. The new rhythm added would be 'beefier' meaning its bass was in a louder volume (Knuckles, 1990). For example, the theme song for The Warehouse, 'Let NO Man Putasunder' by First Choice (Salsoul,1983) was successfully cut up and restructured. These tracks were created specifically for The Warehouse and played on a reel-to-reel tape recorder, a method which he still employed in 1994.[8] This style, the layering of sounds by the DJ, the special restructuring of songs as well as the mixing of techno pop with, for example, Salsoul classics is what was first termed house music in the phrases 'that shit like they play in The House' (Fleming, 1995, p.235) and 'this could be played in the "house"' meaning in The Warehouse club (Tong, 1990). Another explanation for the occurrence of the word 'house' and certainly for its staying power is that a 'house' is also a group of partying people. For instance in voguing[9] competitions, one belongs to a 'house' (Ninja, 1994), which is illustrated in the lyrics of Jack and Jill, 'Work it girlfriend' (Strictly Rhythm Form, 1993), where it is stated that one wins 'prizes in . . . the houses'. A club can also be a 'house', like in the term 'burn the house down', which can be found on many dance records as early as The Trammps' 'Disco inferno' (Atlantic, 1977).[10] Whichever way, the term became a marketing tool for the dance music styles that developed in Chicago.

Dance club The Warehouse is worth mentioning in some greater detail, since it seems that its atmosphere, attitude and music, as well as its setting in the urban layout, were seminal to many later house music parties in one way or another. It was away from any mainstream leisure area of Chicago, and its management policies and audience showed an attitude which enhanced its special and underground character. The entertainment was specifically aimed at young homosexuals, male and female, who were mostly from an African-American and Latino background. The management allowed for an interracial gathering, which was quite unusual in Chicago. Like a New York underground dance club, it provided the punters with non-alcoholic drinks ('Juice Bar') and snacks ('munchies'), which according to Frankie Knuckles was never done before in Chicago; up till then, clubbers used to go out to drink until 2 a.m. In terms of space, Frankie Knuckles has described it as:

> a three storey building [which] sits in the western part of the Loop. Now the Loop in Chicago is the main down town area and the western part is more of an industrial loft area and at that time it was pretty desolate and there was really not that much around there, so it was like the perfect place for if anyone wanted to take a loft and . . . build a night club then it was a perfect area to do it. Now it, it's like prime you know, it's prime real estate now, I mean there are major high-rises over there and all those lofts have been turned into apartments, but, the building itself was a three storey building, it was about nine thousand square feet. At that particular time it was a pretty big club . . . for Chicago you know with three different floors. The dance floor was like in the centre floor and then there was like the lounge area . . . on the upper floor. (Knuckles, 1990)

The upper floor had a trap door that let you down to the centre dance floor; the action of having to go down the steps enhanced its underground 'feel'. Apparently, the heat of the dancing bodies would rise up. The rather low entry fee of four dollars meant that you did not have to be rich to go there. Elsewhere, Frankie Knuckles said:

> It wasn't a polished atmosphere, the lighting was real simplistic, but the sound system was *intense* and it was about what you heard as opposed to what you saw. Comfortably, the place held about 600, but coming and going we did about two thousand to two and a half thousand people. The crowds came in shifts. (Garratt, 1986, p. 21)

The dancers were 'jacking', while at times holding on to the drain pipes that led diagonally across the walls (Walters, 1989). 'Jacking' is a term specific to the type of sexualized dance movements made to the music. People were interpreting the music and moved to and fro, up and down, wheeling their bodies around and against the rhythms, mostly in couples but also on their own. The dancing crowd were in the club from midnight on Saturday until Sunday noon, losing themselves in an ecstatic, frenzied dance. Hodge and Kress (1988) remark that 'Night is a special time . . . There are times when social syntagma lose their force' (p. 73), whereby 'the availability of these oppositional practices is mapped on to social time and space, organised into a system of domains' (p. 78).

One could therefore claim that, in this isolated twelve-hour frenzy of the night, in the middle of the weekend, new identities could be forged that were not necessarily there to be sustained throughout the rest of the week. The

dance, the music, even the club itself were built for that moment in the weekend, to disappear once it had occurred. However, the sense of community
and of a shared 'conspiracy' it created, as well as the force of the experience,
could give you a greater confidence in a private identity constructed outside
a 'mainstream'. Marshall Jefferson, producer of 'The house anthem' (Vax
Records, 1986) exclaimed to an English journalist in 1986: 'You'll leave there
a changed person. You might go and seek religion afterwards! You'll love it.
It's gonna be hot, it's gonna be sweaty, and it's gonna be great! (Garratt,
1986). This was not a political movement with manifestos in print. It was an
ephemeral cultural event which was experienced through the movements of
the body, its sexuality and its emotional reserves.

The contents of the lyrics of Chicago house music were often sexually
explicit. There was also a celebration of purely being alive in these hedonistic, frenzied dance gatherings. Perhaps one could claim that religious
sentiments, as can be found in the gospel impulse (Berry, 1992), were translated into sex talk, thereby drawing the crowd of dancers even closer together
in a sense of community, as though they were attending a religious gathering. Jamie Principle, for example, was very much responsible for setting
such a trend. He was a vocalist who worked together with Frankie Knuckles
when the latter had left The Warehouse to work at The Powerplant. This
club catered for a 'mixed' crowd, meaning a mix of sexualities. Jamie used
to sing to tracks for Frankie – tracks which were specially created for his
audience. At first Frankie Knuckles was bothered about the sexual explicit-
ness of Jamie's lyrics:

> [He] fantasized about what he wants to do and he wants to say stuff like that.
> He set the groundwork for that you know, then all of a sudden different little
> cult records started coming up like 'Sensuous Black Woman' and 'Sweet Pussy
> Pauline' and these different little house records have you know, heavy rhythms
> underneath it and all this sexual whatever going on the top of it. (Knuckles,
> 1990)

A tradition of 'sleazy' tracks with highly sexualized lyrics had established itself
on the house scene. In night clubs which catered to dancers who enjoyed
experimenting with their sense of sexuality, these often melancholic tracks,
driven by deep rolling bass sounds and filled with sentiments of desire and
lust, fitted perfectly. 'Feelin' sleazy' by Fingers Inc. (Jack Trax, 1988), Liz
Torres' 'When you hold me', vocalized by Master C & J, and 'What you
make me feel' (Jack Trax in 1987), as well as the much later 'French kiss' by
Lil Louis (ffrr, 1989) are just a few of many examples.

Often the lyrics of Chicago house music portrayed a sense of hope for the
community as well, much in the way that gospel lyrics do (Berry, 1992).
Many of the American singers of the house music genre, such as Shawn

Christopher, Daryl Pandy, Keith Nunally and Robert Owens, were trained
in gospel church choirs. As Marshall Jefferson put it: '[House] is more like a
feeling that runs through, like old time religion in the way that people just
get happy and screamin'.'

For a group of mainly urban African-American youths, who wanted to
transcend the oppressing boundaries of a racist, homophobic and sexist
world, these parties and clubs were a haven, a night-time church if you like,
where a sense of wholeness could be achieved. The social structure of
Chicago lends itself especially well to the development of a distinct style
within one social group; people from Chicago I spoke to confirmed that this
city has an active policy of segregation (Blanchard, 1992; Smooth, 1992;
Cooper, 1992; Joshua, 1992; Lash, 1992). The house scene was a closed one,
which mainly involved people from the African-American as well as Latino
(Berry, 1992) communities, who like to live on the edge of being sexually
adventurous, where 'it's hip to be gay' (DJ Pierre, 1992). In this specific
cultural space, an idiosyncratic language in dance music developed which is
now called house music.

It may be suggested that in the sense that 'it was hip to be gay', African-
Americans created their own 'bohemia', on the margin of the 'mainstream'
African-American community, which had a different taste in music and
entertainment (O'Connor, 1993). Within the African-American cultural
tradition, blues was seen to be for an older generation and R & B was too
slow in tempo for this hedonist night club crowd; rap was originally created
by and for non-'gay' New Yorkers and go-go was specific to the big bands
of Washington. The notion of 'bohemia' is interesting in itself. While it
cannot be identical to youth, often the two groups do overlap (Mailer, 1959).
In the case of the emergence of house music, this bohemia was based on a
redefinition of sexual identities within the African-American community.
Although this redefinition is critical, it has been argued elsewhere that this
'bohemia' kept close links to the African-American community at large
through the church and its gospel influence (Berry, 1992; Thomas, 1989).

In the early eighties, loft parties developed within this particular African-
American scene or cultural space. 'Mad' dance gatherings in people's houses
and in derelict areas proliferated, inspired by a style of presenting dance music
which DJs like Frankie Knuckles, Ron Hardy or Farley Jackmaster Funk had
developed into a sophisticated form. Maurice Joshua of I-D Productions said
it was 'the best club scene ever was possible' (Joshua, 1992). DJ Pierre
commented on this subject:

> Yeah, like, a few years ago it used to be like huge. Man, we had our own type
> of dress, we thought house music, we thought, 'That's just a way of life man!'
> We used to walk around . . . Parties – oh! 48-hour marathon parties at Ron
> Hardy's . . . a whole weekend straight, non-stop. (DJ Pierre, 1992).

The regular parties had resident DJs and names like The Loft, The Playground, The Sowers, The First Impression or Joe Smooth's East Hollywood. This party scene reached a peak between 1984 and 1986.

A problem for Chicago club DJs was the lack of availability of dance music (Moulton, 1975). This was partly alleviated by the development and avail-ability of relatively cheap Japanese electronic instruments around 1982. Records heard on the radio or at the parties could be reinterpreted, recorded, pressed to vinyl and played at your own party. Hereby the ephemeral DIY sensibility of house music is stressed; rather than being occupied with a sense of purism, the production of house music is about what is at that moment the most effective on the dance floor to make people lose themselves, within the restrictions of the available means, economically, technically and in the sense of skill. An example of this is 'On & On' by First Choice (Salsoul, 1979), which was re-recorded by Jessie Saunders and Vince Lawrence. Released in 1983 on Trax Records, this became the first house track which was commercially available (Lawrence, 1992).[11] Tracks were tools for DJs to be able to boost their performance. There was hardly any song structure to them; they consisted of mainly a rhythm track generated on a drum-machine,[12] a simple yet powerful bass line, some keyboards based on Latin American rhythms (mainly salsa)[13] and, when released commercially, perhaps with the addition of a sparse gospel-based vocal. The drum machine was especially useful, since it could play a steady tempo without changing the speed or needing a break, which would be necessary for a real drummer. Using a drum-machine on a record made the job of mixing two records together much easier for the disco and house DJ, since this requires a consis-tent beat. Within European forms of disco similar technologies were employed, as opposed to New York club music, which preferred the sound of real drummers; so it was the former material that gained popularity in Chicago (Berry, 1992). Avant-garde electronic dance music such as Kraftwerk, Depeche Mode and Quando Quango and European disco such as 'Dirty talk' by Klin & MBO (Baby Records, 1983) were therefore employed within the mix. However, European voices were not liked by the African-American house audience, so it was the instrumentals of Euro-disco tracks which became important (Berry, 1992). As the competition between the DJs increased, so did the urge to be different. E Smoove, who has been a DJ since 1982, said that they 'all made tracks to play at parties, to be one above the rest' (Smoove, 1992). In this way the aesthetic of house became more strictly defined.

According to Frankie Knuckles, it was 'Baby wants to ride' by Jamie Principle (Trax Records, 1984) which broke the concept of house music to a larger audience. In the early to mid-eighties, Jamie had become a popular vocalist within the house scene of Chicago; he was paid $1,500–2,000 for performing just one or two songs in a club. Some years after 'Baby wants to ride' had been written, Frankie sent a copy of it to his colleague of yester-year,[14] Larry Levan, who at that time DJed in the New York underground dance club Paradise Garage. According to Frankie Knuckles, 'Larry flipped over it and started playing it at the Garage . . . and everyone that went to the Garage was like demanding this record . . . New York City made it, you know' (Knuckles, 1990).

Presided over by DJ Larry Levan, the club Paradise Garage had been responsible for its own brand of club music.[15] Slower and more soulful, this was a sound-track for a more upmarket 'gay' crowd in New York, where people cared just a little bit more about their appearance than the wild crowds in Chicago's Warehouse. However, some of the music which was played at 'the Garage', otherwise known as garage music, did cross over with what was played at house events in Chicago and vice versa. Although the speed of the records danced to in New York was slower than in Chicago, there was, for example, a sharing of a love for Italian disco records, although those were ultimately more popular in Chicago. As a member of an electronic dance outfit, Quanto Quango, I had first-hand experience of the atmosphere in this huge club, in which my band performed three times in 1983. It had a custom-built Richard Lund sound system (Harvey, 1983) and catered for 'gays' mainly from African-American and Latino-American backgrounds. The crowd was frantic (on stimulants like cocaine and ecstasy), not like anything seen in England before 1988, which leaves one wondering about the frenzy at the Chicago parties, which was reported to have been even more intense. In this atmosphere, Chicago house crossed to a New York 'gay' crowd, where its form still has its male homosexual connotations.

The music became more widely known to the outside world around 1986, when a host of Chicago house artists presented their work at the New York annual music business conference, the New Music Seminar or NMS. Artists from the Chicago label DJ International were especially well represented. This larger independent Chicago dance label hosted a special party during the NMS in New York's Better Days club. With the attention of the English press that this event attracted, Americans more widely began to gain interest, which meant that Chicago house finally got some radio play outside of Chicago. An indication of its local popularity is that in 1986 Farley Jackmaster Funk attracted 2,000 people at La Mirage on both Friday and Saturday nights, while both Ron Hardy and Frankie Knuckles attracted capacity crowds (Garratt, 1986) at The Music Box and The Powerplant respectively. In September 1986 the energetic and soaring 'Love can't turn around', produced by Farley Jackmaster Funk and featuring male 'diva'[16] singer Daryl Pandy (London Records, 1986), reached number ten in the British national chart (Cheeseman, 1993) and number one in the DMC UK dance chart[17] (*Mixmag*, 1986). In the same dance chart there were other Chicago luminaries, such as JM Silk, with 'Jack your body' (US

Underground, 1986) and also 'No way back' by Adonis (Us Trax, 1986) (*Mixmag*, 1986). Garage act Colonel Abrahams entered this same chart with 'Over and over' (MCA) in 1986.

Given this information, one is forced to consider the racial segregation at work in Chicago and elsewhere, which disadvantages non-'whites' as well as homosexuals who would like to have a greater success in their artistic endeavours. House music had to wait for the attention of Europeans, and in particular of the English, for it to have a wider popular and therefore financial success. As an aesthetic, house music started as an effect of the positive power of a sense of community and a particular style of musical presentation that was specific to a dance floor, not radio listening. However, it is also the effect of the negative power of racial and sexual segregation. Perhaps seeing its existence as a pure act of African-American 'bohemia' would be romanticize its political context. In an act of desire for 'the Other', bohemian young 'white' Europeans, and in particular the English, were keen to buy in on the sense of strength of resistance as well as the musical energetic power that this underground scene and its music showed.

In the Chicago outside of this scene, no one wanted to know about it, and when I visited Chicago in 1992, most people there were still ignorant of its existence. If anything, as the house scene briefly appeared from its underground existence, it was eventually perceived as 'trouble'. For example, in 1987, residents of neighbourhoods which accommodated some of the dance parties started to complain about loud youths leaving rubbish like chicken bones on their lawns. This happened to some of the parties which Detroit-based Vick May and Kevin Saunders BA organized in Chicago (Blanchard, 1992). Although for a while the Chicago authorities seemed to have ignored the illegal tapping of electricity from street lighting and the cutting off of electricity by rival party organizers (Elliott, 1992), this time the police put a ban on after-hours parties. They also withheld late-night licences from house music related clubs (Blanchard, 1992). DJ Pierre argued that it was not only official harassment which stopped house parties from continuing:

> It was more than the police though. Like one of the radio stations, [102.7] WBMX[18] went off the air.[19] That stopped, 'cause . . . [inaudible] . . . used to play a lot of house music, and he was really the only house jock that played the type of music that we liked, right. So, when that went off, that was the end of that. Frankie Knuckles moved to New York, that destroyed it . . . [Ron Hardy] self-destructed, you know, between drugs and other things, you know. (DJ Pierre, 1992).

After 1987, without a party scene, the development of Chicago house music became stagnant.

Although the house party scene in Chicago was stifled, in 1988 house music became an institution in the mainly 'white' heterosexual club world in Europe, especially in England, Holland, Germany, Belgium and Italy. In Europe this musical form gradually lost its African-American sensibilities. Categories like rave, techno and trance house mainly share with house a use of similar production technologies, DJ techniques, the characteristic of a 4/4 beat at 125 bpm or over and their technologies of consumption. At times European house music styles seem like sparse pastiches of what in Chicago was based in a long-lived African-American cultural history. In Europe the term 'house music' has acquired a different meaning, where its own sensibilities have been added, such as its legacy of an electronic avant-garde. European house music styles have been exported back to the United States in the shape of German and Dutch hardcore super speedy tracks, which the Americans call techno-rave. There, European-American youth went wild at Euro-styled rave parties in the suburbs of the larger American cities, such as Washington, New York, Los Angeles and Chicago.

Conclusion

Using Foucault's terminology, certain procedures have been laid down locally which qualify what is included and excluded from its body of aesthetic and ethical knowledge, in the process defining what is house music and what is a house scene, incorporating the positive power of a rich tradition of African-American culture, such as gospel. This process may have started as a reaction to a sense of exclusion or negative power caused by racist and homophobic discourses in American society. Thereby a play with identities based on race and sexuality and perhaps a play with the notion of being 'the (bohemian) Other' has ultimately created a discourse of its own, with its own 'platform'. This process is in line with an observation by Foucault:

> We must make allowance for the complex and unstable process whereby discourse can be both an instrument and an effect of power, but also a hindrance, a stumbling-block, a point of resistance and a starting point for an opposing strategy. (Foucault, 1981, p. 101)

As has been shown, in the Chicago house scene of the eighties, the 'opposing strategy' was not one of manifestos, beyond some of its more explicit lyrics. Rather, the participants of the party and club life surrounding the musical discourse of house music were empowered by the celebration of a sense of community, which shaped identities that were excluded from, or given less power by, the world in which they were administratively ruled by government and mass media. The very existence of the house scene as a space for the bonding of 'alternative' identities was therefore 'a starting point for an opposing strategy'. Interestingly, although the British house scene was not centred around the politics and power struggles surrounding the forging of racial and sexual identities, the British government seems to have understood the format of house music parties as a threat when, during the nineties, it started to legislate against the development of a house music scene in Britain (Redhead, 1993; Rietveld, forthcoming).

This chapter is adapted from the forthcoming book, *This Is Our House* (Arena).

1 bpm is an abbreviation for beats per minute.
2 Sequencers are electronic composition tools.
3 Synthesizers are electronic sound generators.
4 Samplers are electronic devices which enable the recording, manipulation and replay of parts of existing sounds, such as past recorded music.
5 Even though African-American musical forms like jazz, blues, soul music and funk have been eagerly consumed by some Europeans, European contexts of consumption have changed some of the meanings which were generated within African-American historical, political and cultural contexts of production and consumption.
6 For example, hardcore techno, which traces its historical connections with electronic trance and with electronic body music, or break beat rave music and jungle, which in England often carry an African-Caribbean 'accent' with stylistic devices such as raggamuffin talkovers.
7 See also Pratt, 1990.
8 I have witnessed him working as a DJ several times, both in New York and in the UK; the last time I saw this was in March 1994 at Soak in the Corn Exchange in Leeds.
9 'Voguing' is a type of dance which enacts the posing by photo models (Ninja, 1994). The striking of poses is done in a fluent and almost acrobatic manner, whereby any role model can be taken for the outfit and pose, from film star to business man. This type of competitive dancing stems from the New York African-American 'gay' scene. See, for example, the film *Paris is Burning* (ICA, 1991).
10 This track can also be found on the movie sound track for the film that celebrated disco music and its culture, *Saturday Night Fever* (RSO, 1977).
11 With everyone in Chicago claiming to have been the first house protagonist, it is difficult to verify reports. Phil Cheeseman claims that Jessie Saunders' Project Z Factor was first, but not on Trax Records, with either 'Fantasy' or 'I like to do it in a fast car' (Mitchball, 1983). According to Adonis, Jessie Saunders 'bootlegged' Jamie Principle's Waiting on your angel' by re-recording it for Larry Sherman's label, Precision (Cheeseman, 1993).
12 A drum-machine is a sequencer with pre-recorded drum sounds, which can be sequenced by a programmer.
13 Some of the piano riffs of eighties Chicago house music, as well as of similar forms from New York and especially Miami, seems to follow and/or work around the clave rhythm of salsa. For those who are interested in the rhythm figures of salsa music,

Charley Gerard and Marty Sheller's account may be of use (Gerard and Sheller, 1989). An argument could be made for the central importance of the piano rhythms in salsa (Doerschuk, 1992), which in turn have influenced a lot of the early house tracks, such as One on One Crew 'Give it up (piano mix)' (Jack Trax, 1988), culminating in the piano frenzy of mostly Italian, but also English, house productions ('piano tracks') during the early nineties.

14 In the early seventies they both worked at the Continental Baths in New York (Smith, 1992).

15 'Club' is one of the purposefully indefinable terms for dance music in the underground dance clubs of New York. It is, in many ways, related to the initial ideas of both house and garage music, which articulate sensibilities from the African-American and 'gay' communities.

16 Daryl Pandy is a passionate singer with a 'gay' sensibility.

17 This chart is based not on record sales, but rather on the popularity of a record on the dance floor. It is established by letting club DJs fill in chart return lists each week.

18 This was the radio station which featured Farley Jackmaster Funk and the Hot Mix 5 with Mickey Oliver, Ralphy Rosario, Mario Diaz, Julian Perez and Steve Silk Hurley every day after midnight (Cheeseman, 1993).

19 In 1988 (Martin, 1992).

20 DJ Pierre's full name is Pierre Jones. However, within the dance music industry he is known as DJ Pierre; I therefore kept this name for references.

References

Berry, Glen A. (1992) 'House music's development and the east coast underground scene', unpublished paper, University of Wisconsin-Madison, Madison, WI.

Blanchard, Burt 'Non-Stop' (1992) Interview with the author, Chicago, June.

Cheeseman, Phil (1993) 'History of house DJ supplement', *DJ*, no. 87, 22 April – 5 May.

Cooper, Tyree (1992) Interview with the author, Chicago, June.

Cosgrove, Stuart (1988) Sleeve note to *The History of the House Sound of Chicago*, NCM Records, West Germany.

DJ Pierre[20] (1992) Interview with the author, New York City, June.

Doerschuk, Robert L. (1992) 'Secrets of salsa rhythm: piano with hot sauce', in Vernon W. Boggs (ed), *Salsiology: Afro-Cuban music and the Evolution of salsa in New York City*, Westport, CT: Greenwood Press.

Elliott, Kevin (1992) Interview with the author, Chicago, September.

Fleming, Jonathan (1995) *What Kind of House Party is This? History of a Music Revolution*, Slough: MIY Publishing.

Foucault, Michel (1981) *The History of Sexuality, Vol. 1 An Introduction*, London: Peregrine.

Garratt, Sheryl (1986) 'Chicago house', *The Face*, no. 77, September.

Gerard, Charley and Marty Sheller (1989), *Salsa! The Rhythm of Latin Music*, Crown Point, IN: White Cliffs Media Company.

Harvey, Steven (1983) 'Behind the groove: New York City's disco underground', *Collusion*, no. 5.

Hodge, Robert and Gunther Kress (1988) *Social Semiotics*, Oxford: Polity Press.

Joshua, Maurice (1992) Interview with the author, Brookfield, IL, June.

Knuckles, Frankie (1990) Transcribed research interview conducted by Jon Savage for *Rhythm Divine*, Channel 4 (London).

Lash, Scott (1992) Conversation with the author, Manchester, October.

Lawrence, Vince (1992) Interview with the author, Chicago, June.

Mailer, Norman (1959) 'The white Negro', in *Advertisements for Myself*, London: Andre Deutsch.

Martin, Terry (1992) 'Knuckles' Chicago, *Crossfade*, no. 3, November.

Mixmag (1986) 'DMC's UK dance chart' *Mixmag*, no. 44, September.

Moulton, Tom (1975) 'Disco action', *Billboard*, no. 43, 10 February.

Ninja, Willis (1994) 'Not a mutant turtle', in Andrew Ross and Tricia Rose (eds) *Microphone Fiends, Youth Music and Youth Culture*, London: Routledge.

O'Connor, Justin (1993) Conversation with the author, Manchester, March.

Pratt, Ray (1990) *Rhythm and Resistance: Explorations in the Political Uses of Popular Music*, London: Praeger.

Redhead, Steve (ed.) (1993) *Rave Off: Politics and Deviance in Contemporary Youth Culture*, Aldershot: Avebury.

Rietveld, Hillegonda (forthcoming) *This Is Our House*, Aldershot: Arena.

Sherman, Larry (1992) Interview with the author, Chicago, June.

Smith, Richard (1992) 'Going back to my roots', *Mixmag*, vol. 2, no. 17, October.

Smooth, Joe (1992) Interview with the author, Chicago, June.

Smoove, E (1992) Interview with the author, Brookfield, IL, June.

Straw, Will (1991) 'Systems of articulation, logics of change: communities and scenes in popular music', in *Cultural Studies*, London: Routledge.

Thomas, Anthony (1989) 'The house the kids built: the gay black imprint on American dance music', *Out/Look* (US), Summer.

Tong, Pete (1990) Research interview conducted by Jon Savage for *Rhythm Divine*, Channel 4 (London).

Walters, Barry (1989) 'Burning down the house', *Spin*, June.

9 Cocaine Girls:

Marek Kohn

One evening in April 1916, around ten o'clock, Willy Johnson was standing on the corner of Lichfield Street and West Street, off Charing Cross Road in the West End of London. A woman passed by and he accosted her, making her step into the street to avoid him; he approached a second likewise. At that point the two police sergeants who had been watching him pounced. 'I am only trying to sell cocaine,' Johnson protested. As he spoke, he dropped a woollen bag containing eleven small boxes of the drug. Only trying to sell cocaine, as distinct from succeeding in doing so, was not against the law, and Johnson was acquitted. If he had been found guilty, the maximum penalty he could have faced was a £5 fine, a sanction intended for shopkeepers rather than street hustlers. A couple of months before, Harrods and the pharmacists Savory & Moore had incurred such penalties, for selling preparations containing cocaine and morphine.

Johnson's arrest and acquittal was, in fact, a formative moment in the constitution of the British drug underground during the First World War. The case helped to provide the police with a platform upon which to campaign for the criminalization of drug use. They were rapidly successful: within a few weeks, the authorities had introduced the regime of drug control which persists to this day.

The first glimpses of the British drug underground had appeared around the end of 1915, exotic flowers blooming in wartime soil. The initial anticipation, in August 1914, of a campaign 'over by Christmas' had yielded to a recognition of what modern total war meant. It demanded the mobilization of the nation as a single, efficient machine; and this required moral efficiency. Lloyd George declared drink a more deadly foe than the Germans, mainly for its effects on industrial production. Under the catch-all emergency powers of the Defence of the Realm Act, pub opening hours were restricted; and the 'Beauty Sleep Order' obliged restaurants and hotels to close at 10.30. Finally, a campaign by *The Times* extended the net to night-clubs in November 1915. The immediate result was a spawn of illegal clubs: by the end of the year, there were 150 in Soho alone.

In this new, semi-clandestine zone, encompassing both illicit dives and venues that obeyed the letter of the law but not the spirit of patriotic disci-pline, new mutations were observed. At the turn of the year, Quex, the gossip columnist of the *Evening News*, referred to 'the growing craze for opium smoking'. 'West End Bohemia is hearing some dark stories of what is going on', Quex warned.

> But still more prevalent is the use of that exciting drug cocaine. It is so easy to take – just snuffed up the nose; and no-one seems to know why the girls who suffer from this body and soul racking habit find the drug so easy to obtain. In the ladies' cloakroom of a certain establishment two bucketfuls of thrown-away small circular cardboard boxes were discovered by the cleaners the other day – discarded cocaine boxes.

Within a few weeks, the terms of Britain's first drug panic were defined. Among the thousands of Imperial troops stationed in southern England were Canadians, men with a reputation for toughness in combat and disorder-liness off duty. Their ranks included numbers of soldiers who had come into contact with the United States drug underground, already established among the delinquent classes. A small 'sting' operation in Folkestone resulted in the capture of a petty West End criminal and his prostitute asso-ciate, both of whom sold cocaine to a soldier working under cover. The woman said she bought her supplies from a man in a West End pub – 'He sells it to all of us girls.' The problem thus appeared as a threat posed by women of a certain class, aided by male criminals, to the soldiery. Here was an extreme moral opposition, between the epitome of what was deplored in womanhood, and the epitome of what was valued in manhood. It posed a threat precisely to those on whom national survival was believed to depend.

Drugs – and especially cocaine – were thus marked as both subversive and feminine; they were Other. They were also alien, said to have been brought to Britain, at this moment in which the external threat was never graver, by foreigners – the handful of Chinese in the docklands with their opium, Canadians, Continental rogues driven across the Channel by the German advance, Americans associated with the entertainment industry.

In the spring and early summer of 1916, assisted by American films with titles like *The Curse of the Poppy*, the popular press inflected the drug story with the hysteria of wartime: 'Vicious Drug Powder – Cocaine driving hundreds mad – Women And Aliens Prey On Soldiers . . . LONDON IN THE GRIP OF THE DRUG CRAZE . . . SECRET "COKE" PARTIES OF "SNOW SNIFTERS".' Headlines like these helped turn the drug underground into an explicitly criminal one.

However, the connection between moral panic and the passing of new laws was not as strong as might be expected from a modern viewpoint. Sir Malcolm Delevingne, the keenest anti-drug campaigner at the Home Office, admitted that legislation might 'be difficult to get and would possibly not be regarded as uncontroversial'. Emergency powers were used instead. Under the Defence of the Realm Regulation 40B, enacted on 28 July 1916, the possession of cocaine or opium (except by authorized professionals) was made illegal. DORA 40B was subsequently incorporated into peacetime law, forming the basis of the Dangerous Drugs Act, 1920.

This was one of many instruments adopted by the state during the Great War, and thereafter accepted as a permanent fixture. When conscription was introduced in 1916, the Home Secretary resigned because he regarded the measure as an unacceptable infringement on liberty. Although social mores were far more conservative than in even the middle part of the century, and freedom of expression far more circumscribed by censorship, the right of the state to control individual behaviour was in other respects less established than it is today. Though drug use met with strong disapproval – once it was seen to be practised by people of whom the élite disapproved – the idea of prohibition, as distinct from stricter control, did not spring immediately to the minds of those in positions of power or influence.

A cocaine economy had undoubtedly sprung up in the wartime West End. Its dynamics and personae were exemplified by Willy Johnson's case. He had been drawn to the attention of the police by informants, who identified themselves as exiled Belgian detectives. Despite the clumsiness of its English, their letter speaks eloquently of a West End of Continentals, petty criminals and prostitutes: a West End teeming with Others, who mixed promiscuously with the troops arriving or departing from France, via Victoria and Waterloo. 'There is more than ten boys who sell cocaine to the girls', they warned, naming Johnson first of all, and describing his activities on the pitch he had taken outside the café where he had formerly worked as a porter, until it was closed after the proprietor was convicted for allowing prostitutes to gather and remain on the premises.

Johnson, aged 26, turned out to be a petty criminal who lived nearby with a prostitute; empty cocaine boxes were found in their room, and the police thought she was under the influence of the drug during the raid. 'Willy's woman named Phyllis also sells it in the public house, the Provence, Leicester Square', claimed the Belgians, referring to the Hotel Provence, a famous venue for off-duty soldiers and prostitutes. They also pointed the finger at 'four Jewish boys, always in the sandwich shop at 89 Shaftesbury Avenue'.

The police found this place to be 'patronised chiefly by prostitutes and Continental undesirables'.

The cocaine economy was, by today's standards, a lightweight affair. Johnson bought his supplies for ninepence a box, and sold them at two shillings and sixpence. His source, a petty crook called Alfy Benjamin, obtained the drug from a shady chemist in Lisle Street, just a few yards away from Johnson's pitch, who in turn would have paid twopence-halfpenny for the amount contained in one of Johnson's boxes (assuming it was uncut). The pill-boxes hawked around the West End probably contained between a tenth and a sixth of a gram, quantities geared to casual or light users only.

The culture supported by this trade is less easy to assess. These were not people to leave personal papers, like Lady Diana Manners, the leading socialite of the day, who in December 1915 wrote to Raymond Asquith, the son of the prime minister, of how she and Raymond's wife Katharine had lain 'in ecstatic stillness through too short a night, drugged in very deed by my hand with morphia'. Texts like this, and other examples of the high-Bohemian genre of drug literature, have been used to characterize the original British drug underground as an essentially upper-class phenomenon. This, I believe, misses the crucial point of the West End scene. As a compact and close zone of social promiscuity, principally dedicated to the pursuit of pleasure, it allowed rare vertical sections to be cut through a horizontally stratified society. Street prostitutes were part of a stratum reliant upon tempo-rary, largely informal sources of income, some legal and others not. A woman in this milieu might earn a few pounds as a dressmaker here, a few more as a servant there, and sell sexual services at other times.

A significant proportion of women charged with prostitution described themselves in court as 'chorus girls'. Here the chain of association up the social scale begins to become clear. Street prostitutes shaded into the lower reaches of the theatrical milieu; chorus girls mixed with higher-rank actresses, who frequented the more prestigious nightclubs, which were patronized by affluent (and sometimes titled) sensation-seekers. The prosti-tutes in the pubs, asking each other for 'snow', shared a culture with the women who discarded their pill-boxes in the nightclubs that Quex moni-tored. How far this went beyond the sharing of drug argot is hard to say, but it seems reasonable to regard the cocaine-takers of the West End as partici-pants in a hedonistic local culture that embraced values rejected by society as a whole. Bohemia had its upper and lower classes.

Historians and other commentators have tended to neglect this Greater Bohemia, a marginal zone which blurred boundaries and defied categories. Its upper echelons have been subsumed into the bourgeois tradition of lives and letters; its lower orders neglected by the chroniclers of labour, with their preference for the respectable proletariat. Nor do feminist historians seem to show much interest in the women of the period who were not munition workers, 'conductorettes', or Suffragettes.

The 'dope' drama acquired a tragic heroine in November 1918. The day after attending a Victory Ball to celebrate the Armistice, a rising young actress called Billie Carleton died of a drug overdose; it was ascribed to cocaine, though what is known of the circumstances suggest this was unlikely. The ensuing scandal made notorious a circle of theatrical types, centred on a louche and sexually ambivalent costume designer named Reggie de Veulle, who gathered in Mayfair to hold all-night opium 'orgies', wearing chiffon nightdresses and pyjamas. (De Veulle's wife Pauline insisted, with a dress designer's professional precision, that the women had actually worn crêpe de Chine tea gowns and chiffon dresses trimmed with lace. She also claimed that, though she had tried smoking the opium pipe, she had not inhaled.) Racial boundaries as well as those of sex and class were crossed: the opium was supplied by the Scottish wife of a Limehouse Chinese man; the West Enders also travelled to Limehouse – or sent their servant – to obtain the drug.

Billie Carleton, the illegitimate daughter of a chorus girl, was modern in her attitude to pleasure, but old fashioned in her way of seeking it. She was 'under the protection' of a rich, middle-aged playboy, and her closest relationships seem to have been with older men, including de Veulle. Her goals were luxury, glamour and fame, not independence and the right to vote. But her fate was construed as an awful warning for young women who tried to defy any aspect of convention. According to one article arising from the Carleton case, and published a few days before women voted for the first time, the 'woman dope fiend' was to be found in Chelsea, Mayfair and Maida Vale. 'An obscure traffic is pursued in certain doubtful teashops. The sale of certain beauty specifics is only a mask for the illicit traffic in certain drugs.' The article described how 'a young and attractive girl deeply interested in social conditions and political economy' was introduced to drugs by another woman. She soon became 'a confirmed haunter of a certain notorious café', ended up 'acting as a decoy for a notorious gambling hell' and was dead within nine months. 'The queer, bizarre, rather brilliant bachelor girl is a frequent victim to the insidious advances of the female dope fiend', it concluded.

The moral of this story was that young women might have recently developed an interest in politics, or demonstrated the ability to drive ambulances under fire, or performed the kind of factory work hitherto reserved for men, but they remained in essence the frail creatures that the Victorians had insisted they were. The court proceedings that followed Billie Carleton's death offer ample evidence of her vivacity, obstinacy, ambition and manipulativeness. As rewritten by the press, however, her complex and troubled identity was reduced to a 'fairylike figure and face', 'a frail beauty and delicate art . . . all of that perishable, moth-like substance that does not last long in the wear and tear of this rough and ready world'. Years after her death, she would be recalled as 'bright, beautiful Billie Carleton, flitting through life on butterfly wings, fragrant as a lovely flower, but all the time a child gripped in the fiendish clutches of the devil of cocaine'.

The metaphor of butterfly or moth was rooted in the Victorian stereotype of the frail woman-child, but it also alluded to the decidedly unethereal 'flapper', a species which had entered popular parlance shortly before the war. The term denoted a young, foolish, pleasure-loving and fashion-conscious woman. It carried a strong connotation of emotional and intellectual immaturity – the successful legislative move to extend the franchise to women under thirty, passed in 1927, was derided as the 'Votes for Flappers Bill'. But it also suggested vitality and activity. A flapper was not merely what would later be called a bimbo. She was more closely equivalent to the male types – narcissistic, pleasure loving, conspicuously free from responsibilities, devoted to style and appearance – known at various times as 'dandies', 'knuts' or 'swells'.

The flapper came into her own in the aftermath of the Great War. She defined the period; brittle, hedonistic, determinedly superficial. Underneath lay depths of trauma, turbulence and despair. Young women seemed to be the principal beneficiaries of the slaughter, overturning the fundamental law of patriarchal order, which is that inheritance goes to sons rather than daughters.

Part of this inheritance was a new world of mass entertainment. One of the most spectacular features of the war's aftermath was a dance craze, which extended the nightclub world Billie Carleton had enjoyed to her suburban sisters. Clubs and dancehalls sprang up to cater to a new, less exclusive clientele. Many of them, particularly in the West End, immediately became the focus of moral anxiety, and police scrutiny. The limits were tightly drawn: if a woman sat on a man's lap, the venue's licence was in jeopardy.

Nonetheless, prostitution and illegal drug use were intimate features of the club scene. Undercover officers were deployed against them, in top hats and evening dress. Sergeant George Goddard told a court that, according to notes made on the cuff of his shirt, he had observed precisely 292 women of the unfortunate class leaving a particular club in Leicester Square. In 1929 he was jailed on corruption charges, having accumulated £18,000 in savings, a luxury car and a large house in Streatham, although his wages were only £6 15s a week.

Jailed with him was Kate Meyrick, the most notorious nightclub entrepreneur of the 1920s. One of her innovations was the 'dance instructress', a dancing partner who received a small wage and whatever she could get in tips. Like an aspiring actress, her fortunes depended on looks, charm, stamina and male favour. She had to be able to draw attention to herself, dance all night, and be charming as long as she was awake. It is easy to imagine that such a young woman might come to depend on 'snow' to get her through the night.

For Freda Kempton, cocaine was also a final solution. She worked as a dance instructress at Brett's Dance Hall, a club founded by Mrs Meyrick, in a Charing Cross Road basement. 'Freda was a clever dancer, though personally I used to think her steps of an exaggerated type,' an acquaintance condescendingly remarked later, according to the *Evening News*. 'Always full of energy, even at four or five in the morning she would still be dancing and showing very few signs of fatigue.' As she danced, she chewed gum to mask the involuntary grinding of her teeth.

Off stage, so to speak, she revealed a bleaker face. In the first weeks of 1922, she had testified at the inquest on a friend who had killed herself, and remarked afterwards how funny it would be if she committed suicide as well. Her family background had been blighted by her father's dissolute behaviour; more recently, she had suffered some sort of sorrow in love. She seems to have been prone to melancholy – the kind horribly exacerbated by the after-effects of stimulant drugs like cocaine. She once showed her friend Rose Heinberg thirteen packets of cocaine in her powder puff case, which suggests that she was either using quite large quantities or selling it herself. On one occasion, her landlady's daughter encountered her when she got home at six in the morning, her jaw twitching: she was forced to claim she might have been drugged without her knowledge.

At midnight, one weekend early in March, she left the Westbourne Grove flat where she lodged, and went to Brett's, where she met Rose Heinberg. At half past three, they and a couple of male friends moved on to the New Court Club, off Tottenham Court Road, for breakfast. Finally, they went to a Chinese restaurant in Regent Street, one of the first in the West End, where they finished off the night with whiskies. At about eight the following evening, Freda emerged from her room, crying in agony, then dashing her head against the wall. After an hour, she went into convulsions, and died with her head resting on her landlady's arm.

Such a torment is typical of a cocaine overdose. It appeared that she had deliberately taken her life by swallowing a considerable quantity of the drug. At the inquest, Rose Heinberg testified that in the taxi that morning, Freda had announced her intentions. Heinberg also claimed that Freda had left the Chinese restaurant with a bottle of cocaine supplied by the restaurateur, Brilliant Chang.

A press campaign against 'dance dens' began within a few days of the tragedy, with Chang placed – albeit anonymously – at the centre of the scene. The *Daily Express* special correspondent described how a female companion had taken him, one Sunday night, out of the West End to 'a forbidding neighbourhood not very far from the Marble Arch'. The clandestine mood is set as the woman stops the taxi and they walk through the backstreets, past rows of stables and carter's vans, to the door in the wall of some industrial premises, where a sinister figure in black relieves him of £2 and bundles the pair of them into a large unlit building. In today's idiom, it was a warehouse party. At the end of a dark passage, they descend to the cellar. Here a genuine den is revealed, dimly lit, smoky and 'decorated on the incoherent Futurist lines usual in such places'. But the correspondent approves of the band, which 'crashed out a really good foxtrot . . . My companion slipped off her cloak and we danced. Round us danced the same old sickening crowd of under-sized aliens, blue about the chin and greasy, the same predominating type of girl, young, thin, underdressed, perpetually seized with hysterical laughter, ogling, foolish.'

This 'predominating type' was also depicted by an *Evening News* reporter, in an article which appeared the same day as the *Express* piece. In the words of the headline, this correspondent had found 'Cocaine Girls In The West End'; three of them, in a club off Shaftesbury Avenue. 'One was a frail-looking creature of about twenty in a flimsy frock that left three-quarters of her back bare. During the intervals of her vivacious dancing in an underground room, she gave herself over to almost hysterical attacks of inane, purposeless laughter, and now and then stroked the man sitting with her.'

Read through the words of more recent panics, it is possible to identify ironic similarities between then and now, in the common elements of anxiety about youth, stimulant drugs, illegal nightlife, dancing and hedonism. These parallels are not illusory. A distinctive feature of the 'dancedope' agitation was that, for the first time, a modern concept of youth emerged. The conflict between postwar hedonism and Victorian reaction was seen as a clash between the young and the old; with the young having a perspective, even a world-view, peculiar to themselves.

For the British, the dance craze was also the first mass encounter with a black culture. Notwithstanding the evening dress and the foxtrots, and the early attempts at syncopation that make a modern military band sound like a Memphis rhythm section, young Britons were getting their first taste of swing. To the curling of conservative lips, the most fashionable venues imported black American musicians. The *Observer* quoted a definition of jazz as 'a number of niggers surrounded by noise'.

The themes of youth and race are clearer in the light of our own recent history. At the time, the 'cocaine girls' were seen as a refraction of the trauma of the war. The hysteria and purposeless laughter echoed the hysterical derangement of shell-shocked men. Hedonism was more than indulgence; it was a reaction to a profound crisis of values, and the vertiginous conviction that any sense of purpose, national and personal, had been shown by the war to be meaningless.

The sexual forwardness attributed to the cocaine girls was of a piece with their thinness and frailty. This was the tubercular stereotype, of wan but erotic morbidity, combined with a highly strung, nervous temperament. The cocaine girls expressed the idea of a living-dead culture which appeared vibrant on the surface, but was profoundly pathological. It was also racially dysgenic. The flower of British manhood was dead; young womanhood, drugged and dance-crazy, was consorting with 'sickening', 'under-sized' aliens.

In the case of Brilliant Chang, the dancedope scene appeared not just as a potential threat to the quality of racial stock, but also as a culture of sexual perversion. Back at the warehouse party near Marble Arch, the climax of the *Express* correspondent's tale was the entry of a 'Chinaman'. This was not the stereotype of popular fiction, the writer emphasized, 'a cringing yellow man hiding his clasped hands in the wide sleeves of his embroidered gown', but a well-tailored figure with long, manicured hands and manners 'too perfect to be described as good'. Immediately a 'young girl' ran up to him with arms outstretched. In the sense that he was the centre of attention and epitomized the spirit of the occasion, he was the life and soul of the party. This figure was obviously Chang, although his name had yet to merge. To conjure up a more impressive threat, and perhaps to deflect the threat of litigation, the journalist claimed that he was a member of a species. 'Who are these smiling yellow men?' he asked; 'and why are they so popular with frail white women?'

This question became more acute when Chang, a playboy scion of a wealthy mercantile family, surfaced in daylight to refute allegations made by Rose Heinberg at the inquest on Freda Kempton. Not only was he Chinese, but he was little more than five feet tall. Despite being so antithetical to the ideal of English manhood, he seemed to exert a magnetic attraction on young women. After his appearance at the Kempton inquest, it was reported, 'some of the girls rushed to Chang, patted his back, and one, more daring than the rest, fondled the Chinaman's black, smooth hair and passed her fingers slowly through it'. The thick black hair, the blue overcoat with its luxurious fur collar, the grey suede shoes; all were noted, all added to a potent aura of sensuality. There was a subtle link between them and the *Express* man's references to the long manicured hands and the embroidered gown.

Though Chang had adopted western dress and manners, it was implied, his racial character shone through all the same. And this character was a profoundly feminine one. In British eyes, Chinese culture and civilization were unmanly; China's weakness as a power arose from the insidious effects of effeminacy. The *Express* account has the Chinaman making a dramatic entrance at the top of the stairs. The theatricality of the scene emphasizes the implication that he was in costume, acting a part. The hands, and the punctilious manners, were the giveaway. He was a transvestite. Drugs, therefore, caused not only racial but sexual perversion. Their effects, and those of the modernity of which they were a part, were profoundly anti-natural. And whereas the sexuality of the black man was also seen as threatening, it was construed as a straightforward animal phenomenon. An Englishman might not like it, but at least he felt he knew what it was about. The sexuality of the Chinaman was alien in the sort of sense more recently found in narratives about beings from other planets. Perhaps the erotic allure was produced by drugs, or perhaps drugs were a symptom of a greater and more mysterious threat.

These occult anxieties were expressed not only in popular journalism, but in novels and films. Avowedly fictional narratives linked 'dope' and Chinamen, as well as working numerous variations on the theme of the great oriental conspiracy, headed by an evil genius. There was something of Fu Manchu in Brilliant Chang, who was eventually crowned 'Dope King' by the press.

Dope narratives had a less obvious affinity with another genre: the vampire story. There were echoes of it in the living-dead eroticism of the 'dope girls', their nocturnal and clandestine activities, the gathering of female disciples around a charismatic male figure whose own sexuality was potent yet morbid; and, of course, death. Popular journalism and popular fiction combined to produce the Brilliant Chang that the public came to know in 1922. In at least one instance, the interaction was direct. A film entitled *Cocaine*, completed in six weeks and released two weeks after Freda Kempton's death, told the tale of an innocent young woman introduced to the world of nightclubs and drugs by an actress friend. At the club, according to the *Daily Express*, the women saw 'sleek young men and thinly clothed girls (many of them the "real thing") jazz and shimmy and fox-trot under the influence of late hours and excitement, nigger-music and cocktails, drugs and the devil'. The actress is already a cocaine addict; the young woman is induced to try it, whereupon she abandons herself to the predatory manager of 'The Limit'. One of the principal villains is a Chinese drug trafficker, played by a white man affecting a limp; 'a walking embodiment of evil', the *Express* said.

Cocaine was banned in London but shown in Cardiff, where a local Chinese man complained to the Chinese Consul-General that a cinema had advertised it with 'newspaper cuttings of the dancing girl and Mr Chang's photo'. The complainant was interviewed by a police inspector, who reported that offence had been caused to the Chinese community, whereupon the chief constable banned the film.

The evidence in the Freda Kempton case was insufficient to lead to charges against Chang. Perhaps because of this, he became the focus of intense attention from the police. Several of the employees at his restaurant were arrested for selling drugs to women on the premises and in nearby Soho streets. Forced to abandon his stake in the business, he set up a nightclub in

Gerrard Street – it may have been the first Chinese-run business in what would much later become the heart of the West End's 'Chinatown'. Six months later, he quit and headed out to Limehouse, the only Chinatown London then boasted.

Here Chang was a fish out of water, having nothing in common with the Chinese seamen and traders other than race. It is said that he was feared and disliked by his compatriots, partly for the unwanted police attention that followed him. He remained at liberty, however, while the police carried out an effective campaign against street dealers up West. His style was cramped, but it was not extinguished. In his room he kept a stock of identically worded letters addressed to 'Dear Unknown', to pass to women who caught his fancy. One police raiding party found two chorus girls in his bed, but no drugs.

Eventually, in 1924, Chang's luck ran out. After the arrest of a companion, a failed actress and addict called Violet Payne, he was charged with possession of a single packet of cocaine. It was alleged that he insisted on sexual favours from white women, as well as cash, in exchange for drugs. The press eagerly elaborated on this theme. Chang's trial was the nearest thing to a grand finale that the 1920s drug flap had. By the middle of the decade, police action had curbed street dealing, and the scene appeared to die away.

A generation later, after the Second World War, a new drug panic arose. This time it was 'teenage' girls, black men and marijuana, rather than flappers, yellow men and cocaine, but the racial and sexual tales it told were much the same.

Note

Marek Kohn's book *Dope Girls*, from which this chapter is adapted, is published by Lawrence and Wishart.

10 In the Supermarket of Style

Ted Polhemus

1947. French fashion designer Christian Dior unveils the 'New Look'. Feminine curves, luxury, Paris, the war is over. Fashion is back on course and within a few years – despite rationing and austerity – this New Look 'trickles down' the social strata to alter radically the appearance of the average woman in Europe, Britain and America. This is the essence of fashion: celebration of the new, conformity to a singular 'direction', the wealthy avant-garde setting the pace.

1964. Mods and Rockers invade British seaside resorts. Two tribes have gone to war. The Mods are in smart Italian-influenced suits and elegant casualwear. The Rockers are identified by their American biker-influenced leather jackets, jeans and motorcycle boots. The contrasting images also belie differences of attitude – the Mods' hankering after upward social mobility and European sophistication versus the Rockers' working-class pride and gruff machismo. The orientation of dress in both cases is subcultural – appearance signalling group membership and symbolically expressing group values. Everyone knows what side they are on.

Today, as we anxiously approach the start of a new millennium, nothing is quite what it seems.

In Paris, Milan, London and New York the 'fashion industry' – despite all the razzmatazz it can muster – year after year fails to put its finger on some definite New Look which will take the world by storm and cause the majority to jump on its bandwagon. Instead of the consensus of a single 'direction', a glut of alternative possibilities threaten sartorial anarchy.

Which distinctive look is *the* New Look? Which designer has his or her finger on the pulse? Those who would follow fashion splinter off into alternative camps – styletribes – where the 'signature style' of the tribal leader

(Armani, Saint Laurent, Versace, Montana, Westwood, Gaultier, Lauren, etc.) overrides change for the sake of group identity and classic continuity. Fashion becomes style in all but name. Avoiding the pitiful plight of the 'fashion victim', most people take it all with a large pinch of salt, preferring to sample and mix their own, personalized style 'statement'.

Graphically illustrating and celebrating change, progress and the promise of the future, fashion arose as the ultimate expression of modernism. Its decline in the *post*modern era seems hardly surprising. But how are the heirs of the Mods and the Rockers faring in this new/old world (dis)order?

Certainly a superficial, media-inspired perusal of such subcultures suggests that this group-oriented approach to appearance has proliferated geometrically as a host of recently defined styletribes like Technos, Riot Grrrls, Ravers, Modern Primitives, Cyberpunks, Raggamuffins, Acid Jazzers, New Age Travellers, Zippies, Cuties and so forth rub shoulders with Neo-Mod, Neo-Rocker, Neo-Beat, Neo-Punk, Neo-Glam, Neo-New Romantic and other nostalgia addicted revivalists. Closer examination, however, suggests that, despite this apparent cornucopia of tribal identities, as profound a sea change has occurred on the street and in the clubs as has occurred on the fashion catwalks. As with fashion, this change permeates beneath superficial appearances, signalling a radically different approach to style and identity even if, in some cases, the look remains the same.

Back in 1964 you *were* a Mod or a Rocker. Today, you're *into* Techno, Ragga or Acid Jazz. It's the difference between swimming and sticking your foot in the pool to checkout the temperature – an exploratory dalliance versus immersion and commitment. In researching the 'Streetstyle' exhibition (which appeared at the V & A in late 1994 and early 1995) and the book of the same name (Polhemus, 1995), I discovered that the nearer I got to the present day, the harder it was to find young people prepared to label themselves. I couldn't find a single person prepared to say, for example, 'I'm a Techno', 'I'm a Raggamuffin', 'I'm a Raver', 'I'm a Cyberpunk', 'I'm a Traveller', etc. Everyone, it seems, is 'an individual'. One expects that on Brighton beach in 1964 things would have been different.

To be sure, the lines of demarcation between today's Neo-Mods and today's Neo-Rockers are as stylistically distinct as those that existed between their sixties precursors. But here another dalliance – that of playing with history – subverts subcultural identity. It is no longer 1964. The historical circumstances which generated the original Mods and Rockers have been swept away, and the revivalists, however accurate their outfits and scooters/bikes, etc., cannot but reside in a sort of streetstyle theme park where true authenticity will always be an impossible dream. Cruising history, the denizens of style world have no here and now to hang their once street-credible hats upon.

But perhaps what really sets our age apart from the golden age of subcultures is the sheer proliferation of options. We now inhabit a Supermarket of Style where, like tins of soup lined up on endless shelves, we can choose between more than fifty different styletribes. Jumbling geography as well as history, British Punk circa 1976 sits on the shelf next to 1950s American Beatnik or late Jamaican Ragga. You name it, we've got it. You too can be an anarchic Punk, a bohemian Beatnik or a bad ass Raggamuffin. If only for a day.

And stacked next to the revamped youth-oriented streetstyles are the more upmarket products which bear on their label the word 'fashion'. Of course, these days, when even the most expensive designers find their inspiration on the street, and ghetto kids make copies of catwalk creations in a never-ending cycle, it can be difficult telling the two apart. Indeed, the whole notion that streetstyle and 'fashion' are distinct entities seems increasingly suspect.

To add further to the delightful confusion, there are those who playfully sample and mix from different looks. Mocking previously hard and fast distinctions – Streetstyle/High Fashion, Mods/Rockers, Punks/Hippies, The Old/The New, Good Taste/Kitsch, Respectable/Perv – these eclectics delight in incongruity and the unexpected. In the end, in the mix, the possibilities are unlimited: an Armani suit worn with back-to-front baseball cap and 'old school' trainers, a 'Perfecto' black leather jacket worn with tartan flares, a Hippy caftan worn with rubber leggings, DMs and a Chanel handbag.

Be confusing. Make a statement. Get a life.

Of course, the flipside of such choice and freedom is fragmentation and inauthenticity. In the Supermarket of Style everything and nothing is The Genuine Article. Bereft of consensus – either that of fashion's direction or of tribal identity – everything is possible but nothing connects. Outside of history (jumbling together eighteenth-century corsetry and twenty-first-century sci-fi) and defiant of geography (Tokyo Mods dressed in original London sixties gear), where and when dissolve into a space-time continuum. Natural symbols become arbitrary signs: Gay Skinheads, Haute Couture Grunge, Techno Hippies, Pervy Puritans, TV Babes with Stubble, Futuristic Revivalists, Bikers For Jesus, *Femme Fatale* Feminists.

In the Supermarket of Style, everthing is possible and nothing is quite what it appears. As old meanings are trashed, new, unexpected ones are created in a process of semiological terrorism which can be traced back to gay hyper-macho imagery (The Village People), punk pastiche (school blazers worn with tattered fishnets and handcuffs) and, ultimately, surrealist subversion of meaning. While fashion celebrated change and subcultural style celebrated group identity, the inhabitants of Styleworld celebrate the truth of falsehood, the authenticity of simulation, the meaningfulness of gibberish.

What to wear in the third millennium? Go for something that makes sense by making nonsense. Be out of it – out of time, out of place, out of context.

2019. Blade Runner pointed the way with everyone dressed like a film extra out of some other movie. Lots of different movies. All from different eras. All rubbing shoulders in a synchronic orgy where humans as well as replicants use their style to play with time, space and the chimera of reality. There is no discernible fashion direction, but neither is there a sense of subcultural identity. Everyone is a 'Clubber' at a fancy dress party. Different fancy dress parties, each with its own theme. The invitations must have got mixed up in the post.

Who is real? Who is a replicant? Who cares. Enjoy.

Reference

Polhemus, Ted (1995) *Streetstyle*, London: Thames and Hudson.

11 The Love Factory:
[1] The Sites, Practices and Media Relationships of Northern Soul

Katie Milestone

Friday 20th of October, northern soul at the Saints Club, Saint Helens, special guest DJ Brian Rae plus Baz Muleedy and Flanny coming soon there as well the next modern and seventies soul night that's on Saturday the 28th of October, the Saints club, Dunriding Lane, St Helens. 8 through late every third Friday of every month, where quality counts. Also this coming Friday I'll be over in Burnley with Ginger Taylor, at the Kestral suite. An excellent venue, late licence as well. 9 through 2. £3 admission before 9.30. The best in northern in Burnley this Friday. A night of soulful nostalgia at the Pavilions club, Sandy Lane, Runcorn, Cheshire this coming Friday the 13th of October, local DJs playing top soulful sounds from the sixties, seventies and eighties. The first anniversary all-nighter at the Cottons takes place next weekend. Saturday into Sunday the 14th/15th of October, 2–9, guest DJs Ady Croasdale, Pete Hollander, Sos, Sooty, Bob Hinsley and Paul Kidd. £8 admission. Also next Saturday in West Yorkshire an all-nighter at the ballroom of the Griffin Hotel, city centre Leeds. Nine soul-packed hours from 10 till 7 with a top-quality DJ line up . . . (Richard Searling, Jazz FM 100.4, Sunday, 8 October 1995)

Introduction

Richard Searling's weekly one-hour *A Cellar Full of Soul* radio programme is currently a central and important point of information for the large British network of northern and rare soul fans. Each Sunday afternoon the dates, times and venues of on average at least twenty weekly rare soul events are announced at various places in England's north and midlands.

The northern soul scene is one of the UK's longest surviving subcultures. Originating out of the ashes of the first mod scene, the northern or rare soul scene began to consolidate itself in the late 1960s. When, during this period,

London clubs began to move away from prioritizing US soul music and turned increasingly to newer forms such as progressive rock, fans in the north and other 'regional' areas maintained a commitment to soul music in the network of R & B clubs based in many British towns and cities. For most of the 1970s, the UK regional soul scene continued to develop and certain key venues were established, such as the Torch in Stoke-on-Trent, Samantha's in Sheffield and the Wigan Casino.

There are certain key attributes of the northern soul scene: an emphasis on rare records, a maintained commitment to 1960s and early 1970s soul, the willingness of the fans to travel some distance to clubs and a focus on all-night dancing sessions.

The northern soul scene has been in existence for about twenty-five years – the current scene is still made up largely of fans and DJs who joined the scene in the 1970s,[2] as well as people who have drifted on to the scene more recently. The loyalty of the fans and the longevity of the scene is startling. Although the venues have moved over time and the trousers have become less flared,[3] the participants of the scene (many of whom are approaching middle age) maintain a commitment to northern soul that can be compared to that of the 1970s.

Key events in the northern soul calender are the 'all-nighters', which frequently take place on Saturday nights (or on Sundays before bank holiday Mondays, so that people have time to recover from them before going back to work). All-night dancing sessions began to be a feature of R & B clubs during the 1960s. This was particularly true of clubs such as the Twisted Wheel in Manchester, and it was after a visit to this club in 1970 that the music journalist Dave Godin came up with the term 'northern soul' as a device to distinguish music favoured in the north from that of the south. There are those would take issue with the accuracy of this term because there were rare soul clubs and fans in the south and, although many of the clubs may be concentrated in the north, the fans were dispersed over a wider geographical area. This is problematized even further when we pause to remember that the music does not originate from the north or anywhere else in the UK, but from North America. The music cherished by northern soul fans has got to be rare. Because of a seemingly inexhaustible supply of US soul music that never achieved commercial success or never got further than demo stage, the northern soul scene has so far been able to avoid becoming stagnant, and to this day 'new' tracks are still 'discovered'.

Rapidly the 'northern soul' soundbite was adopted by the fans and DJs, and a whole scene developed around the notion of there being a specific regional quality in terms of the listenership of the music. Although there had been a rare soul scene since the mid-1960s, the act of naming a specific facet of it catalysed the development of this subgenre.

A History of the Northern Soul Scene[4]

The Twisted Wheel was the first northern soul venue although shortly after gaining this distinct identity it closed down and reopened as Placemate's disco. Artists who were played at 'the Wheel' included Etta James, Brenda Holloway, Earl Van Dyke and the Impressions. The club was situated across the road from a police station and was frequently raided by the drug squad and fire officers. Drawing on research by C.P. Lee (1995), it is important to note that from 1965 Manchester's R & B clubs and 'coffee clubs' were systematically closed down by the police on the orders of the then chief constable A.J. McKay.[5] A club such as Twisted Wheel, with its associations with drugs and black culture, was doomed to a short lifespan, and after its closure Manchester had no comparable club for quite some time.

The period in which the northern soul scene was 'born' coincided with a period in which it became possible to buy American soul music on import labels, and this should not be estimated as a major factor in why the scene developed in the way that it did. Prior to 1968, people in the UK could only get hold of British issues of US soul music (unless perhaps they were friendly with someone at a British US airbase). As Dean Johnson points out (Johnson and Searling, 1993) the arrival of imports opened a floodgate for people in the north who had run out of records to get because black America had stopped making them; or, if they were making them, they were not hits or, if they were records released on very small labels, they didn't have the economic strength to make it into the charts. Where previously there had been a limit to the amount of rare soul that people could gain access to, all of a sudden a new and seemingly inexhaustible supply of 1960s soul emerged. This meant that the rare soul scene could reinvent itself, discover new sounds and avoid growing stagnant.

Johnson also argues that the rare soul scene began to grow particularly strong in the north and midlands in 1967 partly as a working-class rejection of the growing middle-class culture of hippies, acid and progressive rock:

> The northern soul scene developed because the aesthetic angle up here was not into the summer of love. Nobody wanted to see the Temptations wearing headbands, nobody wanted to 'freak out'. Everyone wanted to be neat, sharp, urban – they wanted to look good and they weren't going to be hippies. (Johnson, 1992)

The next nightclubs which emerged on the circuit of this new northern soul scene were Up the Junction at Crewe and the Torch in Tunstall, which although open for only eighteen months as a northern soul venue[6] has remained a significant point of reference for the subsequent scene. Like the Twisted Wheel, the Torch held all-nighters and was closed down because of pressure from the police and Stoke-on-Trent city council because it was a club in which drug taking was known to take place. Tracks that were being played at this venue included the Exciters' 'Blowing up my mind' and J.J. Barnes' 'Real humdinger', which was on 'Ric Tic', one of the first big import labels.

Although the northern soul scene predominantly centres around vinyl, there is an element of live music in the scene, where US artists who have long fallen into obscurity in the States are invited to play at soul events in the UK. Major Lance, for example, made many visits to England during the late 1960s and 1970s, and in 1972 Major Lance's performance at the Torch was released on John Abbey's Contempo label.[7] In recent years, artists such as Doris Troy, Eddie Holman and Tommy Hunt have been brought over to England. Edwin Starr was such a major 'live' force on the northern soul scene that he includes a song in his current repertoire called 'I remember Wigan'!

Wigan Casino, which opened on 23 September 1973, provided the new home for the northern soul scene, which had been rendered temporarily homeless by the closure of the Torch. In terms of numbers of participants on the scene, it was at Wigan in 1975–6 that its membership peaked. There were 20,000 members of Wigan Casino, many of whom travelled great distances to the club. With its proximity to the M6 motorway and vast urban conurbations, the club was ideally placed. It was also within reasonable distance of Scotland and attracted fans from places such as Edinburgh and Dundee. During the Wigan Casino period of the northern soul scene, it became customary for the DJs to play the same three records at the end of the all-nighters – this was called the 'three before eight'. These records – 'Time will pass you by' by Tobi Legend, 'I'm on my way (back to the city)' by Dean Parrish and 'Long after tonight is all over' by Jimmy Radcliffe – all express themes of the transience of time and space, and remind the northern soul fans that they will soon have to return to their everyday lives.

The popularity of Wigan Casino signified the commercial height of the northern soul scene and, many argue, its aesthetic lowpoint. As DJ Richard Searling put it, the Wigan scene attracted lots of 'sightseers' – people who weren't interested in the music itself, but merely in the beat that it provided. Rather than maintaining a commitment to rarity and quality, some of the DJs at Wigan began to play '100 mile an hour stompers' as a backdrop to frenzied dancing and drug taking.

Stuart Cosgrove has written about the connections between drug taking and northern soul, and makes reference to 'early deaths remembered in dedicated records over the sound systems of all-nighters' (1982). The letters pages of back issues of mid-1970s Blues and Soul magazine also reveal that at this time there were drug-related fatalities occurring on the northern soul scene. Stuart Cosgrove also points out, though, that the scene is not predominantly a hard drug scene, but one in which amphetamines are used to allow people to stay awake during the all-night dancing sessions, and to 'induce people to talk (and overtalk) and thus forge friendships with people of other towns' (1983).

In 1975 records by white artists – 'blue-eyed soul' — began to be incorporated into the scene (much to the horror of many people), purely because they had an 'acceptable' beat. Such tracks included those by Paul Anka and Bobby Paris. It is reputed that even Gary Glitter's 'Rock and roll (part 1)' was played at the Catacombs in Wolverhampton a year before it achieved mainstream chart success, purely because it had a sound that blended in with the northern soul that was being played at the time. Worse still, 'British' northern soul acts began to be promoted by virtue of the fact that they were based in Wigan.[8] It was almost as if during this period people had forgotten that northern soul was really the sound of black America and were starting to believe that soul came from Wigan![9]

It is easy to criticize some of the things that were happening at Wigan and in the mid-1970s, but as Richard Searling points out, there was also still a lot of brilliant soul music being played. Also, it was certainly not the case that the Casino was the only soul club during this period. Blackpool Mecca catered for the more avant-garde side of northern soul, and DJs such as Ian Levine and Colin Curtis began to delve into early 1970s soul music for their repertoire. Levine had a relative in America, which meant that he could search for rare soul in its country of origin, and he brought back thousands of records that no one had heard before. Records that defined the sound of the Mecca included James Fountain's 'Seven day lover' and the Montclairs' 'Hung up on your love'. The Mecca was not an all-night venue – it was open until 2 a.m. The organization of the scene was so tight that it was common for transport to be provided to take fans from one club to another, and a bus left Blackpool at 1 a.m. for people who wanted to go on to Wigan Casino.

Magazines such as *Blues and Soul* and *Black Music* (during the seventies) provided a space for debates about the northern soul scene in letters pages or in articles by writers such as Tony Cummings and Dave Godin (see, for example, Cummings, 1975). Much of this debate centred around what constitutes 'northern soul'. In an article called 'Northern soul at the cross-roads', in the March 1977 edition of *Blues and Soul*, Dave Godin reflected on the scene he 'invented': 'For the record, we should perhaps reiterate that "Northern soul" was simply a term I coined to describe records which were made in the mid-60s (generally), and which became popular in the North about five years later' (Godin, 1977).

Godin went on to describe the rift that was occurring in the rare soul scene in 1977 between 'traditionalists' (who maintained a commitment to 1960s soul) and 'progressive' DJs such as Blackpool Mecca's Ian Levine and Colin

Curtis, who were also playing funk and disco. So massive was the rivalry between the two soul factions that a petition was circulated at this time to 'reclaim' the Blackpool Mecca for 'pure' northern soul. Ironically, in this article Godin admits that for several years he had been urging DJs to 'stop hunting elusive sounds from the past' and to introduce more contemporary black music into their repertoire. In this respect, then, the same person who had originally defined the concept of 'northern soul' was in some people's eyes part of a 'progressive' faction which threatened to destroy the original scene.

Although Stuart Cosgrove (1982) argues that northern soul was a culture of cities, most of the locations for northern soul nights were in small towns such as Wigan, Blackburn, Morecambe, Cleethorpes and Tunstall. The northern soul scene therefore tended to be located in what Rob Shields (1991) describes as 'places on the margin': in areas that were peripheral to the concentration of economic and cultural power in city centres. There was no apparent logic to why it was located in some places and not in others: for example, although the scene was strong in parts of Lancashire, Cheshire and Yorkshire, there was very little activity in the north-east or what is now Merseyside.

Perhaps northern soul can be understood partly as an attempt to cope with the experience of living in an urban, industrial area which is *not* the city, but the edge of the city; an urban landscape *without* a cultural infrastructure. It can be considered an attempt to insert a sense of the cultural exchange found in the city, into the confines of depressed peripheral urban areas. It is no coincidence that black soul music, which emerged from the huge US cities of Detroit and Chicago, should be used for this purpose – a music which not only came from the city (and was industrially produced), but whose lyrics also constantly referred to the experience of living in the city.

Despite being an avowedly working-class, masculine subculture which revolved around records with lyrics concentrated predominantly on hetero-sexual love, it was a scene in which gay men felt comfortable, as Dean Johnson (1992) points out: 'It was OK if you were gay because there wasn't a big emphasis on copping. Half the people on the northern scene were very gay because you could hide away quite merrily without any great social pressure.' This lack of pressure to conform to heterosexual definitions of masculinity is also implied in a one-off article on northern soul in *Fact* maga-zine,[10] in which Steve Strange of Visage and David Ball of Soft Cell both reminisced about their years as participants on the northern soul scene. It is also worth noting that Soft Cell achieved a number one hit with a cover version of Gloria Jones' northern soul 'classic' 'Tainted love'.

Richard Searling recalls how during the punk era of the late 1970s the management of the Wigan Casino decided to make use of the empty club in the time before midnight by holding punk nights. He recalls 'ugly scenes' as the punks were thrown out, only to be greeted by queues of northern soulies. Some northern soul fans abandoned the scene when punk arrived, and in *Subculture: The Meaning of Style*, Dick Hebdige suggests that there were certain influences of the scene on punk:

> They eventually couldn't find stompers any more so they moved the goal posts. The whole thing got slower so there's a lot of mid tempo and even slower than that records played. It couldn't be compared to the rock and roll scene. At least northern soul does reinvent itself. (Johnson and Searling, 1993)

This sort of move was not welcomed by all those in the rare soul fraternity. As Searling recalls of the Ritz in the late seventies, there were big rivalries between fans of 'pure' northern soul and those who were prepared to embrace 'Modern soul'. As Colin Curtis finished his set, the floor would empty, only to be replaced with an entirely different set of dancers who were there to listen to the 1960s soul played by Searling. This split was so intense that occasionally sixties fanatics would throw fresh fruit at DJs who seemed to be threatening the 'true' northern soul scene!

Also in the later part of the seventies there was an emerging soul/disco split which can be traced in the weekly editions of *Blues and Soul* magazine. People were concerned that some seventies soul was sounding too similar to what was seen as mindless, tacky and soulless disco music, which the northern scene wanted to distance itself from.

In the 1980s, and especially after Wigan's biggest tourist attraction, the Wigan Casino, was knocked down in 1981 to build a multistorey car park, new venues sprang up in places such as Rotherham and Morecambe.

We could perhaps have expected that, as the participants of the northern soul scene grew older, the demand for gruelling all-night dancing sessions would subside. This has not been the case and in the 1990s a number of solid all-nighter clubs have emerged, such as those in Keele, Blackburn and the Ritz in Manchester. We could also perhaps expect the style of dancing that has been developed to accompany rare 1960s soul music to have been tamed. This has not always been the case either, and perhaps one of the most incredible things about a contemporary all-nighter is the fact that people in their early forties still dance for several hours in one go. Furthermore, there are still many people who engage in the spectacular, energetic styles of dancing associated with the seventies northern soul scene. 'New' tunes are still also being discovered, and coach parties of young mods from London regularly come up to Blackburn and the Ritz, to what is still considered to be 'the heart of soul'.

Has there ever been anything comparable to a northern soul scene anywhere else apart from the UK? According to Richard Searling (1992), there have been patches of interest in the northern soul scene among people from Holland, Belgium and Japan. He also said that there was something vaguely similar to the northern soul scene in Pittsburgh and that the South Carolina 'beach' scene plays some sixties soul, although it's not generally as rare or esoteric as that of the British scene.

To explore the relationships between the northern soul scene and media forms is crucial in attempting to describe how the scene's history has unfolded and developed. First and foremost, northern soul rejects mass media flows and the formal organizational structures of the record industry by deliberately avoiding records that have achieved commercial success. This is not to suggest (as has sometimes been the accusation) that these records were financially unsuccessful because they weren't any good, as Stuart Cosgrove points out: 'Despite the Northern Scene's undeserved reputation as a subculture which sticks rigidly to old and inferior versions of the Detroit sound, there is in fact a massive range of Northern records which defy this reputation' (1982). Occasionally, in a quest for rarity, issues of quality have become secondary, and, as Cosgrove goes on to argue, sometimes records may be played not so much for their intrinsic qualities as for their potential to contribute to the atmosphere of an all-night session. For the most part, though, it is the devastating beauty of these records that has inspired the fanatical record collecting, intricate dancing styles and longevity of the scene.

In many cases, a record company or indeed the artists themselves have been unaware that people are interested in, or buying, their records. This 'ignorance' is a two-way process – just as the original producers of the music have little way of knowing about the existence of their British fans, so too are the fans/consumers starved of information about the US artists and record companies. This is partly because of the time lapse that occurs when records are 'discovered' on the northern soul scene years after they have been produced, and partly because the small US record companies from which these tracks emerged often had short lifespans themselves and were swallowed up by larger and larger companies. Although the northern soul scene builds its own media infrastructure surrounding the UK scene, this has not always been the case with regard to media about the original soul music itself: 'People collected artists they'd never seen a picture of. There was no media, no information for these people. They had to dig, they had to root. It wasn't easy – it wasn't laid on a plate.' (Johnson and Searling, 1993)

Over the years, dedicated collectors and music journalists have gradually built up biographies about the original artists, which have been disseminated in fanzines and the specialist soul music press. Northern soul, then, is not just centred around searching out rare soul, but also about excavating histories of the now obsolete Detroit[11] labels and the artists who worked for them.

Listening to, dancing to, buying and selling rare, black American soul music from the 1960s and 1970s is the focus and catalyst of this club-based scene, which is sustained through networks of information such as Searling's radio show, specialist soul magazines, fanzines and flyers distributed in specialist record shops and at soul nights. As Sarah Thornton (1994) points out, every music scene has its own specific set of media relations, both in terms of 'micromedia' and 'niche' media, which is produced by people closely allied to a particular music culture, as well as mass media (mis)representations of subcultural movements. By building its own distinct, concealed media network, the northern soul scene has never needed to be (or been) accepted into larger-scale music media,[12] and this must be acknowledged as an important contributing factor to the northern soul scene's ability to remain 'underground' for so long. The exception to this emphasis on subterranean media flows is with respect to Searling's current radio show, which is broadcast on a commercial station, Jazz FM,[13] which repeatedly constructs itself as being respectable, safe, middle class and middle aged. It is a 'black' music radio station, but one whose DJs and listeners are predominantly white. The only reason northern soul has been 'allowed in' is probably because of its age (in terms of both the music and the fans), which has enabled it to be objectified and distanced from its original point of reference.

The relationship between mainstream media and northern soul has never been close, and the few articles that have emerged have either been in a 'moral panic' vein or display fundamental misunderstandings of the scene. As Cosgrove argues: 'For Northern soul the mass media is something to be ridiculed, a cross they have to bear when white rock fails to produce good copy' (1982).

In December 1977 the north-west's regional independent television channel, Granada, broadcast a thirty-minute documentary about Wigan Casino as part of its *This England* series. This was one of the few times that this underground British club scene found its way into the mainstream. The Granada documentary makes much of the connections between the Wigan Casino and the industrial working-class culture in which it is based. Excerpts of folk music, Victorian photographs of young mine and mill workers and shots of factory production lines are interspersed among the segments depicting aspects of the northern soul scene. Apart from the references to the Wigan of the past, the documentary is also cut with 'contemporary' shots of 'backward northerness' – undernourished children playing on wastelands, rag and bone carts, cobbled streets and pit heads. These juxtapositions work to imply that northern soul offers a form of escape from the turgid drudgery of a decaying regional town. The final lingering shot of a rag and bone cart would also seem to suggest that northern soulies, like rag and bone men, find value in other people's discarded junk.

As Joanne Hollows has argued (Hollows and Milestone, 1995), the northern soul scene 'was not simply a watered down version of a southern scene but "produced" within the north'. In this respect 'northern soul rejects the legitimacy of more powerful taste formations (whilst also being unable to displace them)'. Drawing on the work of Rob Shields, Hollows goes on to argue that:

> the urban sites associated with northern soul, reaffirm and celebrate what Shields (1991) calls the 'place image' of 'the North' as 'The Land of the Working Class' and the industrial slum. Northern soul appropriates a vision of 'the North' in which, in Shields' words, 'The past hangs . . . like factory smoke must once have.'

Although the narration of the Granada programme is left to two participants of the scene, the visual depictions of the Wigan Casino during the documentary frequently portray it with much the same bleak dourness as the rest of Wigan. Unusual camera angles distort and objectify the dancers and (the lights being on) the camera focuses on 'working-class signifiers' such as muscles, sweat and tattoos. Rather than the all-nighter looking fast and exciting, it seems strange, dreamlike and suspended in time.

The lights are full on during the shots of the all-nighter, which is 'unnatural' and completely distorts the atmosphere (the atmosphere is drastically altered in most nightclubs at the end of the night when the lights are suddenly turned on). In his work on youth and surveillance, Hebdige argues that a subculture is formed 'in the space between surveillance and the evasion of surveillance' (1988). These brightly lit shots of scenes which should be dark implies that a process of surveillance is taking place here – the northern soul fans are literally 'hiding in the light'. In a subculture which comes alive only in the dark and which, as Cosgrove argues, 'thrives on images of darkness' (1982), it is doubly strange that the programme's makers have chosen to represent the scene in such a way.

Rarity and Aura in Northern Soul

As has been implied through out this chapter, the rarity of records is central to the northern soul scene. There is a desire not only for rare, obscure tracks, but also for issues that are on the original labels. Collectors are prepared to pay vast sums of money to own originals – in the mid-1970s James Fountain's 'Seven day lover' changed hands for around £200, and by the 1990s the value placed on some of the discs had soared into the thousands. That fans are prepared to pay 'over the odds' for original vinyl, even when there are cheap reissues available, implies that the concept of aura is crucial to the way in which the northern soul scene operates. Although Walter Benjamin suggests that the aura might 'wither in the age of mechanical reproduction' (1973), it is also clear that we can apply his claim that 'the presence of the original is the prerequisite to the concept of authenticity' to mechanically

reproduced vinyl in the context of northern soul. This is made possible by
the very fact that, although the music defined as northern or rare soul is
reproduced, it is distinguished by the fact that it has not been *mass* produced
– sometimes there are northern soul tracks of which there is only one original copy.[14]

There is other material that we can appropriate from Benjamin's essay
'The work of art in the age of mechanical reproduction' and apply to the
example of northern soul. For example, Benjamin argues that 'in permitting
the reproduction to meet the beholder or listener in his own particular situation, it reactivates the object reproduced' (1973). It is clear with the case of
northern soul, where a 'local' culture has been produced which centres
around things that have been created in a space thousands of miles away (and
which as far as most of the people who produced the original vinyl are aware
have never moved out of that space), that these commodities have been
'reactivated' in the listener's 'own particular situation'. Vinyl that had apparently been destined for obscurity is given new life and meaning.

Within the northern soul scene there have frequently been concerns about
moves which threaten to destroy the aura of the records. First 'cheap' reissues
of rare tracks on labels such as Pye's Disco Demand in the 1970s pose a threat.
For example, Dave Godin talks about people who buy inferior versions and
pirate copies in the following terms: 'just as one might settle for a reproduction antique if one couldn't afford the real thing, so they want the sound
they get hooked on' (1977). He goes on to argue:

> Only those DJs who can honestly say that they have never ever spun an EMI-
> disc or a pirate pressing can claim to have kept the faith with Northern or
> Rare Soul, for without their spins, the pirates would be bereft of customers.

Bootlegging, where illegal copies of a rare record are pressed, was common
during the 1970s when people thought that a lot of money could be made
out of northern soul. The DJs and collectors were quick to respond to this
and used 'cover-ups', the retitling of rare records, to fox would-be pirates.
New titles or even new names for the artists would be invented.

The terms 'oldies' and 'newies' are used to describe the records played on
the northern soul scene. If a record is an 'oldie', it means that it has been
played at a soul venue in the past, if a record is a 'newie', it is still a 1960s
recording, but one that has only recently been unearthed by an enduring DJ
or collector. Several of the records have only a short lifespan because as soon
as a record becomes popular it will be 'bootlegged' and consequently lose its
exclusive status.

It could be argued that the loss of the aura in northern soul has been
furthered with the increasing number of British labels which put out compilation albums of rare 1960s soul, such as Kent, Goldmine and Soul Supply.

Issues of ownership emerge in this context – occasionally the tracks used on compilation albums may not have been officially licensed for the simple reason that no one can track down the original owners or producers. Also large record companies, which have bought out and swallowed up small independent soul labels over the years, may have no idea what they have in their back catalogues. At a recent conference, a couple of delegates from North America said that one of the only ways in which they can get hold of rare 1960s soul is by buying these types of British compilation albums.

Dean Johnson argues that the rare soul scene has been profoundly influential on later dance music subcultures and styles:

> People who ask, 'What is northern soul?' are really missing the point. The most important thing from a cultural point of view is the rare soul scene. If you want to know what the difference about this is, northern is a very specific place and time. Rare soul is a thing that grew up in the sixties and still exists today. Without rare soul you wouldn't have a club scene, you wouldn't have a rave, you wouldn't have Andy Weatherall remixes, you wouldn't have hip-hop, you wouldn't have Latin clubs. (Johnson and Searling, 1993)

The northern soul scene has certainly had an impact on a number of DJs and musicians. As the eighties progressed and the club DJs introduced more and more underground black American dance and soul music, people began to go to clubs such as the Haçienda to dance. There was a change in attitude towards dance music in the underground as the decade progressed. Where once there had been a big split between what was seen as frivolous, commercial and tacky disco music and more serious and esoteric rock, punk and new wave, people other than those heavily involved in the rare soul scene began to realize that there was a more experimental and innovative edge to dance music. Many of the Haçienda's early DJs had been participants in the northern soul scene – Rob Gretton, Mike Pickering and Graeme Park – and had retained a commitment to searching out rare black styles. John Berry, one of the founders of Manchester's Eastern Bloc Records[15] also talks about the impact of northern soul: 'Northern soul and the dance scene now are very similar. They were making it very rare and hard to get hold of and you have to be one of the boys to get it'.

Non-Stop Dancing . . . [16]

The Northern soul style of dancing needs comment as it is a central feature of club events. This distinctive, acrobatic style of dancing involve spins, handsprings and backdrops. The best way to describe it would be to compare it to break dancing, although because northern soul dancing is performed on the dance floor, among other dancers, people have only a limited amount of space. Stuart Cosgrove writes:

> One of the consistent features of the rare soul scene has been its ability to reproduce superb dancers who can predict almost every beat and soul clap in a thousand unknown sounds. But Northern soul dancing is not only the back-drop, swallow dives and spins that catch the eye of the onlooker, it is more importantly the ritual elegance of a dance style that refuses to adopt a name. (1982)

Although the style has often been described as 'frenzied' (especially during the Wigan Casino phase of the scene), because it has to be contained within a certain space a degree of command and restraint is required. In this context it might be useful to draw upon Wouters' (1986) notion of the 'de-controlled control of the emotions', which he argues is a process of the relaxation of emotional controls that took place in the 1960s, but which also brought about, as Mike Featherstone notes, a 'calculated hedonism' and 'calculation and mutually expected respect for other persons' (1992).

Incorporated into the northern soul scene is the ritual of dancing competitions. The balconied ballrooms so often chosen as venues for all-nighters provide an ideal space in which skilled dancers can perform to the onlooking crowd. Incredible though it may seem, people in their late thirties and forties (people who have remained participants of the scene from its inception to the present day) still engage in this spectacular and extremely energetic form of dancing. In Andrew Davies' research into working-class leisure in Manchester and Salford in the period from the turn of the century until 1939, it is clear that the importance of spectacular and competitive dancing within the northern soul scene finds part of its roots in the northern dance hall tradition that preceded it:

> In some contrast to the cinema, dancing provided an opportunity for working-class youths to develop skills of their own. Accomplished dancers were highly respected, and could gain considerable local reputations, so it is perhaps un-surprising that many people devoted a good deal of their leisure time to the hobby. (1992)

It is interesting to note other ways in which some features of this earlier live-music-based, dance hall culture spilled over into recorded music club scenes. Within the northern soul subculture it is customary to clap after each record has been played (depending, of course, on whether or not the crowd likes the DJs' choice) and to use traditional ballrooms and dance halls as venues for all-nighters.

It is a regular feature of an all-nighter for people to buy and sell records, and there are often several stalls set up for the purpose of doing this. At a large all-nighter there can be anything up to twenty separate stores, mainly selling records, but often tapes, fanzines, videos and T-shirts as well. The stalls will often have small crowds of people huddled around them. The nightclub partly becomes transformed into a market place – the carnivalesque. Again this tradition for the street market to become a focus of leisure echoes earlier working-class leisure activity. Andrew Davies notes the important role that Manchester's Shudehill and Salford's Flat Iron market had to play as the highlight of Saturday night leisure time: 'The market remained a Saturday night mecca for working class youths during the 1920s and 1930s, attracting young people of both sexes who were drawn by the "carnival atmosphere of the market district"' (1992).

The song incorporated into the title of this chapter, Eloise Law's 'Love factory', has been used because it refers to themes of industry and production lines which are strongly associated with places like Detroit and the sites of northern soul. The factory and production line are repeatedly represented in the Granada documentary about Wigan Casino, and likewise it is also claimed that Berry Gordy used his experiences of working in the Detroit car industry at Motown.[17] Yet these objectified allusions to the brutal, emotionless sphere of mass production fail to account for the ways in which people resist repetition and standardization in their lives – the love factory can also be seen as a site of the creative production of culture and meaning.

In 1978 *Blues and Soul* magazine had a feature by Frank Elson called 'Two years of Wigan Oldies', part of which reads:

> The most important thing about Wigan Casino Oldies All-nighters for many people has been the way it has attracted so many 'old' faces back onto the Northern Soul scene. People who have married and have been off Northern Soul for years have been attracted back to listen to their old favourites. One Jock was heard to comment that he'd seen as many pictures of babies in the hands of proud parents as had 'rare' Northern Soul originals! (Elson, 1978)

It is startling so many years later to find that the scene is still very active. Some of the proud parents referred to by Frank Elson may even be grandparents now.

Notes

Many thanks to Joanne Hollows and Mike Bull for comments and help with this chapter
1 Eloise Law, 'Love factory' (Music Merchant, 1972).
2 Searling currently announces northern soul fans' fortieth birthdays, and this is the average age of many of the participants.
3 During the 1970s, the fashion for male northern soul fans was to wear very flared

trousers such as 'Spencer bags', which were available mail order through *Blues and Soul* magazine. Likewise the fashion for women was to wear flared, long skirts.

4 This section builds on earlier work by myself and Joanne Hollows (Hollows and Milestone, forthcoming).

5 As Lee notes, 'So concerned was the chief constable that by August 1965 he had almost singlehandedly generated a moral panic sufficiently large enough to warrant the passing of a special Act of Parliament allowing the police sweeping, some would say draconian, powers to deal with the problem created by the so-called "Coffee Clubs"' (1995, p. 7).

6 It had a reputation for being a premier R & B/mod club as the Golden Torch in the mid-1960s, until 1968 when it had a two-year period of stagnation.

7 *Major Lance Live at the Torch.*

8 Wigan's Ovations and Wigan's Chosen Few were the two main examples of this type of group.

9 In magazines such as *Blues and Soul* and on sew-on embroidered patches, Wigan was promoted as being 'the heart of soul music' in the mid-1970s.

10 Issue 29, September 1982.

11 The music that is defined as northern soul does not emerge exclusively from Detroit, as places such as Chicago, Memphis and Los Angeles have also been a source of the music. Yet, as Cosgrove notes, Detroit is firmly established as 'the mythical capital of the scene' (1982).

12 Such as *New Musical Express*, Radio 1, commercial radio and music television.

13 Jazz FM is transmitted throughout the north-west and midlands of England.

14 For example, there is only one copy known to exist of Frank Wilson's 'Do I love you', which was released on a Tamla Motown subsidiary in 1966 and withdrawn almost immediately. This record is currently valued at about £5,000.

15 Eastern Bloc is one of the UK's leading dance music record shops, whose founders include John Berry and Martin Price (also a member of the group 808 State). The shop also licenses records on its own record labels.

16 'Non-stop dancing' (Paul Weller), track on the Jam's *In the City* album (Polydor, 1977).

17 Fitzgerald (1995) challenges Adornoesque arguments about the repeated use of the same formula apparently used in some soul music.

References

Benjamin, W. (1973) 'The work of art in the age of mechanical reproduction' in *Illuminations*, London: Fontana.

Berry, John (1995) Interview with the author, June.

Cosgrove, Stuart (1991) 'Living in the city: a soul essay', talk given at the Manchester Polytechnic Unit for Law and Popular Culture, January.

Cummings, T. (1975) 'Northern soul: after the goldrush', *Black Magic*, November.

Davies, A. (1992) *Leisure, Gender and Poverty: Working Class Culture in Salford and Manchester, 1900–1939*, Milton Keynes: Open University Press.

Elson, Frank (1978) 'Two years of Wigan Oldies', *Blues and Soul*, no. 244, 31 January – 13 February.

Featherstone, M. (1991) *Consumer Culture and Postmodernism*, London: Sage.

Fitzgerald, J. (1995) 'Mowtown crossover hits 1963–1966 and the creative process', *Popular Music*, vol. 14, no. 1.

Godin, Dave (1977) 'Northern soul at the crossroads,' *Blues and Soul*, no. 222, 29 March –11 April.

Hebdige, D. (1979) *Subculture: The Meaning of Style*, London: Methuen.

—— (1988) *Hiding in the Light*, London: Comedia.

Hollows, J. and K. Milestone (1995) 'Intercity soul', paper presented at the BSA conference, 'Contested Cities', Leicester, April.

—— (forthcoming) *Welcome to Dreamsville: A History and Geography of Northern Soul*.

Johnson, Dean (1992) Interview with the author, November.

Johnson, Dean and Richard Searling (1993) Talk given at the Manchester Metropolitan University Institute for Popular Culture, March.

Lee, C.P. (1995) 'And then there were none: government legislation and Manchester beat clubs, 1965–', paper given at the first Critical Musicology Conference, Salford.

Searling, Richard (1992) Interview with the author, December.

Shields, R. (1991) *Places on the Margin: Alternative Geographies of Modernity*, London: Routledge.

Thornton, S. (1994) 'Moral panic, the media and British rave culture', in A. Ross and T. Rose (eds), *Microphone Fiends: Youth Music and Youth Culture*, London: Routledge.

Wouters, C. (1986) 'Formalisation and informalisation: changing tension balances in civilising processes' *Theory, Culture and Society*, vol. 3, no. 2.

12 DJ Culture

Dave Haslam

There are parts of cities like Manchester, Liverpool and London where more young kids in the early teens want to be DJs than popstars, their ideal birthday present not a guitar but a pair of Technics turntables. From warehouse ravers in the early days to the so-called superclubs of today (like Cream in Liverpool, and the Ministry of Sound in London), since the late 1980s the dancefloor has consolidated its position as the focus of British youth culture. In the early 1960s Manchester was renowned for its nightlife, its beat groups and its basement venues, with nearly thirty clubs successfully operating in the city centre; Manchester still has its pulse on the rhythm nation, but the thousands who now go out on the town are listening to DJs not live bands.

In the last decade DJs have become some of the most highly paid people in the entertainment world, and have enjoyed a burgeoning profile in the media and the record industry. The kind of fees DJs can attract has gone sky-high, with top British DJs attracting in excess of £2,000 (plus VAT) a night, and, following a renewed interest in the American underground house sound, American DJs like Danny Tenaglia and Todd Terry getting 'a grand or two' more than that. Radio 1's famous shake-up in the mid-1990s reflected a need for the station to attract club-based DJs on to the roster, the kind previously only used on pirate radio and specialist dance stations like Kiss FM. Marketing departments in record companies have taken to employing DJs to remix their releases for the dancefloor. In fact, record companies are now staffed and even run by DJs: Pete Tong at London Records, Paul Oakenfold at Perfecto, for example.

The DJ lifestyle is now prized, packaged and sold, in true late twentieth-century consumerist style; in June 1994 *Details* magazine latched on to DJs' bags, 'originally designed for DJs to jockey their twelve inch vinyls from club to club', claiming that their use had broadened, with 'regular folks co-opting the square satchel as a new-school urban briefcase'. Embossed with record company label logos, these tools of the DJ trade are selling at fifty dollars a bag. Meanwhile, the DJ is currently considered at the cutting edge of popular music. DJ-ing provides a career opportunity, and a lifestyle to aspire to. How did this happen? Why?

Clubbing has a fantastic attraction. Going out to clubs gives punters the chance to forget mundanity and dress to impress; and a chance to meet, let go, relax, pick up, chat up. Ultimately, though, clubbing is music driven. In Manchester – a city with a highly developed musical conscience – even more so. If you let the music lift you up, a great record played at the right time in the night by a good DJ can sound like the finest four minutes of recorded music in history and the greatest four minutes of the week. I might be thought melodramatic, but there are people who come to Saturday night at the Boardwalk in Manchester who have gone without a meal or two so that they can afford a proper night out. They live for the weekend. Everything you need to know about this is enshrined in the 'Let the beat hit 'em (part 2)' single by Lisa Lisa and Cult Jam, produced by C&C Music Factory. (I can't stop recommending tunes, by the way; it's part of the job.)

DJ-ing is evangelism; a desire to share songs. A key skill is obviously not just to drop the popular, well-known songs at the right part of the night, but to pick the right new releases, track down the obscurer tunes and newest imports, get hold of next month's big tune this month; you gather this pile, this tinder, together, then you work the records, mix them, drop them, cut them, scratch them, melt them, beat them all together until they unite. *Voilà*; disco inferno.

Music-loving dancefloor DJs in Britain have roots in the early sixties, when music from overseas – rock 'n' roll, R & B and reggae – was in big demand. The black community longed to stay in touch with music from Jamaica, and looked to the sound system DJs to find the hard-to-get imports, and play them on behalf of the community. White youth, meanwhile, were eager to get R & B from the USA, but the key tunes were only available on import to a select few. One of the reasons why there were so many live groups in Manchester in this period was poor supply (in record shops and on radio), which failed to match the high demand for the new pop sounds, so most groups were making a living doing cover versions (as indeed the Beatles and the Rolling Stones began their careers doing). Many had nothing inspirational to add to the original, but got work solely because the crowd wanted to hear the song; the crowd would have preferred to hear the original in many cases. Jimmy Saville – then working in Manchester's clubland – realized this, and instituted what were called Disc Only Sessions. He dispensed with the bands and, improvising with two record players, proceeded to pack the Plaza on Oxford Street. Imports have always been important to DJs, and whether it's Airwaves in Shepherd's Bush supplying soul in 1976, or Spin Inn bringing electro to Manchester in the early 1980s, the mutually beneficial relationship of record shop and specialist DJ is integral in keeping scenes alive.

Despite the existence of coteries of credible dancefloor DJs in Britain for decades, most continued to serve specialist communities (in Manchester, in the early 1980s, for example, there was Colin Curtis at Berlin playing jazz, Hewan Clarke at the Reno playing back street sounds, and Greg Wilson at Legend playing electro). When I first started DJ-ing in the mid-1980s, DJs in general – and certainly in the mainstream – weren't considered to be at the cutting edge of cool. Most discothèques employed 'personality' jocks, (although any casual investigation would reveal that, among the chest wigs, silver lamé suits, wet T-shirt competitions and dolly birds, what personality these DJs had was deeply flawed). I didn't have any role models when I started DJ-ing. I started DJ-ing because I loved music. And because I was a mug; people promoting gigs paid me £20 to play records before and after bands. It was a good way to learn the craft and pressures of DJ-ing; your music simply had to stop people going home when the group was finished. I was so into the thrill of it all that I would probably have done it for 20 pence, in fact. I started out doing this kind of DJ-ing at the Man Alive, the Venue and the Haçienda.

At the Man Alive, the group Big Flame used to promote the Wilde Club on Thursday nights in 1985. The Man Alive was a Caribbean-owned club. It hadn't got a stage; it hadn't got anything much except big bass bins and a small kitchen churning out chickens and patties. There was room for about 150 in the club, including ten on the dancefloor (which doubled as the stage when the band played). They put on the likes of the Wedding Present, Chakk, That Petrol Emotion, the Age of Chance, and – about every three weeks, it seemed – Big Flame. I was supposed to play Go-Go records, and electro, and stuff like Nuance's 'Loveride'. Even when the promoters lent me records, we could only afford about four import records a week between us, so I had to mix it up a bit with all sorts of other stuff; On-U label material, and old James Brown records especially.

The combination of live indie guitar janglers and a Go-Go and funk disco might seem a bit strange, but it didn't to us. In fact, Dill and Greg out of Big Flame scolded me if I played anything remotely jangly. I think I was allowed to play stuff by The Pop Group and the Fire Engines, but that's as guitary as it got. They were right, but it's almost the only time I've ever listened to club promoters, managers or owners. The only other time I had to justify my playlist was in March 1986 when I was asked to do a new Thursday night at the Haçienda called the Temperance Club. Paul Mason, the Haçienda's manager, read a list of my choice tracks; I'd included this fabulous funk record on 4th & Broadway by Donald Banks called 'Status quo'. '*I don't think rock like that will be appropriate,*' he said. I guessed afterwards that he must have misread and assumed that there was a song called 'Donald Banks' by Status Quo. Since then I haven't debated what I was playing with anyone.

In its early years the Haçienda was a live venue, first and foremost. Andrew Berry used to DJ band nights, and he was by no means as conscientious as me; he'd arrive late, or leave early. I imagine he had better things to do than spend hours in the Haçienda trying to get 150 people who'd come out on a rainy Friday to see Bourgie Bourgie and to dance until the bar closed. Sadly, I hadn't, so he sometimes used to let me play. But by the end of 1985 I had graduated beyond DJ-ing on band nights; I'd been given the chance to do a Friday night at a small club about 100 yards from the Haçienda. Over the summer of 1985 some friends of mine who ran a fly poster business round town – Mike and Vini Faal and Jimmy Carr – had briefly taken over the running of the club, and had named it The Wheel; Jimmy had been a massive fan of the Twisted Wheel, Manchester's famous soul and R & B club. They asked me to play on Friday and Saturday nights, but the ads soon got more and more hopeless, and the poster boys were losing interest, so the club owner decided to rename the club The Venue and install me as the resident weekend DJ. I soon gave up Saturdays (Dean Johnson took over, playing jazz, rare groove, old soul and Latin) and concentrated on Fridays, and it worked. By this time the Wilde Club had come to an end. Some of the Wilde Club boys and girls carried on coming to hear me play, and at the Venue I still played anything that turned me on. It was a unique mix; I suppose there wasn't another dancefloor in the world which filled to the first Primal Scream 7", the Jackson Five, the Smiths, Joyce Sims, and just about anything produced by Adrian Sherwood. On a good night in the autumn of 1985, there were queues up the road and past the Haçienda staff entrance. This alerted the Haçienda to my existence (my clandestine appearances courtesy of Andrew Berry hadn't), and pretty soon came the offer of a Thursday night.

When Jimmy Saville was at the Plaza, he was actually the manager of the club. He would have seen what was obvious; if you can make a night featuring a DJ work, then there's more money to be made than booking bands with all their equipment, soundchecks, guest lists and mithering managers. The DJ is the economic choice. At the Man Alive the disco was occasionally more successful than the groups anyway; at the Venue invariably so. The simple idea was to sack the bands. The same thing happened down the road at the Haçienda: under new manager Paul Mason (who joined the club in January 1986) the large opening costs for band nights, and the rarity of bands filling the cavernous old yacht warehouse with poor sight-lines and a reputation for dodgy sound, made a change of direction financially necessary. He decided to go for club nights Thursday through to Saturday, the success of which wasn't by any means assured, given that the Haçienda wasn't renowned for welcoming the mass youth of Manchester. It was any arty hangout, with a discernible us-and-them attitude to the rest of the city. Nevertheless, for me the offer of a night there was irresistible.

The Temperance Club started on May Day 1986. I played whatever I liked, from the Smiths and sixties girl groups, to Motown, New Order and hip-hop. Mark E Smith bought me a pint because I played 'Little doll' by the Stooges. I remember Morrissey coming one evening and settling himself down in the DJ box. I was all fired up; I pulled out that classic electro track 'Hip hop, be bop (don't stop)' by Man Parrish. 'Remember this?' I yelled to him. He didn't, of course, and he didn't seem impressed. I didn't see why he wouldn't like the records I played; after all, I liked the songs he sang. Who knows what could have happened if I'd managed to turn him on that night? Imagine if he'd gone round to Johnny Marr's the next day and said, 'I heard this great record last night, all drum machines, no guitars, no lyrics. Sack this gloomy rockabilly-tinged balladeering, we're going hip-hop.' It was not to be.

At this time I didn't have any sense that as a DJ you would even want to limit yourself, label yourself. I understood the attractions for Colin Curtis playing to the right seventy jazz aficionados at Berlin, but I wanted the buzz of changing minds, breaking barriers. Sometimes this evangelism works. When I DJ-ed at a Sonic Youth gig at the New Ardri Ballroom in Hulme in June 1987, and played hip-hop for two hours, Thurston Moore asked me to make a tape for him; ironically, most of the stuff I'd been playing probably came from his native New York, of course. But more important than how a few professional musicians react to your music is, of course, what your audience makes of it; your regulars. Most satisfying is when a record builds up a groundswell of support on the dancefloor without any kind of outside commercial pressure or influence. Sometimes records grow huge on the dancefloor without ever getting any commercial success: Young MC's 'Know how', Charles B's 'Lack of love' and 'Dreams of Santa Anna' by Orange Lemon. There are other records that are dancefloor smashes way ahead of commercial release; subsequent radio play cements their appeal and sends them chartbound. At the end of August 1995, Blur and Oasis entered the pop charts at one and two; those two bands had benefited from thousands of pounds of advertising, hundreds of column inches of pre-release hype, front-page profiles in the national and music press, and TV news coverage, as well as having enjoyed previous hit singles, major tours and industry accolades. But the way The Original's 'I luv you baby', which had been placed in clubs (in various mixes) from February 1995, charged straight in at number two just a week or so earlier, almost solely on the back of club play (with no tours, press interviews or previous form, no industry encouragement and little radio play until the final weeks), tells us more about British pop than the contrived duel between Blur and Oasis. Records bursting high into the charts – on the back of little more than sustained DJ play – is a unique feature of modern pop culture.

In the summer of 1986 the Temperance Club was working well. On Thursday, 28 August 1986 the club was full; the first time since the Haçienda opened four and a half years earlier that the club had been full on a club night. It was to be the first, though, of hundreds. Mike Pickering's Friday Nude Night was now massive, but Paul Mason's first attempts to launch a club night on a Saturday had failed throughout the first half of 1986. In something approaching desperation, I should think, the management asked me to work Saturdays as well, starting in July 1986. I suggested they poach another graduate from the Venue and employ Dean to play his esoteric soul, funk and jazz cuts, alongside me playing whatever I thought would fill the dance-floor, from 'Sleep talk' to 'Backstabbers'. In recognition of our attempts to yoke such disparate music together, the night was called Wide Night. Wide thrived.

At the Temperance Club I was witnessing the bridging of the biggest gulf in music: the one between dance fans and rock fans. The breach may have begun in the late 1960s when white youth took to lying in fields listening to guitar solos rather than crowding into basement clubs for rhythm-heavy soul or R & B. I've always maintained that it was a generational thing. The punk generation had considered punk to be a reaction against dinosaur rock acts like ELP and Pink Floyd, but shared rock's traditional disdain for disco music. Punk was an excluding movement; despite a nod towards reggae, it sneered at anything outside its values (Tony Parsons has described it as 'Stalinist'). Those whose mindset was formed during that era – among whom I would include Morrissey and Tony Wilson – found it hard, or even impossible, to see any positive values in dance music. But the generation after punk – my generation – we didn't run with that punk thing, we were a little less uptight, a little less prone to conform to punk's wholesale rejection of disco. Sometimes this was hard; in about 1979 I remember trying to justify in my mind why – against the grain of my friends and *NME* (which I had become addicted to) – I preferred The Real Thing's 'Can you feel the force?' to Generation X's 'King Rocker'.

The punk against funk battle was fought all through the early part of the eighties in the music papers, and in the clubs. For instance, the two dominant club nights in Manchester in the couple of years up to 1985 were Goth nights and black dance nights. Goth music was an obvious evolution from punk, and Goth nights were miserable affairs featuring hours of Spear of Destiny, the Cramps and 'Should I stay or should I go?' by the Clash. The busiest club night at the Haçienda up to 1985, incidentally, was The End on Tuesday nights; 'No Funk Night' it was called (an echo, perhaps, of the anti-disco discos at Liverpool's famous punk club Eric's in 1977). The battle was irrelevant to me; mine was a pluralistic mind. And, although the battle was also still being fought in the mid–1980s, with the fires regularly stoked by Morrissey's pronouncements on discos and dance music, there was a genuine change of attitude among those going out in Manchester. It wasn't just evident at the Wilde Club, you could sense it too in the way New Order had co-opted the sounds of New York for their hits 'Blue Monday' and 'Confusion' in the early 1980s, with help from Arthur Baker. The dormant strand – the one where musical miscegenation was welcome – began to reassert itself once the authority of the punk generation began to wane.

Black dance music made extraordinary advances in the early 1980s, flinging out ideas, discovering and using new technology – samplers and drum machines – in ways that the more technophobic rock artists failed to do. The British dance scene was changing in the early 1980s, too, as electro, hip and hop and harder sounds made an impact, putting the established dance hierarchy on the defensive. Mike Pickering sensed this street energy surfacing way back in June 1987 when he told me: 'There's still all that smoochy stuff, with all those British bands still going with tacky wet-look haircuts and lamé suits. That's gradually changing and you can tell that by the dance night at the club; the younger people, and the whole atmosphere is a lot tougher.'

The big change in the club from 1986 to 1989 was so obvious that the old–guard dance heads and rock's punk generation could no longer ignore what was filling the floor. On Saturdays at the end of 1987, my set at the Haçienda would include Maceo and the Macks, the O'Jays, hip-hop like 'Talkin' all that jazz' and 'It takes two', remix records like 'Paid in full' and New York stuff like 'Let the music play'. At the same time, Mike Pickering's Fridays, which had always included harder, more street sounds, had become the first night in Britain regularly to programme the first beginnings of Chicago house in 1986. His own interests in house had already seen him form T-Coy, and release the seminal Latin House track 'Carino' in July 1987. And Wednesday was Zumbar, a prototype of the famous gay Flesh nights launched in 1991; playing party music to an up-for-it fashion crowd. My Thursdays at the end of 1987 were still mixing and mashing the genres; if Morrissey couldn't cope with the idea of the Smiths back-to-back with Public Enemy, I found that the ordinary indie fans could. It was then that I knew the old punk generation had had its day; in August 1987 – perhaps with less fanfare than the notion, it was to turn out, deserved – I suggested in the *NME* that the Happy Mondays were turning the phrase '24-hour party people' into a slogan for a generation, and recommended people to join them.

In a sense, a revolution had already begun: the dancefloor had already reasserted itself as the focus of youth culture in Manchester; new technology was releasing new creativity; black and white records were getting played in a deghettoized way; music from urban black America (hip-hop and disco from New York, house from Chicago, Go-Go from Washington) was huge; a younger generation of clubgoers had embraced the sounds of a new era; DJs were making and remixing records; and all this even before house music began properly pouring through to us from across the Atlantic to change Manchester indisputably and for ever.

The revolution wasn't plotted, not even expected or defined. Labels came later; acid, balearic, indie dance; I can remember Jon Da Silva in about November 1987 (before he'd become a DJ at the club) congratulating me on 'that last half-hour of acid'. I really didn't know what he was talking about. I didn't recognize the labels. I was making it up as I went along. The house music boom which swept the city was exciting precisely because it was out of control. We were in an era when there weren't just new great records released every week, but new styles and ideas. The vocabulary of sounds and the grammar of music making was being revised; we rocked the disco-text.

1988 was the watershed, the First Summer of Love. House music became the sound of now, the bona fide party sound; Zumbar turned to Hot, and Wednesday nights became the airborne madness; Dean's Latin jazz and soul got drowned in the cascades of house, and Jon Da Silva took over playing Saturdays with me; Nude night exploded into the most important club night Manchester has ever staged. Up until 1988 house had been coming into Britain intermittently. There was hip-hop and hip-house, Chicago-style jacking records and Detroit-style spectral techno, but we didn't really know where all this was going. As it turned out, it was going overground. 1988 was the year 'acid' house hit the tabloids, 'We call it acieeed' went Top 20, and in Britain the media and the mainstream discovered house. And more house. And ecstasy. There is no doubt that the entry of ecstasy into house clubs gave the scene a huge boost, loosened the crowds, fed the atmosphere and contributed to the staggering rise of house music. Long term, you could certainly argue that E narrowed club music to certain bpms and a circumscribed sound, but 1988 was all innocent excitement, and an authentic, original movement in a wholesale pop revolution. 1988 was the year of 'Big fun', and 'You're gonna miss me when I'm gone'.

The vibe was so intense, the club so packed, the music just so pure, fresh and mindblowing; DJ-ing at the Haçienda in 1988, 1989 and 1990 was fantastic. It was an unmedicated experience. It didn't feel second-hand, it wasn't forced, it had no models, it wasn't faked, it wasn't ritualistic; it was immediate. This was Manchester. Nobody was excluded: shop assistants, secretaries, dole-ites, plasterers, thieves, students. I felt at the centre of the pop world, that's one thing, but better still was that I felt in the middle of a huge explosion of energy. Everybody danced; on the stairs, on the stage, on the balcony, and at the bar. They danced in the cloakroom queue. For all I know, they were dancing in the street outside.

I didn't care if the music was from Chicago or Manchester or Italy or New York; if it rocked the house, it got played. Seven years down the line we've all seen house music mutate, replicate, evolve, survive. It's been through phases of gross commercialization, but that's somehow just added to the fun. There's always something new, underground, different to play; that's the way DJs love it. Great dancefloor sounds have a direct, visceral appeal. Generally the identity of the music-makers is of minimal interest. Imports and white labels, major label releases, indie promos; it was all the same to me. People used to say 'faceless techno'; but that missed the point. The best thing about it is the fact that it's faceless. The music industry believes in selling us stars, encouraging hero worship and blind devotion. In rock music the front man is all, but none of them was my hero; I wasn't going to the ends of the world for Lou Reed, Bob Dylan, Joe Strummer or any of them. The dancefloor, on the other hand, is no respecter of reputations. Even techno innovators like Derrick May and Kevin Saunderson have no divine right to fill a dancefloor, eight or nine years down the line, and ultimately that's liberating.

In fact, I did have a bias – towards Manchester groups. This was part of the chemistry of clubland in the city. From the first, house influenced Manchester musicians just as R & B had in the early 1960s, and electro in the early 1980s. Mike Pickering recreated Nude night with T-Coy (and, much later, M-People). A Guy Called Gerald could be in the club one night and in the studio the next day. Next weekend there'd be a cassette of the track in the DJ box, followed by a test pressing a fortnight later, bedlam on the dancefloor for two months, and then, at last, the video on *The Chart Show*. That was a sign it was all working well, that Manchester wasn't just passively sponging up new American dance sounds, but was making versions and hybrids of its own; even the guitar bands felt the need to acknowledge the music they were hearing in clubs. The audiences at that time were filled with future DJs: Justin Robertson, Peter Heller, Sasha. And music makers: A Guy Called Gerald, of course, and 808 State, Happy Mondays, Johnny Marr, Bernard Sumner from New Order, Johnny Jay of the Development Corporation, Baby Ford and the Chemical Brothers. As a DJ, I certainly felt the urge to champion music from the city. And I didn't stop playing it when the music started changing. The charts didn't really matter to me, and still don't. A good record transcends chart placing, press hype or any of the other hullabaloo. I'm not one of these DJs who stop playing a record when it isn't underground any more. I'm not one of these DJ's obsessed by the authentic, purist sounds. I always loved classic Italian house of 1989–1 and played it to death; it was very impure, raw and unsubtle.

It was not as cool as New York, and not as credible as Detroit, but Italian house had more to do with the rise of rave and the broadening of house music's popularity in those years immediately following the First Summer of

Love than any amount of authentic techno. Piano breaks and screaming divas – the staple of classic Italian house – formed the basic sound at Shelly's in Stoke (where Sasha started DJ-ing) and Quadrant Park in Liverpool. In the same years breakbeat-based hardcore rave multiplied house music's audience. By the end of 1990, the Haçienda monopoly was well and truly dead. At the time when the club closed because of gang trouble, there was only one busy night. By then I'd left; I wanted to avoid the inevitable nostalgia, and to find a new mission for myself well away from my progressively poor relations with the club's management and owners. As the house scene drew more people, the gangsters discovered it (people always think that gangsters are cool, but I tell you, they're always the last people to find out where the action is). Now there are more than 5,000 people going out every week, but they're not all going to the Haçienda; clubs have multiplied in Manchester in the years since the Haçienda's first era, as house music has renewed itself and diversified. Unfortunately, proportionately larger numbers of dealers and gangsters now bring their bad vibes and moody attitudes into Manchester clubs. That's two undoubted changes in Manchester clubland since 1988: there are more roughnecks in Manchester clubs now, and there are more than half a handful of DJs making a living.

The extracurricular activities of DJs have increased too, as dance music has boomed. In the late 1980s, tracks that were being played in discothèques started turning up high in the charts in numbers never previously known. They hit the chart as if from nowhere (the traditional channels of media hype, press photos, bands demoing, going on the road, etc. now all redundant), and the record companies wanted a piece of the action. A record's dancefloor appeal can't be faked, as any DJ knows. A record's either got the power or it hasn't. The record companies went straight to the DJs to find the key. DJs had recorded and remixed before: sound system guys like Duke Reid had put big Jamaican records out in the early 1960s; there'd been special one-off dub plates in reggae circles; Larry Levan and Shep Pettibone had remixed New York disco in the early 1980s. DJs had remixed live for years: mixing two records together, cutting drum breaks, dropping an a capella on to an instrumental track, and so on, was what launched hip-hop culture. As the dancefloor sounds of 1988 onwards took over, the DJs were seen as tastemakers; DJs were recruited to A & R labels (Mike Pickering had great success launching DeConstruction Records on the back of Back Box's 'Ride on time'); and DJs like Paul Oakenfold and Andrew Weatherall were recruited to make the songs of guitar bands Happy Mondays and Primal Scream more dancefloor friendly. Although Primal Scream milked their dancefloor connections only to go back to being the Rolling Stones, the experiments with technology and the cross-fertilizations of 1989 and 1990 – the legacy of which was laying foundations for the success of later bands like the Stereo MCs, Orbital and Portished – were thrilling.

What the British remixers like Oakenfold and Weatherall did was a lot more drastic than what Larry Levan or Shep Pettibone had done. It wasn't so much remixing as rewriting; new drum patterns and bass lines were introduced, choruses and verses rejigged. The remix principle has overrun British music in the last few years. Now it's not unusual to receive double- or triple-pack promo records with eight or ten mixes of a song. Even acts with no previous interest in the dance scene – indeed, even acts who've openly despised the dance scene in the past – now employ DJs as remixers, to give them a badge of credibility and a boost in the clubs.

The remix explosion has thrown up a few ironies though. Even artists who have a great dancefloor pedigree are overshadowed by the remixers, like when Soul II Soul's 'Love enuff' is given a house treatment by Todd Terry and Roger Sanchez (and the original isn't even included on the promotional records sent out to DJs). The replacing of original R & B rhythms with bog-standard house mixes is especially pernicious (Uno Clio remixing Brownstone's 'I can't tell you why', for example; again with no original mixes on the promo). What can it all mean? Obviously the remix boom has changed the nature of DJ-ing. So younger DJs like Elliot Eastwick and Miles Hollway, just months after first making names for themselves DJ-ing, get down to remixing records. Or writing songs, which is just one stage further, after all. Italy is full of DJ songwriters (such as Alex Natale, Claudio Coccoluto and Paolo Martini). It's as if DJs are now as at home in a recording studio as in a club. With his record company and remixing duties mounting, Paul Oakenfold, I hear, is saying that he only DJs in his 'spare time'.

One commentator has described how, in recent years, the cult of the DJ has achieved 'priestly proportions'. Whether a DJ is a priest or a prostitute, I don't know, but DJ-ing is certainly a great buzz. The significant chemistry of clubland isn't the ecstasy doing strange things inside people's brains. The important chemistry is the reaction between the music and the crowd; and the DJ is somewhere at the centre of it all, a catalyst. Ecstasy without music is a worthless thing; you're just running round hugging trees and grinning at bus drivers. But a drug-free dancefloor still kicks. Witness one of New York's star dancers, Willi Ninja, talking about feelings out on the floor: 'How the DJ clips the music – certain combinations – can totally inspire you. Sometimes people think I'm on major drugs because when a song clicks, I am gone. I mean I don't see, hear, smell or taste no one. I get such a high from dancing.'

To get that right, to work those dancers, is the DJ's dream. You can tell the difference between a good and a bad DJ: do they move a crowd? Once you've accepted those differences exist, then you accept a hierarchy; hence the inflationary fees that the DJs with the best reputations can pick up. But the growth in the status of DJs in recent years is also down to the fact that the music press and the record industry need DJ stars; club culture is no respecter of artists, but it needs something to sell, icons and a commodity. DJs have become a commodity, a name on a flyer, an investment.

As demand for good DJs has multiplied, DJs have also started touring in a manner not known five years ago, travelling the motorways and railways of Britain; Bristol one week, Wolverhampton the next. Now London, now Leeds. DJ-ing is a proper job now. The old informal routes are gone. The competition is fierce; there are technical skills to master, demo tapes to record, a heavy investment in decks and records to make. It's a big thing. I learned the rules as I went along. I've DJ-ed overseas dozens of times – in Detroit, Boston, Paris and Geneva, for example – and I love getting paid to get on a plane and play my favourite records to a bunch of enthusiastic strangers; it's a lucky life. But I love the special relationship with a crowd that having your own residency brings. I've been at the Boardwalk over five years, with two full nights, and I play what I like and love what I do. The nights depend on my performance. I am instantly accountable to the audience; if I fuck up, they don't come. If people have paid £6 after queuing for half an hour in the rain, they demand something good. If I don't provide it at the Boardwalk, they'll go somewhere else in Manchester, Leeds, Sheffield or Liverpool. I get all the attention and all the pressure. And I get people bugging me all night, 'The cloakroom's full, can you look after my jacket?'

The last twelve years or so are confused. I just do it. Retrieving all this and trying to recall how it happened, and when, and why; it's harder work than putting one record on after another, hearing yells of joy, watching the arms in the air as the piano break kicks in. That's podium heaven. The whys and the wherefores are yesterday's news. The time is now. This weekend, next weekend.

Plates

Plates 1 to 7 were taken at Flesh, a gay club event at the Haçienda, Manchester (the pictures were taken between winter 1992 and winter 1995).

Plates 8 to 11 were taken at the Northern Soul Reunion 'all-nighter' at the Ritz, Manchester (Boxing Day, 1995).

Plates 12 to 16 were taken at the Bad Manners gig at Witchwood, Ashton-Under-Lyne (December 1995).

Photos by Patrick Henry.

THEORY 2

13 The Post-subculturalist

David Muggleton

This chapter explores the implications of the postmodern for 'spectacular' subcultural style. My remarks on postmodern subcultures are deduced from a 'double comparison' with the modern and with 'conventional' style. The chapter is in large part a review of other writers' assertions followed by my own deductions about possible occurrences made on the basis of such arguments. There is, however, an unfortunate lack of availability of studies which privilege the actual practices, meanings and experiences of consumers themselves. I do aim eventually to provide data of this kind through my own interviews with 'spectacular' stylists. During this fieldwork I will be treating part of the material in the final section of this chapter as a series of hypotheses to be subjected to empirical test, for it is only by the provision of evidence based on the values, meanings and motives of the subculturalists themselves that we can progress beyond the sterility of previous approaches and add to our knowledge of this phenomenon. In the meantime, many of the more theoretical claims made here must be regarded as conjectural.

The Paradoxes of Modernity: 'From Modern Styles to Postmodern Codes'

In a postmodern culture typified by the disappearance of the Real and by the suffocation of natural contexts, fashion provides aesthetic holograms as moveable texts for the general economy of excess. Indeed, if fashion cycles now appear to oscillate with greater and greater speed, frenzy and intensity of circulation of all the signs, that is because fashion, in an era when the body is the inscribed surface of events, is like brownian motion in physics: the greater the

velocity and circulation of its surface features, the greater the internal movement towards stasis, immobility and inertia. An entire postmodern scene,
therefore, brought under the double sign of culture where, as Baudrillard has
hinted, the secret of fashion is to introduce the appearance of radical novelty,
while maintaining the reality of no substantial change. Or is it the opposite?
(Kroker *et al.*, 1989)

The cultural logic of modernity is not merely that of rationality as expressed
in the activities of calculation and experiment; it is also that of passion, and
the creative dream born of longing. (Campbell, 1987).

Despite those theories (Bell, 1976) which stress the contradictory relationship which exists between a rational economy organized on the basis of
efficiency and a hedonistic culture ruled by the principle of self-gratification,
it is possible to posit puritan-rationalism and romantic-hedonism as
contrasting cultural traditions of modernity locked together into a symbiotic
relationship (Campbell, 1987). While the sphere of modern hedonistic
consumption obtains its dynamic from pietistic puritanism, romanticism and
an ethic of sensibility, the origins of modern production lie in ascetic puritanism, founded upon rationalization, utilitarianism and regulation. The
rational precepts of production thus appear Apollonian in character
compared to the Dionysian dynamics of consumption. This remains the case
if we switch from the 'idealism' of Weber to the 'materialism' of Marx. In
Frisby (1985), for example, we read of modernite: the sense of flux, rapidity
and hedonism resulting from immersion in the nascent world of nineteenth-
century consumer culture. Yet we are issued with a warning: to remain at
the superficial level which is the fragmentary and ephemeral experience of
aesthetic modernity is to risk being stranded on the ideological surfaces of the
world of commodity fetishism; for situated below the dynamic of
consumerism is stasis, the structure of fixed and definite social relationships
of production 'that assumes . . . the fantastic form of a relationship between
things' (Marx, 1976).

   Yet as Berman (1987) realizes, it is paradox which is the true key to the
understanding of modernity, for every set of concepts contains within itself
the germination of its opposite. It is this sense of paradox which allows us
to comprehend how a unificatory, rationalist and foundationalist
Enlightenment modernity could provide the driving forces of disintegration
which lie behind modernization – the growth and development of industri-
alization, science, technology and urbanization associated with
unprecedented levels of rapid social change and the sweeping away of
traditional economic and cultural structures where 'All that is solid melts into
air'. The series of contrasts implicated here, between stasis and dynamism,
unificatory and fragmentary, rationalist and aesthetic, puritan and hedonistic,

are particularly pronounced within the paradoxical phenomenon we call fashion. On the one hand, such upheavals and dislocations, the rapid pace of change in both the spheres of production and consumption, have defined an insecure epoch of modernity in direct opposition to the stability, certitude and predictability of traditional society. As Wilson (1985) puts it: 'the colliding dynamism, the thirst for change and the heightened sensation that characterize city societies particularly of modern industrial capitalism go up to make this modernity, and the hysteria and exaggeration of fashion well express it'. But if Wilson sees a congruence between this 'aesthetic modernity' and the phenomenon of fashion, there is the other modernity: a modernity of certainty, universalism and immutability built upon bedrock principles of rationality, science and technological progress, and opposing the pre-modern 'irrationalities of myth, religion, superstition' (Harvey, 1991). It was this 'Enlightenment modernity' which was the provider of the dominant conceptions of modern fashion in the period from the late nineteenth century until the 1960s.

> Of course, the history of fashion does have a significant and well-attested modernist phase. The insistence on purity and function, along with the hatred of superfluous ornament, that are expressed in the work of architects like Miles van der Rohe, artists like Piet Mondrian and theorists like Alfred Loos, resulted in attempts to rationalize dress, and figures like Victor Tatlin, Kasmir Malevich, Sonia Delaunay, Walter Gropius and Jacobus Ord were all interested in extending the modernist revolution in the arts to matters of clothing. It is even possible to conceive of the invention of something like a 'modernist body', the slim and functional female figure of the 1920s, liberated from the corset and the paraphernalia of female ornament. (Connor, 1991)

I consider it instructive to preface a discussion on modern fashion with the above quotation because, interesting as such an analysis is, it places emphasis on the particular historical movement of 1920s and 1930s artistic modernism rather than the broader epoch of modernity, and therefore focuses on avant-garde high culture rather than popular culture, and without considering the dissemination of the former into the latter. Moreover, although the relationship of artistic movements to broader economic, cultural and social structures is obviously complex, modernism contains elements which are symptomatic of both Enlightenment and aesthetic strands within modernity. Connor himself draws attention to Wollen's (1987) article which details 'an alternative history of dress design to be discerned in modernism, a history of a continuing infatuation with decorative excess and stylistic extravagance' (Connor, 1991). Modernity, in the epochal sense of the term, was also a witness to decorative trends in fashion not usually associated with 'high modernism', including that of women's dress in the Edwardian era: exactly that excess of ornament which the inter-war female figure was 'liberated from'. Indeed, one might go further and hypothesize that, since both a rationalist–utilitarian and a Romantic–aesthetic ethic are implicated in the development of modernity, fashions throughout this epoch would emphasize both of these tendencies, but alternatively, in a cyclical pattern.

The sociological variables of class and gender must, however, be considered in any such analysis. Fashion, in the sense of aesthetic display and rapid change, is a gendered term in the empirical history of conventional modern dress: women have 'fashion'; men, sober, sombre and static, have 'style'. This gender division, which is predicated upon the relationship of masculinity to a puritan business ethic (Flugel, 1930; Konig, 1973; Wilson, 1990) and the linking of femininity through romanticism to consumption (Campbell, 1987), is also cross-cut by the cleavage of social class. Historical accounts (Steedman, 1986; Holdsworth, 1989) have shown how the dimensions of middleclass/workingclass have tended to work themselves out along the axis of decoration–fashion/utility–necessity. Yet, despite this presence of a decorative–aesthetic element, it is the functional and utilitarian axis of modern dress codes which appears to possess a particular affinity with the rational precepts of Fordist mass production techniques. Utilizing Taylor's principles of 'scientific management' (which paradoxically entailed a fragmentation and differentiation of tasks), Fordism is seen to have generated a relatively standardized set of products tied to mass markets; the phenomenon of mass consumption was the inescapable corollary of such a system (Harvey, 1991, ch. 8; Crook *et al.*, 1992, ch. 6). As Urry (1990) has said within the context of a sociology of tourism, 'Central to modernism is the view of the public as an homogeneous mass, that there is a realm of correct values which will serve to unify people.' So while it is correct to note that 'the clothing industry could never be as Fordist, as concentrated and as Taylorist as most other sectors because it entails a much higher turnover of styles' (Lash and Urry, 1994), the prevailing image of conventional fashion in the period of modernity after the change from liberal to organized capitalism (Lash and Urry, 1988) tends to be one of uniformity, predictability and conformity, its usage governed by the dictates of a functional–rationality.

Yet it is precisely this dominant conception of Enlightenment modernity which the postmodern is said to herald a break from. For when viewed from the perspective of a paradoxical modernity, postmodern dress articulates its increasing detachment from Enlightenment precepts, while displaying an intensification of those traits which characterized aesthetic modernity along with its burgeoning consumer culture, and which stretched to embrace the alternative history of modernism. In contrast to a modernism of purity, functionality and utilitarianism, to be fashionable in postmodernism is therefore to involve oneself in aesthetic play, with the focus on hedonism, pleasure and spectacle, 'a return to ornament, decoration and stylistic eclecticism' (Connor, 1990). A modernity of Fordist uniformity, linear rationality and stability has likewise given way to what, according to Harvey (1991), 'appears to be the most startling fact about postmodernism: its total acceptance of the ephemerality, fragmentation, discontinuity and the chaotic that formed the one [aesthetic] half of Baudelaire's conception of modernity'. Wilson (1985), in agreement, acknowledges how: 'fashion does appear to express such a fragmented sensibility particularly well – its obsession with surface, novelty and style for style's sake highly congruent with this sort of post-modernist aesthetic'.

Contemporary debates have also cited the development of flexible forms of technology and the associated shift from Fordist to post-Fordist production techniques as responsible for an increasing acceleration in the emergence of new fashions; turnover time in consumption has speeded up correspondingly as consumers have eagerly availed themselves of this ever-expanding 'emporium of styles'. Yet, in addition to expansionism, the decline of Fordism also entails the fragmentation of mass identities (Lash and Urry, 1988) – the paradoxical proliferation of disintegration characteristic of aesthetic modernity. With the advent of 'specialized consumption' and 'market segmentation', 'lifestyle enclaves' are said to be losing their correspondence to, and indeed superseding as a basis for social stratification, modernist grids of class, gender, age and ethnicity (Evans and Thornton, 1989; Crook *et al.*, 1992, Nixon, 1992). 'Modernist styles', once firmly structured along these traditional lines of demarcation, become 'postmodernist codes' (Jameson, 1991) available for the pleasure of the (apparently ironic, reflexive and knowing) postmodern consumer who wishes to construct his or her own identity through the wearing of stylistic 'masks'. The prevailing mood of the times is best captured through the slogans of Ewen and Ewen (1982): 'Today there is no fashion, only fashions.' 'No rules, only choices.' 'Everyone can be anyone.'

As 'evidence' of these changes, Evans and Thornton (1989) chart how 'since the decline in the 1960s of a seasonal "look" of which women could be sure, mainstream fashion has deliberately constructed itself as a variety of "looks". But in the 1980s the turnover of looks speeded up hysterically.' Connor (1991) also views the sixties as being something of a watershed, citing 'the abundant multiplicity of styles and accelerated rhythm of fashion from the prosperous years of the 1960s onwards'. Similarly, for Wilson (1990), 'the "confusion" that so puzzled fashion writers in the 1970s, the apparent ending of the orderly evolution of one style out of another, is explicable once it is seen as part of postmodernism'. Kaiser *et al.* (1991) claim that now even the last bastions of puritanism are susceptible to a decorative impulse:

The tendency towards a breakdown of conventional rules may be found in a much more limited extent in the American business world . . . Even in some professional contexts, in a subtle manner within conventional bounds, men as well as women seem to have more freedom (if they are so inclined) to experiment with color and accessories (for example, braces or suspenders for men, brightly colored suits for women).

Elsewhere, in a comparison with the modern, Lash (1990) manages to capture together both sensibilities of postmodern dress – the fragmented and the aesthetic:

Consider for example a photo of British football supporters in the interwar period. The similarity and 'mass-ness' of their dress is striking to the contemporary observer. Compare this, then, with the very diversity of clothing styles and associated subcultures among British working-class youth in more recent times . . . the shift has not just been of one from mass-ness to specialization but also from a focus on function to a concern with style.

While Lash looks at soccer supporters, my own example focuses on the outfits worn by the players. Whereas twenty years ago, British soccer club strips were relatively plain, unadorned and functional, today we find a strange combination of lurid colours (fluorescent salmon pinks and lime greens) arranged in intricate designs using a plethora of decoration (motifs, numbers in imitation 3-D, superimposed letters). We even have instances of 1920s pastiche with lace-up V-necks. Furthermore, whereas team designs used to remain comparatively stable over a number of seasons with only minimal changes, clubs today issue radically new versions of their kit at a much faster rate, with manufacturers and retailers only too eager to announce the arrival in the sportshops of this season's new Manchester United, Arsenal or Liverpool third-choice away strip.

Our views of modern mainstream fashion consumption tend to be defined negatively against what is perceived to be the active consumer of postmodernity. Certainly, given the dominant conception of modern fashion as uniform, massified and predictable, it is easy to understand how it might be consumed 'passively': that is, for outfits to be taken over 'wholesale' without the need for much symbolic creativity by consumers. One might think here of the mass-produced 'ready-to-wear' suit, or the costume with matching accessories. Of course, the aesthetic tendencies of modernity imply a potential over time for increased complexity of arrangements and changes in the meanings attached to particular clothing constructs, and one suspects that, in practice, consumers often fulfilled this potential. For example, Partington (1992) suggests that working-class women actively created their own 'hybrid' versions of Dior's New Look. By selecting, mixing and matching items from both utility and glamour wear, they undermined the dominant expectations of designer dress codes. If we persist, however, in an ideal-typical analysis where an expansion of commercialization and commodification would not disrupt the modernist trend towards regularity, then modernist 'appearance management' would tend towards the uncomplicated, the utilitarian and the functional. In semiotic terms, the codes associated with particular forms of dress would be relatively unambiguous and tied unproblematically to particular contexts: in other words, the mode of signification would be realist.

> Modernist American culture, based on puritanism, industrialism and utilitarianism, has traditionally demanded univocal, rather than ambiguous forms of discourse. The business suit is a prime example . . . this rational, technological ethos of univocality . . . a 'flight from ambiguity'. Postmodern capitalism, however, problematizes this flight. (Kaiser *et al.*, 1991)

This problematization has at its root what might be termed the postmodern expansion of eclecticism: a wider variety of styles now travel at a faster rate than ever before, giving 'active' consumers greater scope for their creative and aesthetic outlets. The result is 'a promotion of do-it-yourself style', where 'postmodern appearance management may be compared with the formal technique of collage' (Kaiser *et al.*, 1991). This trend, towards the construction of complex appearances through the self-conscious act of stylistic *bricolage*, is particularly notable in Willis's study of the 'grounded aesthetics' and 'symbolic creativity' of youth culture:

> Young people don't just buy passively or uncritically. They always transform the meaning of bought goods, appropriating and recontextualising mass-market styles . . . Most young people combine elements of clothing to create new meanings . . . and sometimes reject the normative definitions and categories of 'fashion' promoted by the clothing industry. (Willis, 1990)

While the decoding of modernist style was facilitated by its univocality – a limited availability of signifiers and a stable anchorage in a particular time-space context – it was also assisted by the firm demarcation of specific social groups, each with its own style boundaries; for modernity was an era of clearly differentiated, yet internally homogeneous, collectivities. Postmodernity, however, appears to entail the inverse of this process; internal fragmentation has reached such proportions that the boundaries between established cultural collectivities appear to be breaking down – this is what Lash (1990) has referred to as 'de-differentiation', a reversal of the modernist tendency towards the differentiation of cultural spheres. Perhaps this de-differentiating movement is responsible for what some observers claim is a tendency for designer, retail and street/subcultural styles to merge: a contemporary use of fashion which pays no heed to the once firm and established divisions between high, mainstream and low (Evans and Thornton, 1989). This, if true, is a useful example of how a surfeit of signs and a breaking down of boundaries might problematize the way in which social groups use style as a means of classification and demarcation – a point made by Featherstone (1992). As differentiated unities are replaced by a similarity of difference, 'appearance perception' becomes a hazardous undertaking, an ever-increasing number of interpretations being possible. If modern mainstream fashion 'readerly', then Kaiser *et al.* would appear to see postmodernist style as analogous to Barthes' 'writerly' text (Barthes, 1975), where 'signifiers, it seems, hold a certain privilege over what is signified'.

Subcultural Style: From the Grand Narratives of Modernity to Hyperfragmentation in the Postmodern Global Village

> I see this little group of mates which is like one of those mixed assorted liqueurs, because you've got a rather bad one of everything. There is, for instance, a Nouveau Mass-Mod, 1979 style . . . His mate is Two Tone . . . One girl is plasticine punk . . . And her mate is a high yellow girl with the most enormous bouffant, a B52 . . . And the point is . . . that they're all mates and by any of the laws of nature ought to be at each other's throats, for any of a hundred reasons to do with the old inextricable laws of Teen society and dressing the part. The problem is that the old laws are clearly being mucked around with something criminal. (York, 1980)

At the visible level of 'spectacular' style, the studies of youth subcultures which came out of the 'Birmingham School' (Hall and Jefferson, 1976; Mungham and Pearson, 1976; Willis, 1978; Hebdige, 1979) stressed the subculture's active appropriation and transformation of signs through the subversive act of *bricolage*, contrasting this by implication with the 'passive' consumption of mainstream fashion and, hence, dominant identities by 'conventional' youth culture. Thus, although the wholesale adoption of modern mainstream fashion seems to be defined in contrast to the active and creative postmodern consumer, it also provides the norm of 'passive' conformity to dominant modes against which the acts of *bricolage* by modern youth subculturalists were a form of resistance.

Before considering the implications of the postmodern for youth subcultural styles, it is therefore necessary to emphasize how there is much about this neo-Marxist theory which is derived from the precepts of an Enlightenment modernity: its emancipatory metanarrative which claims to provide a 'scientific' analysis of society – hence its assumed authority to speak on behalf of the excluded Other rather than trust the voices of the subculturalists themselves; its totalizing conception of the social formation within which the specific element under study must be reinstated; the sense of linear time along which these successive subcultures are seen to unfold; the portrayal of subcultures as externally differentiated, yet internally homogeneous collectivities, existing in clear opposition to each other and to conventional style.

Yet while this modernist neo-Marxist paradigm is predicted upon a 'depth model' of the social formation from which a whole host of subcultural oppositions were derived – essence/appearance, unobservable/phenomenal, production/consumption, authentic/manufactured, style-as-resistance/ style-as-fashion, subcultural/conventional, value/image and so on, postmodernity collapses these oppositions. In particular, it undercuts them by problematizing the distinction between representations and reality. For while Marxism was concerned to stress the misleading character of appearances, what is privileged in postmodernity is the absolute power of image. One might begin here with Jameson's (1991) reference to 'a society of the image or the simulacrum', then consider Lash's (1990) contention that communication in postmodernity is becoming increasingly figural as opposed to the discursive nature of modernity, before arriving at our final destination, the wholly artificial yet all-encompassing, hermetically sealed, computer-generated world of virtual reality, prophesied by Kroker and Cook (1991) as the logical conclusion to the encroachment of the visual into the province of the real.

The increasingly central role of the visual media as an image bank from which knowledge of fashion is derived has not gone unnoticed by sociologists and cultural commentators alike (McRobbie, 1989; Savage, 1989; Willis, 1990). Television (particularly MTV), video and the style magazines, *ID*, *Blitz* and *The Face*, which are primarily visual rather than textual in their impact (one cannot 'read' *The Face*), are most usually quoted as the postmodern paradigm case. As Evans and Thornton tellingly comment, 'at the heart of the new magazines was the idea that identity (I-D) is forged by appearance' (Evans and Thornton, 1989). Here, we might discern the homogenizing impulse of such a scenario: the progressive obliteration of cultural difference following the weakening of local powers of resistance to the inexorable stylistic globalizing processes of the mediascape.

Yet an aesthetic, fragmentary tendency is clearly detectable in Jameson (1985), particularly his use of Lacan's notion of schizophrenia to express a form of postmodern sensibility, 'a series of pure and unrelated presents in time'. Such an emphasis fits well, claims Harvey (1991) with the 'ephemerality', 'instantaneity', 'disposability' and volatility which are said to typify postmodern 'fashions, products [and] production techniques'. What faces us is not therefore necessarily the stifling of change by an all-encompassing 'astral empire of signs', but rather the paradox of a McLuhanian global village of ever-fragmenting fashions, 'an eclectic blend of cross-cultural commodities' (Kaiser, 1990), which forces into prominence the proclivities of consumers to become sartorial bricoleurs. As commodity production, exchange and creative appropriation intensify, signs travel towards the point at which they become irrevocably divorced from their original cultural contexts.

> Individuals obtaining ideas about what to wear may neither be aware of, nor necessarily care about the ideology to which styles have originally referred. Hence PLO headscarves become trendy on the streets of New York City, skulls and crossbones become insignia on children's clothing, and Rastafarian dreadlocks are preempted by runaway fashion models and rock (not necessarily reggae) musicians. (Kaiser et al., 1991)

So does the postmodern trend towards stylistic eclecticism, iconic overloading and the destruction of historical referents finally result in the 'death of the social', a total loss of meaning? Perhaps, like their attitude towards God, Baudrillard's masses retain only the image of fashion, 'never the idea' (Baudrillard, 1983a). Similarly, Jameson's 'breakdown in the signifying chain', which leads to the destruction of narrative utterance and its replacement by the intensification of aesthetic 'affect', can be interpreted as having identical consequences for fashion. In both cases, meaning gives way to spectacle. Style is now worn for its look, not for any underlying message; or rather, the look is now the message.

As the above discussion has indicated, narrative meaning is also intimately bound up with questions of temporality. Lyotard's *grands récits* are a testament to the optimism of the Enlightenment project with its progressive notion of history. At an individual and personal level, the deferment of gratification and the construction of lifelong narratives are equally symptomatic of this same modernist confidence, investment and faith in the future. It is therefore easy to associate the postmodern fragmentation of these ongoing, linear narratives with the move from the rationality of 'clock time' to 'instantaneous time', where a projection into the future appears neither possible nor desirable. Rather than wait for an empty promise, we are said to 'want the future now' (Lash and Urry, 1994, ch. 9). Or perhaps, in a postmodern, postindustrial urban wasteland where the atmosphere is heavily charged with apocalyptic fears, hearkening back to a past 'golden age' will always be preferable to existing in a crisis-ridden present. Hence that remarkable surge of contemporary fascination with nostalgia, its visible, stylistic manifestion being:

> that accelerating tendency in the 1980s to ransack history for key items of dress, in a seemingly eclectic and haphazard manner . . . This instant recall on history, fuelled by the superfluity of images thrown up by the media, has

produced a non-stop fashion parade in which 'different decades are placed together with no historical continuity'. (McRobbie, 1989)

Such changes have important and far-reaching implications for spectacular stylists. Once, youth subcultures were able to effect ironic transformations of the most unique, visible and excessive aspects of post-war 'conventional' style, only to see these ritualistic responses rendered harmless by their stylistic and ideological incorporation into the mainstream. But as each successive resolution of this dialectical movement from thesis to antithesis to synthesis hastens the effacement of the mainstream – subcultural divide, the excessive (now commonplace) no longer retains its power to shock; stylistic heterogeneity has been pushed to its utmost limits as the outward apperance of rebellion becomes merely another mode of fashion. At the point when a sartorial norm no longer exists, subcultural attempts to criticize an existing order through the employment of stylistic parody are likely to miss their mark. This is surely Jameson's world of pastiche, 'a world in which stylistic innovation is no longer possible, all that is left is to imitate dead styles, to speak through the masks and with the voices of the styles in the imaginary museum' (Jameson, 1985).

With nothing progressive left to say or do, subcultural stylists draw from and feed off each other in a cannibalistic orgy of cross-fertilization, destroying their own internal boundaries through the very act of expansion. (The resulting mutation, a subcultural hybridity of elements from punk, goth, grunge, new age and traveller, has been referred to as 'crossover-counter-culture' by one of my own respondents.) Alternatively, postmodern youth can indulge in what appears to be a form of nostalgic revivalism of a particular syle: the teddy boy, mod, skinhead, hippy and punk styles have all made their reappearances in the years since the original punk rock explosion of the mid to late 1970s. One must also mention in this context the apparently renewed interest in second-hand dress or 'retro style' (Carter, 1983; McRobbie, 1989). And, as a virtual *bricolage*, a Burroughs cut-up of previous subcultural styles, punk really does seem to have been the historical turning point here. With its inclusion of retro-style elements, its complex clothing collages, the analogy with the poststructuralist writerly text (Hebdige, 1979), punk style defies interpretation, 'refuses meaning' and is said to herald the subcultural break from modernity to postmodernity.

Yet if the post-punk stylistic revivals really are examples of pastiche, then, as Jameson would have it, they are merely 'simulacra', representing nothing more than our 'pop images' and 'cultural sterotypes' about the past, for the peculiarity of postmodern time has now and for ever more precluded any possibility of subcultural 'originality'. The concept of 'authenticity' must likewise be expunged from the postmodern vocabulary. The all-encompassing power of the contemporary mass media has ensured that there can no longer be a sanctuary for the original, 'pure', creative moment of subcultural innovation which preceded the onset of the contaminating processes of commercialization, commodification and diffusion. Redhead appears to be a proponent of a 'weak' version of this thesis, where 'post-punk subcultures have been characterised by a speeding up of the time between points of "authenticity" and manufacture' (Redhead, 1991). McRobbie, however, proposes a stronger version, whereby 'the "implosionary" effect of the mass media means that in the 1980s youth styles and fashions are born into the media. There is an "instantaneity" which replaces the old period of subcultural incubation' (McRobbie, 1989).

One might wish to make two criticisms of this thesis, which proclaims the postmodern 'death' of subcultural originality and authenticity. First, postmodernity entails the active subculturalist reordering existing subcultural items into new and original combinations. Second, and conversely, there never was a privileged moment of 'authentic' subcultural inception untainted by media, commercial and entrepreneurial influences, in the manner that modernist theory suggested, since:

> Media representations provide the ideological framework within which subcultures can represent themselves, shaping as well as limiting what they can say . . . Hebdige claims that the punks did not so much express the alienation they felt from mainstream society as dramatise contemporary media and political discourse about Britain's decline. (Beezer, 1992)

McRobbie's example is also punk, but again her point has a general applicability:

> the very idea that style could be purchased over the counter went against the grain of those analyses which saw the adoption of punk style as an act of creative defiance far removed from the mundane act of buying. The role of McLaren and Westwood was also downgraded for the similar reason that punk was seen as a kind of collective creative impulse. To focus on a designer and an art-school entrepreneur would have been to undermine the purity or authenticity of the subculture. (McRobbie, 1989)

But to concur with these two criticisms does not necessarily weaken the postmodern claim; for modernist subcultural 'originality' and 'authenticity' are defined in terms of an attempted solution to real historical contradictions, and if postmodern theory is taken at face value, there no longer exists outside of the media any province of the real for subcultural styles to be a cultural response to. Following the logic of Baudrillard (1983a, 1983b), if we are indeed no longer consuming commodities but signs, while, furthermore, the referents to which these signs supposedly refer are themselves increasingly comprised of representations, then subcultural styles have become simulacra – copies with no originals. By inscribing visual signs upon their bodies, post-modern youth subculturalists simulate the simulation of the media, becoming mere models themselves. In this implosive move from subcultural production to reproduction, from use-value (authentic-modern) to exchange-value (manufactured-modern) to sign-value (postmodern), subcultural simulacra not only take on the qualities of the real, but become hyperreal as reality is eclipsed. If, following Harvey, styles become subject to time-space compression, a dislocation from their original temporal-spatial origins, then in the wake of the irrevocable loss of these referents we can no longer experience the real, but 'live everywhere already in an "aesthetic" hallucination of reality' (Baudrillard, 1983b).

Take, for example, two contrasting claims which grant only partial recognition to the full implications of the postmodern for subcultural style. The first seeks less to document the change from modernity to post-modernity than to reinterpret modernist theory in the light of the postmodern:

> Clarke understands skinhead 'style' in dress, territoriality, homophobia, racism, and aggression as a 'symbolic' recovery of the values of a disappearing working-class community. Skinhead excesses are explained by the absence of any 'material and organizational' community base . . . Seen through the lens of postmodernization, Clarke's skinheads enter the register of the hyperreal, where the ironic juxtaposition of cultural fragments offers the reassurances of the real. (Crook *et al.*, 1992)

The second claim uses the same subcultural example, but attempts to save the skinhead from the full ramifications of postmodernity, while, at the same time, granting the postmodern thesis legitimacy with regard to other subcultures:

> There has been an overlapping, semiotic deviancy and a generic confusion that, culminating in the self-conscious cut-up style of punk, has displaced clas-sical white, male subcultures from the arguments of exclusion, urban romanticism and stylistic contestation. The firm and exclusive referents that once guided the teddy boys or the mods in their distinctive options in clothing or music are apparently no longer available . . . Only the skinhead – recalling a mythically 'authentic' reality . . . refuses this ironic and facetious relation-ship to the present and past . . . remains a stubborn referent in an increasingly mobile landscape . . . proposes the simple timeless truths and identities: those of the nation, of race, of masculinity, of class. (Chambers, 1990)

Now, if the act of *bricolage* is a coded response to a disappearing, fragmenting material base, then skinhead style may well be defined as a postmodern 'hypersimulated "panic" or "nostalgic" production of cultural reality' (Crook *et al.*, 1992). Yet, by the very same token, this particular, original 1960s 'ironic juxtaposition of cultural fragments' was, according to modernist theory, an 'authentic' response by a specific class fraction (emanating from 'real' underlying production relations) to a real structural contradiction at a particular unique, historical moment unfolding in linear time. To attempt to reconstitute it for postmodernist 'hyperreality' is there- fore to suggest that these modernist structural grids never possessed the validity conferred upon them, to claim that we have always had 'the end of history', that it is only now that we can recognize it. Conversely, today's skinheads cannot be saved for modernism. If referents are no longer avail- able for any other subculture, neither are they available for the skinhead. In 1994, over a quarter of a century after skinheads first made their appearance on English football terraces, Ben Sherman 'originals' made their reappear- ance – in the Manchester branch of Top Man.

The Post-subculturalist?

If we do grant complete acceptance to the full implications of the post- modern, then today's subculturalists are characteristic of Urry's (1990) figure of the postmodern 'post-tourist'. In fact it is probably apt to talk of postmodernity as the era of the post-subculturalist and the fashion tourist. Post-subculturalists no longer have any sense of subcultural 'authenticity', where inception is rooted in particular sociotemporal contexts and tied to underlying structural relations. Indeed post-subculturalists will experience all the signs of the subculture of their choosing time and time again through the media, before inscribing these signifiers on their own bodies. Choosing is the operative word here, for post-subculturalists revel in the availability of subcultural choice. While, for example, modernist theory stressed a series of discrete subcultural styles unfolding in linear time up until the late 1970s, the postmodern 1980s and 1990s have been decades of subcultural fragmentation and proliferation, with a glut of revivals, hybrids and transformations, and the co-existence of myriad styles at any one point in time and individual subculturalists moving quickly and freely from one style to another as they wish; indeed, this high degree of sartorial mobility is the source of playfulness and pleasure. They do not have to worry about contradictions between their selected subcultural identities, or agonize over the correct mode of dress, since there are no longer any cor- rect interpretations. This is something that all post-subculturalists are aware of, that there are no rules, that there is no authenticity, no reason for ideological commitment, merely a stylistic game to be played.

If modern subcultures existed in a state of mutual opposition, with 'members' maintaining strong stylistic and ideological boundaries through expressed comparisons with other such groups (see, for example, Widdicombe and Wooffitt, 1990), then in postmodernity the need for boundary maintenance becomes negligible as the lines of subcultural demarcation dissolve. We should as a result expect to discover that subcultural 'followers', who exemplify ephemeral attachments to a variety of styles, find it problematic to make strong comparisons with out-groups. Following the logic of Kellner (1992), we can therefore understand postmodern subcultural identities to be multiple and fluid. Constituted through consumption, subcultural style is no longer articulated around the modernist structuring relations of class, gender, ethnicity or even the age span of 'youth'. Instead, these modernist looks become recycled as free-floating signifiers, enabling subcultural identity to be constructed through the succession of styles that 'followers' try on and cast off.

But perhaps the very concept of subculture is becoming less applicable in postmodernity, for it only maintains its specificity with something to define it against. When one compares styles from the periphery of the spectacular and the mainstream, it is, of course, still possible to distinguish visibly subcultural and conventional style. But what happens as we move towards the central meeting point where boundaries erode, and where hyper-differentiation in each of these stylistic spheres produces de-differentiation of both the subcultural and conventional and of once distinct subcultural styles? For if it is 'the communication of significant difference' that is the point of spectacular style (Hebdige, 1979), then, as Connor realizes:

> Such an analysis encounters difficulties when faced with the fact that this visibility of diverse and stylistically distinct groups is part of the official or dominant mode of advertising and the media in the West . . . Under these circumstances, visibility and self-proclamation may have become a market requirement rather than a mode of liberation. (Connor, 1991)

And as Beezer (1992) concludes, 'without this surface difference, subcultures slip from view, to the point where their existence can be thrown into question'. While the postmodern 'spectacularization' of style may eclipse subcultural visibility, is there still an analytical distinction to be drawn? It would appear not. For as we have seen, if modernist subcultures were defined in terms of a series of theoretical oppositions to non-subcultural style, then postmodernity dissolves such distinctions. It might even be the case that the postmodern fragmentation of collective identities has advanced to the point at which spectacular stylists, situated on de-differentiating boundaries, begin to espouse an individualistic rather than a subcultural identity.

It remains to be seen what implications this has for subcultures as a struggle within ideology, a battle for possession of the sign. Crook *et al.* feel that 'the critical point is not that style cannot resist, clearly it can in many registers, but contests between resistance and conformity do not conform to a single line between the subordinate and the hegemonic' (Crook *et al.*, 1992). One might wonder when they ever did. A 'pure' working-class subcultural membership was clearly an epistemological, theoretical and methodological construction, less obviously an empirical reality. One thinks also of middle-class countercultural style and the problems encountered by the *Resistance Through Rituals* authors in attempting to accommodate this phenomenon within their Marxist framework.

So in the wake of the collapse of emancipatory grand narratives, does it make sense to talk of style still being able to resist, but at a 'local' level? One should remember that active consumption is not necessarily a form of resistance (Stacey, 1993). For a proponent of an 'optimistic' postmodernism, subcultures are just another form of depoliticized play in the postmodern pleasuredome, where emphasis is placed on the surface qualities of the spectacle at the expense of any underlying ideologies of resistance. For post-subculturalists, the trappings of spectacular style are their right of admission to a costume party, a masquerade, a hedonistic escape into a Blitz Culture fantasy characterized by political indifference. But perhaps this tone is too celebratory, for the carnivalesque is certainly not in keeping with the pessimism characteristic of an alternative, apocalyptic postmodern scenario. Would this landscape be fertile ground for the anarchistic, nihilistic and seditious legacy of punk, or would cynicism breed a figure who 'neither embraces nor criticises, but beholds the world blankly with a knowingness that dissolves feeling and commitment into irony (Gitlin, 1989)?

I would like to conclude by first reiterating that the traits I identify as constitutive of the postmodern are, by and large, not novel. The view that the genesis of the postmodern can be found in strains of aesthetic modernity directly informs my analysis of subcultural style. While modernist theory postulated a succession of 'authentic', discrete subcultures unfolding in linear time, we can also detect in Clark (1976), Hebdige (1979) and Fox (1987) at least some recognition of those (often disregarded) aesthetic characteristics which have always been implicated in the subcultural movement towards commercialization, diffusion and defusion. While the aesthetic remains largely unexamined in the modernist paradigm as a whole, a more complete analysis would necessitate a focus on the dynamic processes of stylistic and ideological transmission, transformation and fragmentation.

A very different picture would then emerge to challenge the modernist paradigm's prevailing view of subcultures as 'static', 'ahistorical essences' (Waters, 1981; Clarke, 1982), captured in their first, 'pure' moment of inception. Redhead in fact wishes to go further by suggesting that subcultural time has always been cyclical rather than linear; his contention is that ' "authentic" subcultures were produced by subcultural theories, not the other way around' (Redhead, 1990). I, too, suspect that 'lived' subcultural experience has always been more complex than modernist theories have been willing to allow, and I suggest that if we talk to some of these pre-punk subculturalists of the past they might remember a change of subcultural allegiance and a degree of stylistic fragmentation which is only (theoretically) accorded to today's postmodern youth.

This brings me neatly to my final, but most important recapitulation: that much of this chapter is theoretical speculation. Although this is a useful starting point, it is my firm belief that the major criterion of theoretical adequacy is that it should be amenable to empirical evaluation. Much has been made of the 'inadequate' third level of analysis in the Marxist paradigm: the level of biography, of phenomenology, of how the subculture is 'lived out', experienced and interpreted by its members (see, for example, the critiques by Cohen, 1980; Waters, 1981; Clarke, 1982; Dorn and South, 1982; Widdicombe and Wooffitt, 1990). In my view these problems are not contingent, but are symptomatic of a realist epistemology and totalizing theory which results in the imposition of an a priori framework upon the phenomenon in question.

What is now required is an approach where the subjective meanings and perceptions of the subculturalists themselves constitute the first, privileged level of analysis. Ideally, these data should be used to test existing theory and to construct further hypotheses which again become subject to empirical examination. In this way our knowledge of this phenomenon is gradually constructed through comparative research. Faced, therefore, with the inadequacies of the previous, modernist subcultural paradigm and the predilection of many contemporary writers merely to hypothesize about the implications of the postmodern, I can think of no more fitting a finish than the following words of wisdom from Mike Featherstone: 'There is nothing wrong with high level speculative theory, except if it becomes presented and legitimated as having surpassed or succeeded in discrediting the need for, empirical research' (Featherstone, 1992).

Note

This paper was written as part of a research thesis supported by an ESRC postgraduate studentship held in the Department of Sociology at the University of Lancaster. I would also like to thank Nick Abercrombie and Steve Redhead for their comments and support.

References

Barthes, R. (1975) *S/Z*, London, Cape.
Baudrillard, J. (1983a) *In the Shadow of the Silent Majorities*, New York: Semiotext(e).
    (1983b) *Simulations*, New York: Semiotext(e).

Beezer, A. (1992) 'Dick Hebdige, *Subculture: The Meaning of Style*', in M. Barker and A. Beezer (eds), *Reading into Cultural Studies*, London: Routledge.

Bell, D. (1976) *The Cultural Contradictions of Capitalism*, London: Heinemann.

Berman, M. (1987) *All that is Solid Melts into Air*, London: Verso.

Campbell, C. (1987) *The Romantic Ethic and the Spirit of Modern Consumerism*, Oxford: Blackwell.

Carter, A. (1983) 'The recession style', *New Society*, 13 January.

Chambers, I. (1990) *Border Dialogues: Journeys in Postmodernity*, London: Routledge.

Clarke, G. (1982) 'Defending ski-jumpers: a critique of theories of youth culture', Stencilled Paper, No. 71, CCCS, University of Birmingham.

Clarke, J. (1976) 'Style', in S. Hall and T. Jefferson (eds), *Resistance Through Rituals: Youth Subcultures in Post-War Britain*, London: Hutchinson.

Cohen, S. (1980) 'Symbols of trouble: introduction to the new edition', in *Folk Devils and Moral Panics*, Oxford: Martin Robertson.

Connor, S. (1990) *Postmodernist Culture*, Oxford: Blackwell.

Crook, S., J. Pakuliski and M. Waters (1992) *Postmodernization: Change in Advanced Society*, London: Sage.

Dorn, N. and N. South (1982) 'Of males and markets: a critical review of youth culture' theory', Research Paper No. 1, Centre for Occupational and Community Research, Middlesex Polytechnic.

Evans, C. and M. Thornton (1989) *Women and Fashion: A New Look*, London: Quartet.

Ewen, S. and E. Ewen (1982) *Channels of Desire*, New York: McGraw-Hill.

Featherstone, M. (1992) *Consumer Culture and Postmodernism*, London: Sage.

Flugel, J.C. (1930) *The Psychology of Clothes*, London: Hogarth.

Fox, K.J. (1987) 'Real punks and pretenders: the social organization of a counterculture', *Journal of Contemporary Ethnography*, vol. 16, no. 3, October.

Frisby, D. (1985) *Fragments of Modernity*, Cambridge: Polity Press.

Gitlin, T. (1989) 'Postmodernism defined, at last!' *Utne Reader*, July/August.

Hall, S. and T. Jefferson (eds) (1976) *Resistance Through Rituals: Youth Subcultures in Post-War Britain*, London: Hutchinson.

Harvey, D. (1991) *The Condition of Postmodernity*, Oxford: Blackwell.

Hebdige, D. (1979) *Subculture: The Meaning of Style*, London: Methuen.

Holdsworth, A. (1989) *Out of the Doll's House: The Story of Women in the Twentieth Century*, London: BBC.

Jameson, F. (1985) 'Postmodernism and consumer culture', in H. Foster (ed.), *Postmodern Culture*, London: Pluto.

(1991) *Postmodernism: or the Cultural Logic of Late Capitalism*, London: Verso.

Kaiser, S. (1990) *The Social Psychology of Clothing: Symbolic Appearances in Context*, 2nd edn, New York: Macmillan.

Kaiser, S.B., R.H. Nagasawa and S.S Hutton (1991) 'Fashion, postmodernity and personal appearance: a symbolic interactionist formulation', *Symbolic Interaction*, vol. 14, no. 2.

Kellner, D. (1992) 'Popular culture and the construction of postmodern identities', in S. Lash and J. Friedman (eds), *Modernity and Identity*, Oxford: Blackwell.

Konig, R. (1973) *The Restless Image: A Sociology of Fashion*, London: George Allen and Unwin.

Kroker, A. and D. Cook (1991) *The Postmodern Scene: Excremental Culture and Hyper-Aesthetics*, London: Macmillan Education.

Kroker, A. and M. Kroker and D. Cook (1989) *Panic Encyclpedia: The Definitive Guide to the Postmodern Scene*, London: Macmillan.

Lash, S. (1990) *The Sociology of Postmodernism*, London: Routledge.

Lash, S. and J. Urry (1988) *The End of Organized Capitalism*, Cambridge: Polity Press.

(1994) *Economies of Signs and Space*, London: Sage.

Marx, K. (1976) *Capital*, vol. 1, Harmondsworth: Penguin.

McRobbie, A. (1989) 'Second-hand dresses and the role of the rag market', in A. McRobbie (ed.), *Zoot-Suits and Second-Hand Dresses: An Anthology of Fashion and Music*, London: Macmillan.

Mungham, G. and G. Pearson (1976) *Working Class Youth Culture*, London: Routledge and Kegan Paul.

Nixon, S. (1992) 'Have you got the look?: Masculinities and shopping spectacle', in R. Shields (ed.), *Lifestyle Shopping*, London: Routledge.

Partington, A. (1992) 'Popular fashion and working-class affluence', in J. Ash and E. Wilson (eds), *Chic Thrills: A Fashion Reader*, London: Pandora.

Redhead, S. (1990) *The End of the Century Party: Youth and Pop Towards 2000*, Manchester: Manchester University Press.

(1991) 'Rave off: youth, subcultures and the law', *Social Studies Review*, January.

Savage, J. (1989) 'The age of plunder' in A. McRobbie (ed.), *Zoot-Suits and Second-Hand Dresses: An Anthology of Fashion and Music*, London: Macmillan.

Stacey, J. (1993) *Star Gazing: Hollywood Cinema and Female Spectatorship*, London: Routledge.

Steedman, C. (1986) *Landscape for a Good Woman*, London: Virago.

Urry, J. (1990) *The Tourist Gaze: Leisure and Travel in Contemporary Societies*, London: Sage.

Waters, C. (1981) 'Badges of half-formed inarticulate radicalism: a critique of recent trends in the study of working-class culture', *International Journal of Labour and Working Class History*, no. 19, spring.

Widdicombe, S. and R. Wooffitt (1990) '"Being" versus "doing" punk: on achieving authenticity as a member', *Journal of Language and Social Psychology*, vol. 9, no. 4.

Willis, P. (1978) *Profane Culture*, London: Routledge and Kegan Paul.

(1990) *Common Culture*, Milton Keynes: Open University Press.

Wilson, E. (1985) *Adorned in Dreams: Fashion and Modernity*, London: Virago.

(1990) 'These new components of the spectacle: fashion and postmodernism', in R. Boyne and A. Rattansi (eds), *Postmodernism and Society*, London: Macmillan.

Wollen, P. (1987) 'Fashion/orientalism/the body', *New Formations*, no. 1.

York, P. (1980) *Style Wars*, London: Sidgwick and Jackson.

14 Reaping Pop:
The Press, the Scholar and the Consequences of Popular Cultural Studies

Steve Jones

Introduction: (Scholarly) Material Girl

One battle in what appears to be a war between the pundit, the professor and the press, recently took place after the publication of Madonna's *Sex* book. An opening salvo in that battle came when some journalists characterized research on Madonna as contemptible. One can find played out within the ensuing debate about Madonna scholars and their scholarship elements Hanno Hardt criticizes for creating a climate that '[equates] the notion of active participation in the social structure with consumption of media presentations' (Hardt, 1993). There is indeed a struggle between scholars and journalists, but it is not only a struggle over the commodities they write about. It is also about the place each holds in the social structure and the relationships thus formed to those commodities, and as such it is a particularly fierce struggle and deserves continued attention as it reveals our investments in our commodities and ourselves.

This study is an effort to gather demographic (and other) information about scholars studying Madonna and related phenomena. It is also a brief critique of the manner in which popular culture is studied and an analysis of the criticism of Madonna scholars. Another way to put the central issue at hand is: what happens when scholars study a popular form, namely, make the popular 'academic'?

Anne Matthews has claimed that scholars and journalists have 'a mutual conviction of self-importance and sense of privileged immunity' (Sahadi, 1994), and finds that there is a 'culture war' between the two groups. Recent debates about the rise of a new group of 'public intellectuals' similarly entail vociferous claims of selling out and transgression. Journalists point out that scholars are encroaching on territories in the popular media once reserved for cultural criticism; some scholars claim that they simply seek to leave their ivory tower, while other scholars criticize those who seek a broader audience. Theodore J. Lowi, for instance, writing in the *Chronicle of Higher Education*, claimed:

> Who . . . is filling the role of the public intellectual? Most such individuals are actually idea entrepreneurs, who take a concept – their own or another's – and focus their energies on popularizing it rather than on analyzing it and coming up with a really fresh way of thinking about the subject. (Lowi, 1995)

Simultaneously, a reporter for the London *Times* can claim:

> The great thinkers of the New World sit around eating tortilla chips and watching pop videos, just like ordinary teenagers. The difference is that while ordinary teenagers consign such information to their mental trash cans, the academics feel it necessary to consign it to their word processors. (Muir, 1992)

If there is a war at hand, it is not simply scholar versus journalist, or even scholar versus scholar; it is often one that scholars and journalists wage internally, as Fernandez describes it:

> While popular-culture studies . . . are gaining more acceptance for blurring the line between highbrow and lowbrow, many scholars seem fearful of sliding into *real* low culuture . . . At the ['Icons of Popular Culture I: Elvis and Marilyn'] conference, one of the ways in which fear manifested itself was in the distinction made again and again between the conference-goer and the 'middle-aged woman with a beehive'. (Fernandez, 1994)

Compelling boundaries are drawn between being a fan, a critic or a scholar, an 'analyser' versus a 'popularizer', and so on.

However, though boundaries exist, the lines that create them are usually less than visible. It is often only when the boundaries are crossed that their place becomes clear, and one such transgression that provides particular clarity is the debate concerning scholarship about Madonna.

Of course, the study of objects popular with mass audiences necessarily resurrects the traditional high culture/low culture debate of the 1950s and 1960s.[1] In that debate, voices championing high culture traditionally have generally come from academia and from particular academic disciplines. The strongest opposition came later, from British cultural studies, including Raymond Williams, Stuart Hall and those at the Birmingham Centre for

Contemporary Cultural Studies, who '[reject] the idea that the media necessarily and inevitably produce rubbish' (Turner, 1991).

Now, in an interesting twist, the increase in scholarship about Madonna
(and related cultural phenomena like music videos, popular music and rap
music) has generated opposition to the study of mass culture from within the
media itself. Daniel Harris, for instance, wrote in *The Nation*:

> If co-optation involves the appropriation of a marginal artist by the main-
> stream, reverse co-optation involves the appropriation of a mainstream artist
> by a marginal group – in this case, the increasing numbers of academics who
> are currently flooding the country's journals and small presses with a glut of
> scholarship on the stylistic flamboyance – the glitz, guts and pure raunch – of a
> celebrity who has borne much of the brunt of the university's restless and
> uncertain engagement with popular culture. (Harris, 1992)

Harris goes on to characterize those studying Madonna (and popular culture
generally) as doing so 'to counteract their own marginality'. Such press
coverage has not, in turn, gone unnoticed by scholars. Cathy
Schwichtenberg, editor of *The Madonna Connection*, an anthology of critical
essays that sparked much of the journalistic writing about the scholarly study
of Madonna, noted that there thus exists an opportunity 'to reveal some of
the ways in which academics are constructed by the press . . . [and] these
constructions further illustrate what the press thinks the common person
thinks about academics and their scholarly pursuits' (Schwichtenberg,
1993a).

This study was in part inspired by Schwichtenberg's claims, and thus I
have made an effort to gather demographic (and other) information to determine what construction (if any, while fully acknowledging the constructed
nature of self-reports and surveys) is made from self-reported information by
Madonna scholars. I also believe that, via critique of the manner in which
popular culture is studied and via analysis of the criticism of Madonna
scholars, it is possible to discern that 'these constructions . . . illustrate' what
the press think of themselves.

And so: what happens when scholars make the popular 'academic'? The
study of popular cultural icons foments a struggle for the power to produce
and reproduce the meanings and typologies of those icons. Thus, another
important question: is it the popular critics, news media or intellectuals who
gain in the struggle to (re)symbolize from the deconstruction of the popular?
That such a struggle exists is evident in the strident character of the media
criticism of Madonna scholarship published in books and journals in the early
and mid-1990s. But *why* a struggle? In *Representations of the Intellectual*,
Edward Said provides good insight into the nature of the tensions exposed
in the criticism of Madonna scholars and their work. Said borrows from

Gramsci to discuss the roles of the 'traditional intellectuals' and 'organic intellectuals', defined in the following manner:

> [T]raditional intellectuals such as teachers, priests, and administrators . . . do the same thing from generation to generation . . . organic intellectuals are actively involved in society, that is, they constantly struggle to change minds and expand markets; unlike teachers and priests, who seem more or less to remain in place, doing the same kind of work year in year out, organic intellectuals are always on the move, on the make. (Said, 1994)

Said sets off Gramsci's duality by contrasting it to Julien Benda's vision of the intellectual as a 'philosopher king': someone able to speak truth to power, a crusty, eloquent, fantastically courageous and angry individual for whom no worldly power is too big and imposing to be criticized and pointedly taken to task. However, Said goes on to write:

> Gramsci's social analysis of the intellectual as a person who fulfills a particular set of functions in the society is much closer to the reality than anything Benda gives us, particularly in the late twentieth century when so many new professions – broadcasters, academic professionals . . . and indeed the whole field of modern mass journalism itself – have vindicated Gramsci's vision.

To see a struggle in the criticism and debate surrounding Madonna scholarship is to witness the fight over fragmented roles and fracturing power, as 'organic intellectuals' raise their voices to new heights to be heard in the din of mass-mediated discourse. Said gives further weight to Gramsci, himself adopting a virtually identical position, when he writes: 'The central fact for me is, I think, that the intellectual is an individual endowed with a faculty for representing, embodying, articulating a message, a view, an attitude, philosophy or opinion to, as well as for, a public.'

From such a position it is easy to see why book, film, music and media critics and others consider themselves intellectuals, and why, moreover, intellectual discourse is played out ever increasingly on a mass-mediated stage. The *raison d'etre* of a newspaper or magazine, a publisher will tell you, is to serve a public: that is, an audience. As that audience is fragmented by strenuous marketing efforts and new audiences/publics are created, more gaps open that intellectuals may fill. Intellectuals seem quite aware of this phenomenon, though they often provide rationale in terms somewhat different from those used in the commercial arena. One journal editor, for instance, bemoaning the difficulty in starting up a new publication, attributed the difficulty to 'The decline of the reading public . . . [and an] audience for educated opinion and analysis of topical issues . . . so small that it does not cast a shadow' (Taves, 1987).

Interestingly, this occurs during a time when it is argued that public intellectuals have virtually disappeared. Russell Jacoby, whose book *The Last Intellectuals* serves as a milestone in that argument, even juxtaposes the intellectual against the media when he writes:

> To declare an intellectual generation 'invisible' is fraught with difficulties. The statement seems to accept the judgment of the 'public sphere' – newspapers, book reviews, talk shows – as truth itself; it risks confounding glitter with substance, TV exposure with intellectual weight. (Jacoby, 1987)

Indeed, Jacoby's own position is quite clear:

> My argument of a missing generation [of intellectuals] might be challenged by proposing that the new intellectuals thrive in journalism. I agree that the new and no-so-new journalism (personal reportage, muckraking, rock criticism) testifies – or once testified – to a vigorous younger generation. Moreover, by virtue of abdication elsewhere journalists have assumed a critical, and increasing, importance. Yet the constraints of living solely from the press – deadlines, space, money – finally dilute, not accentuate, intellectual work.

Yet intellectuals in academia operate within the same constraints. Deadlines for articles and papers are, perhaps, not *daily*, but they do give an important structure to academic life. Space is, of course, an issue, as journal editors, reviewers, publishers and others largely seek to achieve the same ends and economies of scale as newspaper editors. And money . . . well, it would be hard to argue that either journalists or intellectuals are generally well paid.

But it does not appear that Jacoby is interested in savaging journalists, and in fact later in his book he believes he sees a connection between journalists and intellectuals: they both engage in public writing. And, Jacoby goes on, there is evidence of the same pattern among journalists as among intellectuals; once there were many, now there are few, and our society is the worse off for it.

Of course, both groups, journalists and intellectuals, are under attack by the public, and in a later article Jacoby does a much better job of examining the struggle between them although his conclusion, that it is often only a matter of writing styles that distinguishes them, is weak at best. The stronger point Jacoby makes is that 'the lingo of theoretical breakthroughs and explosions partakes of the language of the market because it is a market' (Jacoby, 1993), thus noting that, whether each group once had a golden age or not, both are engaged in activities buffeted, if not driven, by market forces. What potentially occurs, then, is, as with any marketing effort, an attempt to differentiate oneself or one's work from that of others, and in a fragmented market place serving a fragmented audience it is no wonder that the struggle quickly turns to one of 'positioning' and identity (whether by oneself or by others, who position and identify themselves in opposition).

Who's That Scholar?

As Madonna herself moved across various media (first music, then video, then film, then print and photography), her work was encountered by critics specializing in, as Said put it, 'representing, embodying, articulating a message, a view, an attitude, philosophy or opinion to, as well as for, a public' attending to those media. Madonna's use and manipulation of media became clearer over time, and her work allowed for self-reflection by some of those critics, but it also created an opportunity for popular culture to be taken seriously beyond the confines of the mediated object. Thus not only did critics writing in the mass media find themselves shaping a contemporary object of study (Madonna), they also found themselves shaping the discourse about the media, its cultural and political roles, within which Madonna worked.

Along the way, critics began to shape the image of the scholars who were studying Madonna, and were themselves taking popular culture seriously. So, for instance, Harris claims:

> Madonna has been drafted into the staggeringly implausible role of spokeswoman of the values and professional interests of university instructors . . . Just as members of the left often sentimentalize the proletariat, so academics have begun to sentimentalize popular culture by ascribing to it all sorts of admirable characteristics that it does not have – in particular, the potential to radicalize the huddled masses by providing typically quiescent MTV viewers with what it is now fasionable to term 'a site of contention' (or, in Charles Wells' marvellous malapropism, a 'cite of contention'). (Harris, 1992)

Harris' critique combines comments about popular culture that one might expect from cultural criticism with comments about university instructors (itself an interesting occupational description, eliding the label 'scholar' and even that of 'teacher'). That *The Nation* chose this particular side of this battle is itself interesting, given its openness to cultural criticism and its generally 'left'-leaning intellectual position. Laurie Ouellette counters in *On The Issues*:

> What will ultimately emerge is a situation where the right no longer needs to tell those scholars – feminist, gay and lesbian, and people of color – who are not part of the white male establishment that their work is not appropriate for the academy. (Ouellette, 1993)

Others quickly followed Harris and Ouellette. Four letters to *The Nation*'s editors quickly followed Harris' article. Camille Paglia, for instance, in one letter, congradulated 'Harris for his splendid dissection of the pretension and ineptitude of the academic Madonna exploiters, with their comical Rube Goldberg theoretical apparatuses' (Paglia, 1992). (Unfortunately, Paglia does not give insight into her feelings about non-academic Madonna exploiters.) A second letter found a scholar (apparently) distancing himself from Madonna scholars:

> [N]ot all academics do criticism, and of those who do, not all study popular culture. Of those who study popular culture, not all do cultural studies. Of those who do cultural studies, not all are postmodernists, and of the small group of postmodernists doing cultural studies, only a handful study Madonna, and only a few are idiots. (Erlich, 1992)

(One can imagine, someday, the creation of an endowed chair in non-Madonna, non-postmodernist, non-cultural studies, non-popular culture criticism.) A third letter took to 'off-loading' the issue on to students. Its author claimed that scholars must study Madonna because students are familiar with her and her work, and she thus 'get[s] students interested and talking' (Rand, 1992). The fourth letter was from Harold P. Schlechtweg and Schwichtenberg herself, with the postscript, 'Cathy says to tell Dan, "Kiss my grits."' (Schlechtweg and Schwichtenberg, 1992).

Some reviewers of *The Madonna Connection* were cognizant of the tensions between scholars and journalists (in some part probably due to the near-simultaneous publication of Madonna's own *Sex* book). Paul Burston made note, for instance, of the 'apparent tension between the practitioners of slanted journalism (Madonna-haters) and the defenders of unbiased critical engagement (Madonna-scholars)' (Burston, 1992). A reviewer for the *New York Times* found Schwichtenberg's book 'laughable' and 'point[ing] up the distressing state of academic scholarship' (Kakutani, 1992). The reviewer was quick to point out, however, that the book's 'observations could easily be made by any number of Madonna's fans', and indeed many have 'already been laid out – often *ad nauseam* – in the popular press and on television'.

Still other critics found in Madonna scholars the ammunition they needed to load into their anti-higher education *ProfScam* guns and fire charges that anyone studying Madonna has 'too much time on their hands' (Sheldon, 1992) and that the book is 'littered with academic jargon that will make it impenetrable to most *Sex* readers'. *ProfScam*'s author, Charles Sykes, weighed in on the side of Madonna critics by stating that she is 'almost too easy a target' (Bailey, 1992), and Madonna scholarship 'fall[s] under what I would call junk scholarship. You're dressing up very routine subjects in the garb of academic seriousness' (Singleton, 1992).

From these articles and reviews of *The Madonna Connection*, as well as from other articles too numerous to abstract here, a particular image of the Madonna scholar (and the scholar's position in the academy) emerges. Madonna scholars are typically women, feminist, marginalized (such a characterization not without redundancies). That last characterization, as marginalized, in particular speaks to the ways in which the press understands and translates academic debate, as a kind of intellectual wrestling match which, like the World Wrestling Federation, has its share of heroes and losers united via hype, but lacking greatly in actual effect.

Schwichtenberg, reflecting on her experience after publication of *The Madonna Connection*, noted that it is claimed that Madonna scholars are assistant professors in search of something with which to spice up otherwise dreary lives, 'young opportunist[s] . . . supposedly validated by virtue of esoteric theory, jargon, and real world object' (Schwichtenberg, 1993b).

The Immaculate Collection (of Data)

Though surveys have their own pitfalls, assessing not the state of Madonna scholars or scholarship, but their status via demographic information seemed one way to approach an alternative construction to that built by the press. An extensive literature search was conducted using the following keywords: Madonna, videos, MTV, music television, music videos, rap, rap music. Then, bibliographic and references sources and databases were searched between 1980 and 1994 using those keywords.[2] The search resulted in 336 references. The authors from each reference were compiled in a separate list, resulting in 138 individuals' names (since some published more than one article, or had an article reprinted as a book chapter, and the like). A variety of association directories and guides to scholars, and this author's personal sources and resources, were used to find a mailing address for each author.

A questionnaire was developed, asking for demographic information and information about the authors' experiences, attitudes and beliefs concerning their own scholarship and scholarship in popular culture generally. The questionnaire consisted of thirty questions, three of which were open-ended. Then 138 questionnaires were mailed and subjects were given three weeks to respond. In all, 106 questionnaires were returned completed, for a return rate of 76.8 per cent.

Results

Several generalities can be made from the completed questionnaires. Virtually all of the respondents (96.2 per cent) had earned a Ph.D. A slight majority, 51.9 per cent, are female and a vast majority, 95.3 per cent, categorized themselves as white. All of the respondents held an academic post at a college or university. The majority (76.4 per cent) were tenured at schools in the United States of America, at the associate and full professor level. Respondents who held positions in departments of communication outnumbered those in other departments, and if one includes those who reported their positions as being in a department of journalism and radio-TV-film the majority, 74.5 per cent, are communication scholars of one stripe or another. The age of the respondents ranged from 36 to 55 (median age of 42 and mean age of 43.6), with a majority (61.3 per cent) in their forties.

The demographic picture painted by the survey responses hardly coincides with that painted by Harris, which sees them as somehow marginal; nor does it match up with Harris's claim that 'Madonna scholars see themselves as iconoclasts rebelling against the suffocating strictures of High Art, as devilish pranksters shocking prudish humanists who hurl themselves melodramatically in front of the canon in order to shield it maternally from assault' (Harris, 1992). And it particularly does not fit the image portrayed by Henry Allen in the *Washington Post*, who believed that nearly all Madonna scholars are opportunistic assistant professors (Allen, 1992).

Indeed, Allen was probably the Madonna scholars' harshest critic, writing of 'the despair of assistant professors' who live in a world where 'the only people getting tenure these days are Pakistani electrical engineering professors, who have "real world" appeal'. Allen makes clear what other critics and reviewers hint at, that studying Madonna is the potential on-ramp to the tenure highway that all assistant professors seek to navigate:

> It has that sound. That tenure sound. That publish–not–perish sound. Maybe even a get-yourself-on-TV sound, if you use the secret language to write about something people actually care about, something real world like the Material Girl herself, the woman is everything that a despairing assistant professor is not.

Allen thus combines several of the issues currently engaging scholars, journalists and critics, by claiming that assistant professors (1) claim objectivity but want publicity, as, it seems, do journalists, and (2) want out of their hopeless existence, as, it seems, do fans. It simply will not do for an intellectual to be either, Allen seems to be saying, although given that he's circumscribed the extremes, one can hardly find fault with a scholar who falls into the (human) ground in-between.

It is too easy to refute Allen's claims by simply looking at the demographic data collected for this study. The more interesting data, and questions, are related not to the demographic information, but rather to the respondents' comments in answer to questions about their opinion of research in Madonna studies, music videos, etc. A five-point Likert-type scale was used to ask those surveyed to respond to several questions related to their own status and that of the popular cultural phenomena they have studied. More than two-thirds of those surveyed do not believe that their research on music videos, Madonna, rap, popular music and so on is what they are best known for in their field. Also, many more (52.9 per cent versus 22.1 per cent) do not find their research in this area more satisfying than other research in which they are engaged. In regard to the status of research in these areas of popular culture within academia, only 10.9 per cent of the respondents reported that they had been counselled to abandon their research as it would not 'count' toward tenure. Most respondents also believed such research central to the study of popular culture. Interestingly, the respondents seemed only slightly more likely than not to believe that their colleagues had interest in their work in this area.

Perhaps the most interesting results are that, in response to questions about their own consumption of the popular cultural texts they have studied, more (59.4 per cent versus 41.5 per cent) agreed or strongly agreed that they are fans of rock music than that they are fans of Madonna (music videos, MTV and rap music also came in behind rock music, but well in front of Madonna). Four times as many disagreed or stongly disagreed that they are fans of Madonna as disagreed or strongly disagreed that they are fans of rock music (again, Madonna seems to be last among the respondents' choices). Finally, many more of the respondents purchased rock music than had purchased items in the other categories, and nearly half of the respondents reported that they did not watch MTV at all during a typical week.

Discussion: What Becomes a Commodity Most

The picture of popular culture scholars engaged in studying Madonna, music videos, rap music, rock music and the like created by the popular press does not match up to that which can be composited from the responses to this survey. Of course, it cannot be claimed from the survey that critical scholars are not marginalized despite (or become of?) their generally tenured, established academic positions.

But there are still more interesting facets to the picture, one of which is: what prompts academic interest in *any* area?[3] By way of their work, popular culture scholars create second-order commodities from the ones they study. Annalee Newitz believes that:

> intellectual cultural critics['] . . . endorsement[s] of Madonna . . . no doubt
> lend an aura of legitimacy to Madonna's work; and academics such as John

Fiske and E. Ann Kaplan have represented Madonna to their academic audiences as a moment in which popular culture imitates critical theories of history,
knowledge and human identity. (Newitz, 1993)

The obverse seems implicit – 'non-intellectual' cultural critics, the press for
instance, do not legitimize Madonna (perhaps because they strive for 'objectivity'?), and so the press is not a complicit actor in the 'star' system. And yet
the claims by critics in the press seem to imply (at least) that scholars are legitimizing *themselves* via Madonna. Contradictions abound, as Schwichtenberg
noted:

[T]he academic constructed by these journalists is a repository of contradictory directives . . . [and] pilfers in journalistic territory but belongs in the ivory
tower which is irrelevant to life, so that when the academic transgresses and
enters the public arena, he/she is analyzing popular culture for advancement
and social relevance. (Schwichtenberg, 1993b)

Russell Jacoby would agree with Schwichtenberg, and does so in *The Last
Intellectuals*. According to him:

Journalists have sustained – more in their books than in their daily writing –
the general culture . . . As academic life and writing have grown wan, journalism has expanded, appearing bigger than life: vigorous, committed,
public. Journalists themselves have been romanticized in countless movies . . .
Journalists search for truth, for which they risk their lives or careers; they are
unswervingly devoted to a public. They are everything professors are not.
(Jacoby, 1987)

Additionally, Jacoby believes that another struggle, that between print
journalists and television journalists, affects the relationship that journalists
and intellectuals have, and that print journalists feel 'squeezed' on both
sides.

It is interesting, then, not only that academics and journalists are engaged
in a debate about the public intellectual, a debate whose import may have
waned since the 1980s, but that the trajectories of both professions seem to
mirror one another. There are not only the parallels that Jacoby (explicitly
or inadvertently) draws, but ones that are of even greater consequence for
individuals in those fields, such as the increase in freelancers and adjunct
instructors. Why this struggle, why now?

Among the possibilities: it is a struggle for fame by two groups that have
acknowledged the slim availability of fortune (and fame's appearance as a
prerequisite for fortune), a struggle among those whose egos are stroked only
by recognition (hence a need to publish), and/or a struggle to *matter* by those

working in two professions whose influence seems to be on the wane. It may also be a struggle against an enemy without, by professions who have several enemies within. As Jacoby indicated, journalists working in different media are at odds, and academics have their own inside critics in the shape of people such as Charles Sykes and Allan Bloom. And yet, as one study has pointed out, 'public opinion [of universities, higher education and faculty members] has remained consistent, despite criticism in the media' (Land, 1995). How seriously, then, can one take these possibilities? Are intellectuals and journalists either (1) so thin-skinned as to believe their critics and/or (2) out of touch with the public?

It is more likely that the intention of scholars is not so much to legitimize Madonna as to legitimize critical theory. Only two of the respondents to this study's survey expressed that their initial interest in music videos, Madonna, etc. was the result of those phenomena being 'convenient sites' for their theoretical work. Many, many more were drawn to these topics by their own children, or by their students, and several claimed that scholarship in these areas was 'a nice change from other research interests'. None of the responses showed evidence of interest directed forcefully by the ability to publish, gain tenure, gain recognition and the like. In its way, this mirrors rather clearly the *modus operandi* of the popular critic, legitimizing and commodifying social, aesthetic and artistic observation and analysis with references to particular works, events and, ultimately, sources (via quotation) as part of what is understood as the ongoing construction of individual and collective reality. In that sense, both groups can be understood as public intellectuals, or at least may be considered as engaged with intellectualizing the public. As there appears to be less and less of the public (or at least less of its attention singularly forcused) to go around in a fragmented media-world, it should be no surprise that both groups' voices struggle to be heard, though it remains surprising that each is so at odds with the other.

Notes

1 Chapters in Rosenberg and White's *Mass Culture* and *Mass Culture Revisited* provide archetypal examples of that debate. See also Jensen (1991).
2 Many different sources were used, including the Humanities Index 1982–93 and the Social Sciences Index 1982–93.
3 Jacoby (1995): 'academics face a crisis of dwindling materials; classic books have been studied to death. With the added allure of subverting Western hegemony, post-colonial studies opens up a new turn and allows the re-examination of old ground.' This is an ingenuous claim, for it measures the worth of academic work by its novelty, and positions academics as intellectual scavengers (perhaps another inadvertent attempt at a parallel between intellectuals and journalists).

References

Allen, Henry (1992) 'The other Madonna book', *Washington Post*, 1 November.

Bailey, Martin (1992) 'American scholar deconstructs a "metatextual girl"', *Observer*, 15 October.

Burston, Paul (1992) 'Immaterial girl', *Modern Review*, December.

Erlich, Richard (1992) 'Papa don't preach', *The Nation*, 17–24 August.

Fernandez, Sally (1994) 'The iconography of Elvis and Marilyn', *Chronicle of Higher Education*, 27 January.

Hardt, Hanno (1993) 'Authenticity, communication and critical theory', *Critical Studies in Mass Communication* vol. 10, no. 1, March.

Harris, Daniel (1992) 'Make my rainy day', *The Nation*, 8 June.

Jacoby, Russell (1987) *The Last Intellectuals*, New York: Basic Books.

 (1993) 'Journalists, cynics and cheerleaders', *Telos*, no. 97, Fall.

 (1995) *Lingua Franca*, September/October.

Jensen, Joli (1991) *Redeeming Modernity*, Newbury Park: Sage.

Kakutani, Michiko (1992) 'Essays by "Madonna scholars" laughable', *New York Times*, 21 October.

Land, M.J. (1995) 'Critics' use of the media and public opinion of faculty members at universities', paper to annual meeting of the Association for Education in Journalism and Mass Communication, Washington DC, August.

Lowi, Theodore J. (1995) 'Media fascination with self-styled public intellectuals', *Chronicle of Higher Education*, 27 January.

Muir, Kate (1992) 'The face that launched a thousand theses', *The Times*, 8 November.

Newitz, Annalee (1993) 'Madonna's revenge', *Bad Subjects*, no. 9.

Ouellette, Laurie (1993) 'Let's get serious: the attack on Madonna scholarship', *On The Issues*, Spring.

Paglia, Camille (1992) 'Material girls', *The Nation*, 17–24 August.

Rand, Erica (1992) 'Get into the groove', *The Nation*, 17–24 August.

Sahadi, Jeanne (1994) 'Dissecting the culture wars between media and academe', *Communique*, July/August.

Said, Edward (1994) *Representations of the Intellectual*, New York: Random House.

Schlechtweg, Harold P. and Cathy Schwichtenberg (1992) 'Express yourself', *The Nation*, 17–24 August.

Schwichtenberg, Cathy (ed.) (1993a) *The Madonna Connection*, Boulder, CO: Westview Press.

 (1993b) 'The Madonna connection: academics, the press and popular culture', unpublished paper presented at the First International Scholarly Conference on Rock and Rap, University of Missouri, 5 February.

Shelden, Michael (1992) 'Set on dropping her frock', *Daily Telegraph*, 9 December.

Singleton, Janet (1992) 'Celebrity research: some say it's important work', *College Press Service*, 7 May.

Taves, Michael (1987) 'Missing and accounted for: public intellectuals', *Telos*, no. 73, Fall.

Turner, Graeme (1991) *British Cultural Studies*, Boston, MA: Unwin Hyman.

15 Replacing Popular Culture

Lawrence Grossberg

Many writers seem to assume that the rise of cultural studies and the rapid growth of interest in the study of popular culture are inextricably linked if not identical academic developments, as if cultural studies were somehow defined by popular culture. In fact, the two discourses are not the same or even necessarily connected, although they have been articulated together in at least some discourses and networks. What remains unspecified is the precise nature of those articulations, the choices strategically made in specific contexts and enacted in specific critical practices. I want to use this question as an opportunity to reflect on my own work, since my project, begun over twenty years ago,[1] can be situated here: between an interest in the social effects and logics of popular culture, especially rock music and youth culture, and a commitment to the possibilities of cultural studies as a form of progressive intellectual work.

On first glance, my work has followed four trajectories: a rather abstract concern with the nature of cultural studies; a highly philosophical interest in cultural and communication theory: an exploration of the popularity and effectivity of rock music; and an investigation into the apparent success of the new conservative hegemony. In fact, I have never thought of these as separable projects, but as interconnected components of a larger and more pressing attempt to find a critical practice adequate to the challenges of understanding 'the politics of the popular' in the contemporary USA, all the while recognizing that national contexts can no longer be so confidently isolated from the global circulations of people, power, capital and culture. By 'the politics of the popular', I do not mean merely the political inflections of particular texts, or the relations of such texts to ideological positions, subjectives or pleasures. Rather I mean to point to the intersections of popular culture, popular politics (or political identity) and systemic structures and forces of political and economic inequality and domination. It describes what Meaghan Morris (1988) calls the links between the politics of culture and the politics of politics.

The notion of 'the popular' has a long history, although a clear notion of popular culture appeared only in the nineteenth century. But it is important to keep these notions – the popular and popular culture – separated, if only for a moment, so that we can see the consequences of their eventual linkage. As early as the sixteenth century, 'the popular' operated in legal, social and governmental discourses, and in each of these regimes it embodied a particular contradiction: between the people as a whole and the common people (Shiach, 1989). The term has always operated on the boundary of unity and differentiation, pulling simultaneously in both directions. The popular refers to the people, but as all the inhabitants of a nation? Or as the commonality of the people? Or as a particular fraction? While 'the popular' operated differently in different registers, its ambiguity allowed it precisely to place 'the people' within dominant economic and political relationships. Thus politically, the discourse of the popular was aligned with the interests of the state and again any perceived threat to the social order. As Shiach points out, while the people could struggle for the vote, it was not the people struggling for economic justice. But even within such struggles, 'the popular' had yet another exclusionary function and dimension, for there were always those (women, children, the colonized) who were inevitably excluded from any such possibilities.

It is only when the discourse of the popular (and the people) enters the domain of culture that its vector of differentiation becomes transparent and dominant. Popular culture referred to that which was accessible to, comprehensible by, those already excluded from the people – children, women and the colonized. It is not difficult to see how from this beginning the popular could be extended to all those outside the dominant institutions of knowledge and cultural legitimation. And thus the people could be made to refer to that particular fraction, located in the subordinated postition in an economy of differences, referred to as the masses, the multitude, the ordinary, the lower classes, and always assumed to be those with baser needs and desires. That is, within the domain of culture, the positivity of the people – its unity and lack of differentiation – became its negativity: the popular is that which is non-selective, which allows no discrimination and, hence, entails no distinctions of value. But even as this cultural discourse was taking shape, a counter-discourse was also emerging, a romantic discourse which saw in popular culture, at least potentially, the authentic expression of a nation and its people.

Cultural studies has always argued that popular culture cannot be defined by appealing to either an objective aesthetic standard (as if it were inherently different from art) or an objective social standard (as if it were inherently determined by who makes it or for whom it is made). Rather it has to be seen as a sphere in which people struggle over reality and their place in it, a sphere in which people are continuously working with and within already existing relations of power, to make sense of and improve their lives. Cultural studies has questioned the authority of any specific line that can be drawn between popular culture and its Other (whether élite or mass culture). But this does not go far enough, for it potentially leaves in place two problematic assumptions.

Recognizing that the line between popular and legitimate culture is a political struggle, too much work in cultural studies satisfies itself with merely struggling over the line rather than rejecting the very practice by which the line is constituted. While I agree with Hall (1981) that 'The changing balance and relations of social forces throughout . . . history reveal themselves, time and time again, in struggles over the forms of the culture, traditions and ways of life of the popular classes', I am not willing to accept the assumption of a constituted category of popular culture which somehow necessarily corresponds to or even is made to correspond to the ways of life of the popular classes. If there is 'a continuous and necessarily uneven and unequal struggle, by the dominant culture, constantly to disorganise and reorganise popular culture', then it is the very process that must be contested. And that means abandoning the category of popular culture as part of a sociological or normative economy. This, it seems to me, is at least one reading of Hall's warning that to unravel a history of popular culture, one could not begin without talking about many things which usually don't figure in the discussion of 'culture' at all. They have to do with the reconstruction of capitalism and the rise of collectivisms and the formation of a new kind of educative state as much as with recreation, dance and popular song. As an area of serious historical work, the study of popular culture is like the study of labour history and its institutions.

But too much of cultural studies has continued to locate popular culture within two binary normative economies: on the one hand, the popular (as poaching, fragmented, contradictory, bodily, carnivalesque, pleasurable) versus the legitimate (as reified, hierarchical, intellectual, etc.), and, on the other hand, the popular (as stylized, artificial, disruptive, marginal, resisting) versus the mainstream (as naturalized, commonsensical, incorporated, etc.). Even Hall's often repeated warning to approach popular culture as 'the double movement of containment and resistance' has not stopped critics from distributing texts, audiences and reading practices into these dichotomous judgements. Critics divide up popular culture, identifying specific forms as resistance, and relegating all others to a cultural mainstream in which they are 'contained' by the existing structures of power. At best, the 'dialectic' is given a temporal sense (what was resistant is then contained, perhaps later to escape and become resistant again), or a spatial sense (while the practice resists over here, it is contained over there), or it is traced on to different aspects of the form (this element is resistant, that is contained). The real dialectic, the articulation, the relationship between the two movements (which might say that because of its specific resistance, it is also contained, or vice versa), is rarely examined.

Moving beyond this normative and still static model, my own work presupposes a more dynamic model of the circulation of popular practices. Instead of constructing some homogeneous mainstream, I see it as a social pastiche, a structured distribution of practices, codes and effects, constantly rearticulating itself by incorporating pieces of the margins and excorporating pieces of itself into the margins. The distinction between mainstream and margin is then a question, quite literally, of social space, a distinction that does not carry with it any guarantees about either textuality or effects. The mainstream is not a unity, but is marked by differences: it is a collection of overlapping cultural styles, defined by sets of productive and consumptive practices. It is differentiated both through the various local alliances which articulate it to concrete places and audiences, and through diverse fractions which compete for public attention, whether in fact they define the economic mainstream. Thus, for example, in my own work on music, I have always focused on one 'face' of the mainstream: when talking about the sixties, I have been concerned primarily with the counterculture, and when talking about the seventies, with disco and punk, although these were never the centre of success, as it were. Rather they were the leading edge of the mainstream, dominant fractions which were most visible, most influential, which most indelibly marked their social and cultural contexts at that moment.

And the margins are not inherently marginal; they only come to be expelled in this way in the context of the ongoing fluid articulations of the mainstream. Thus my work has always involved a defence of the mainstream of popular culture or, at least, an unwillingness to begin by subdividing popular culture into intrinsically politically resonant categories. I want to defend popular culture not only against those who are hostile to any of its forms (by measuring it against 'legitimated' culture), but more importantly, against those who are hostile to the largest part of popular culture because they champion those marginal trends or appropriations, as in subcultural theories. I am not a great fan of marginality for its own sake or for the sake of the critic's own cherished assumptions. I do not see popular culture in opposition to legitimate culture (it is even possible that 'high' culture is someone's popular culture). Nor do I see a 'co-opted' mainstream against a resistant margin. Instead, I see a complex range of possibilities for the differentially articulated effects of cultural practices. In other words, being 'in the mainstream' is never defined in purely textual terms, nor is it solely a matter of audiences; rather, it is a description of a relationship between cultural practices and their contexts.

But if cultural studies should demand that we refuse to begin which such normative judgements, that we refuse to organize the diversity into predefined opposed unities, the fact is that such judgements are an integral part of the behaviour of those who produce and consume popular culture. And since we too are implicated as participants/consumers of popular culture (in fact, often as fans of what we write about), we face a particular challenge when trying to write as reflective critics: the challenge to postpone judgement until the last instance. Writing as a cultural critic, at least on this model of cultural studies, is not about justifying one's own tastes or the ways they are inserted into one's life. That doesn't mean we don't use those tastes or write about them. Rather, we have to distance ourselves from our tastes (or anyone's for that matter) in order to write about taste itself, to write about what it means to be a fan of different popular cultural practices and organizations, in different contexts. In the end, the question is not whether or how one defends popular culture, but what such practices are doing and what is being done with them. It is not a question of judging people so much as trying to describe how their everyday lives are articulated by and with popular culture, how they are empowered and disempowered by the particular structures and forces which organize, always in contradictory ways, their lives, and how their everyday lives are themselves articulated to and by the trajectories of economic and political power.

The second assumption that I find problematic in much of the cultural studies work on popular culture is that popular discourses can be neatly divided and distributed into domains – the social, the cultural, the political, etc. – with their own specific modes of practices and planes of effects. Popular culture, then, is simply a subsection of the larger category of cultural practices. Obviously, this not only throws popular discourses into the problem of normative differentiation, of discrimination and value, it also locates any attempt to make sense of popular discourses within the logic of the modern concept of culture. According to this logic, culture is the necessary excess filling in for the lack of an adequate instinctual apparatus in human beings. Culture is that which mediates between people and reality, turning chaos into order. Therefore, all cultural practices necessarily involve the production of meanings and representations, of subjectivities and identities (making it into little more than the form of ideology or the content of common sense). This notion of culture as a plane of cognitive meanings makes critical analysis into a question of individuated (often defined through social identities) and psychological interpretations and tastes. Additionally, culture is all too easily assumed to be equivalent to communication, and all discursive practices are treated as instances of the communicational relationship between text and audience.

I have challenged, on both theoretical and strategic grounds, the dominance of such communicational models of culture. I have argued against any analysis which finds meaning in texts, or in an audience's experiences of texts. Perhaps my theoretical antagonism to this model derives in part from my position within the discipline of communication itself. But it seems to me that the so-called linguistic or interpretive turn in contemporary theory is actually built upon an assumed centrality of communication in human life and a very limited set of taken-for-granted but rarely elaborated assumptions about the nature of human communication. Within this 'turn', power and struggles against domination are increasingly displaced into and imagined within a reified realm of culture and communication.[2]

Alternatively, I have attempted to hold on to a contextual notion of discursive practices and effects, arguing that both texts and audiences are themselves located within and articulated by broader contexts that determine the identity and effects of any cultural practice. And while I have never wanted to deny that cultural practices enable us to 'make sense' of the world and our experiences, I do want to contest the reduction of sense making to cognitive meaning and interpretation, and the model of culture as somehow standing apart from another plane which it interprets. I have argued that cultural practices always operate on multiple planes, producing multiple effects that cannot be entirely analysed in the terms of any theory or ideology, consciousness or semiotic. Thus, the problem may be more general, involving not merely the equation of culture and communication, but the very logic of culture itself. Perhaps the problem is the very subsumption of popular discourses into the category of culture.[3]

Consequently, I have never been particularly interested in either cultural texts or audiences, nor have I conceived of the object of analysis as simply the relationship between them. I suppose one could say that I have been investigating the question of taste, but I refuse to see it in individual or psychological terms, or to explain it as an excess of determination. Rather, I began with the question of popularity: what does it mean that something is popular? But I quickly translated the question from an attribution made to a text to a question of the nature of the relationship of fandom. A 'fan' is a particular sort of relationship which can be distinguished from a number of other possibilities. First, fandom is a positive relationship as compared, for example, with an opponent or antagonist. Second, fandom is immediate and, to a certain extent, unreflective, as compared, for example, with a critic. Third, fandom is different from consumption or simply enjoyment (although it may incorporate it) because it involves a certain kind of identification or investment; one can like something (enjoy it, find pleasure in it) without being a fan *per se*. Finally, fandom is different from what I have called fanaticism, by which I mean an (ideological) identification which involves the production of identity. In fanaticism, the investment in particular cultural practices becomes the dominant structure of one's self-imagination (such as in subcultural identities). It seems reasonable to assume that taste describes the quality and quantity of one's relationship to particular practices, that it is a matter of the investment people make in particular things, of the ways they matter. Fandom then describes a particular slice of the range of possibilities for such investments, located largely (but probably not entirely) in what is generally called 'the mainstream'. But fandom is not reducible to a relationship between a text and an audience member, for it involves a more complex set of relations and investments between practices.

But if culture is not simply a matter of meaning and communication, then the struggle over 'culture' is a struggle over the behaviour of the population, especially the different and differently subordinated fractions (which in the contemporary world include the vast majority of the population), and the role of discursive practices in constructing the machinery by which such behaviour is controlled. Is it about constructing the line between legitimate and popular culture? Perhaps that is one of the (increasingly minor) mechanisms of power. Is it about distributing the population into the dominant and the subordinate, about constituting the subject of 'popular culture' as the popular classes (as opposed to the power bloc)? Again, that may be one of the ways in which particular discursive practices of the popular are deployed, but it is not the primary site of the subordination of people or practices, or of their identity as subordinated. We fail if we forget what has always been for me the primary lesson of Stuart Hall's classic article (Hall, 1981): not that popular culture is inherently subordinated or resisting, but rather that it is a force in political struggles. Popular culture is one of the sites where this struggle for and against a culture of the powerful is engaged: it is also the stake to be won or lost in that struggle. It is the arena of consent and resistance. It is partly where hegemony arises and where it is secured. It is not a sphere where socialism, a socialist culture – already fully formed – might be simply expressed. But it is one of the places where socialism might be constituted. That is why popular culture matters. Otherwise, to tell you the truth, I don't give a damn about it.

That is, popular discourse is not about culture, but about the stuggles to articulate the relations between social and economic power, political forms of agency, and modes of discursive pratices. To put it another way, as Shiach (1989) suggests, the rhetorical power of the discourse of popular culture is much greater than its descriptive specificity or, I would add, its political utility. Instead, we might do better by foregrounding the notion of 'the popular' in order to explore the relationships between popular practices, everyday lives[4] and machineries of power.

I have tried to understand the increasing power of a popular conservatism in the USA. In many ways, the challenge of this new conservatism merely recreates the question that has troubled political analysts for so long: why do people agree to their own subordination or, perhaps less judgementally, what is it people are doing when they appear to be acceding to specific structures of inequality and power? How is popular culture deployed not only in contemporary political struggles, but also in the very construction of the crisis which now drives those struggles forward? How is popular culture implicated in the changing and emerging forms of leadership and authority? How can we describe the complex ways in which a new structure of power is being organized, built upon contradictory political, ideological, economic and cultural commitments? How is political power being restructured in such a way that ideological and economic subordination are articulated to certain forms of culture empowerment? How is culture made into the site of the struggle as well as its weapon? Where do contemporary forms of cultural practice engage with the struggle for hegemonic leadership?

In attempting to answer some of these questions, or at least to provide the terms within which such an answer might be given, I have increasingly come to the conclusion that it is impossible to understand the project of the new conservatism, as well as the form and strategy of its success, apart from its relationship to the popular. It operates largely in the realms of the popular and everyday life (although the sites of power from and into which it is reaching are both political and economic). Moreover, its successes depend to a large extent upon its ability to appropriate some of the very 'operational logics' which made post-war popular culture different, and which gave it its central and often threatening place in everyday life, and to make them, simultaneously, into positive and negative allegories for a new kind of political struggle.

In other words, I am interested in the changing relations between the popular and a specific hegemonic struggle in the contemporary nation (and global) context, and in the ways these planes are being rearticulated to reshape the balance of forces in the social formation of the USA. I have a particular reading of hegemony in mind, which starts from Stuart Hall's (1988) notion of the struggle of a power bloc to win the position of leadership over and against 'the people'. Hegemony is a matter of consent and not consensus; and it is a specific, historically recent (since it depends on the emergence of 'the masses' as a political and cultural subject) form of the struggle for power. But I want to go a step further and argue that there are significantly different hegemonic struggles, depending upon the way in which leadership is constituted and won. While Hall's analysis of Thatcherism depends on a struggle over common sense, I believe that, in the USA, the struggle is around a certain 'national popular' which is not the same as, or reducible to, common sense.

The development and increasing urgency of these concerns have always driven my efforts to understand some of the tendencies of postwar American popular culture. If nothing else, this defines for me the difference between doing cultural studies of and with rock, and studying rock as another genre or medium.[5] My project is to understand how the popular defines at least one set of the conditions of possibilities for the increasing appeal of a new conservatism. But certainly, one cannot stop there: one has to transform the understanding of the context as a set of conditions to a more politically productive understanding of the context as a set of possibilities or effectivities. Just as cultural practices are no longer to be taken as merely representational, but rather as productive, so the analysis itself must be seen as not merely reconstructing the context, but as actively producing or fabricating it, as empowering the practice within the context of its own analysis. Or perhaps we can think of this in Gramscian terms: analysis is always an attempt to 'prise open already existing contradictions . . . thereby renovating and making critical an already existing activity'.

Transforming the context in this way requires a detour through theory, and it requires a theory that is adequate not only to our object, but to the question and the context as well.[6] That is, theory cannot be taken for granted, put in place, as it were, before the work of describing the context and transforming that description has begun. Of course, it is never that simple or easy; one always begins within a theoretical discourse which has to be measured by its ability actually to enable the project. But at the same time, such an 'empirico-political' judgement cannot be entirely separated from the ongoing and simultaneous theoretical investigation. Similarly, I believe that political strategy, as well as assumptions about the nature and sites of struggle, has to be deferred until the empirical and theoretical work is actually under way, if not completed. To begin already knowing what and where the real and possible struggles are is to give up what I take to be the responsibility of the political intellectual.

Not surprisingly, I have never been particularly sympathetic to any of the dominant modes of critical practice available for studying popular culture. Although all three claim to contextualize their objects, each has too limited an understanding of contexts.[7]

'Film theory' does recognize – at least theoretically, if not always in its critical practice – that texts exist only in larger contexts or apparatuses which include more than textual and cultural practices and are specific to particular media, social and historical contexts. However, by privileging a particular apparatus (with little or no empirical justification) and assuming an engaged subjectivity concentrating on and absorbed into the filmic world, its interpretive practice ends up returning to a structural interpretation of texts and their relations to subjectivity; and its political practice is often vanguardist and élitist. While it opens the theoretical possibility of recognizing that not all cultural practices are taken up, lived and practised in the same way and to the same degree, it fails to embody that recognition in a critical practice that is flexible enough to be appropriate to the different forces, rhythms and terrains of the popular. British cultural studies (at least as it has been received in the USA) foregrounds notions of contradiction and struggle in economics of power, and undermines the assumption of historical necessity and critical élitism. But because it reduces to ideology the role of the popular in the struggle over power, its notion of culture is flat and passionless, and its use of articulation is abstract and unmotivated. By giving too much power to the audience,[8] it ends up reducing the context which it claims is determinate to little more than sociological position and a cultural identity. And in the name of political optimism, it too easily ignores the macropolitical success of hegemonic struggles in favour of abstract micropolitical struggles. Postmodernism champions multiplicity and dispersion over and against structure and differences, but it fails to recognize the contextual production and power of the latter. And because it absolutizes historical ruptures, it fails to describe the partial continuities operating across and constituting contexts. Moreover, because it often takes singular events as synecdochal figures of the totality, its critical practice becomes little more than a metaphorical reading of texts.

From another perspective, my dissatisfaction with the available models of popular culture analysis is political. Rather than surprising us with analyses of the contemporary context (and of the ways popular discourses are being used to structure, organize and activate specific features of that context) which open up new possibilities for political struggle, and new understandings and enervations of existing struggles, contemporary critical practices are often too caught up proving what we already know. They tell us that our cultural practices are constantly reinscribing us (usually, though, the critic excludes him or herself) in (the same old predictable and abstract) structures of ideological domination (whether patriarchy, racism, etc., or fetishism, hierarchy, etc.) – unless, of course, they are of a different (avant-garde or cosmopolitan-postmodern) sort, in which case they are cosntantly reinscribing us (including the critic) in structures of ideological opposition. Or they tell us that people are not cultural dopes, by assuming that every act of consumption (or pleasure) is an act of resistance; or that every text is contradictory and so may have very different effects (but what the actual effects are and how they are determined is rarely addressed); or that the very scene of politics (e.g. the public sphere) has disappeared. It seems to me that all of these practices miss the very heart of Hall's description of the importance of the popular because they fail to address the actual context of relations, the articulations, between popular culture and systemic politics (or, in my own terms, a context constituted at the intersection of popular discourses, everyday life and the machineries of power).

But accepting the consequences of articulation, of a radically contextualist model, threatens to make all analysis futile. Imagine you are confronted with a box containing the pieces of an undisclosed number of jigsaw puzzles.[9] All of the original boxes are lost, so you don't know what the puzzles are supposed to look like. It is also possible that the same piece will fit in several different puzzles. Thus the identity of each piece is only the set of its possible places in the as yet undefinable contexts. It is its possible functions. Thus you cannot name a piece or describe its contribution before the puzzle itself is assembled, but of course, you cannot know ahead of time what is being assembled. No piece can be taken for granted, and in the end, the significance of any piece – its possibilities for serving a range of functions – might never be exhausted. Yet while there is no necessary correspondence between the surface of a piece and its place, the surface is never blank or innocent, and its function is determined in part by its shape and appearance. It is scarred by traces of its history, a history of functions and effects that mark its emergence and survival and articulation. Read as a signifying practice, any piece can be related to any other piece and interpretation is undecidable or reduced to the 'impossible science of the individual'. Read alternatively as a function that allows and is allowed by particular connections, analysis is a process of mapping the vectors of effects that traverse and encircle any piece as a possible practice. The metaphor of a jigsaw puzzle, however, too easily suggests a static representation (as recuperation) of a real situation, and needs to be replaced with a more active and multidimensional one: a functioning or machinic apparatus. My own cultural practice attempts to map out the lines that distribute, place and connect cultural practices. This form is the import of 'everyday life': a description of the distribution of practices across social space in such a way as to define the differential access which social groups have to specific forms of enactment.

Rather than asking how texts communicate, or how discourses construct subjective identities and experiences, or how people use culture, I want to explore the ways in which everyday life is articulated by and with the specific forms and formations, the material deployment and effects, of popular discursive practices. At the same time, I want to identify the different ways in which volition and 'will' (i.e. forms of agency) can be enacted contextually to construct people's lives and history. This analytic model allows me to try to describe the various ways in which both discursive practices and human actors are effective. Moreover, it now follows that the relations between individuals, culture and reality cannot simply be defined as the necessary mediation of ideological effects. The site of this intersection must also be opened up, and I have used Bourdieu's (1984) notion of sensibilities to describe the specific planes on which forms of cultural effects and agency are produced. Sensibilities empower cultural practices to work in certain ways, and they empower individuals to enact them in certain places. Sensibilities define the dialectical production of active audiences, everyday practices and productive contexts.

This has important consequences for the study of the popular as a sphere in which people struggle over reality and their place in it. I see popular sensibilities delimiting the effects of discursive practices. I have argued that 'popular culture' is characterized by the production of affective logics and relations: that is, relations of volitional power, mood, investment and energization. Obviously, this conclusion has been shaped in part by my concern with popularity and fandom, and by the fact that the object of my analysis, the rock formation, places musical practices at its centre.[10] Talking about the rock formation requires a way of understanding the ability of such sounds both to become the points at which a wide range of practices and commitments can be articulated, and to travel across and into different contexts and configurations. In fact, I disagree with the new (Derridean-derived) common wisdom that the western (logocentric) tradition has always privileged the presence of the aural (speech) over the visual (writing). In fact, Derrida's vision of aurality makes it into little more than writing (meaning) with an excess of immediacy. But that immediacy is never explored – it is simply assumed as presence (more like breath than sound). I want to make the more limited claim that within North Atlantic modernity, the visual (and the legible) has usually been privileged as the model of perception, knowledge and sense making, and hence of our relationship to the world. At the same time, this modernity has recognized that there is something else to human existence beyond the epistemological, but it has quickly assigned this excess to the domain of the irrational, the unstructured, the unmappable (e.g. as desire or creativity). Drawing upon Freud, I began to think about affect as the plan of cathexis (including more than just libidinal modes); drawing upon Nietzsche, I began to think about affect as the plane of cathexis (including more than just libidinal modes); drawing upon Nietzsche, I began to think about affect as the plane of effectivity (the ability to effect and be effected). My dilemma has always been the relationship between these two understandings of affect.

So, using Deleuze and Guattari (1977, 1987), I began to think of affect as a structured plane of effects (investment) which is the very possibility of agency (of acting wilfully). That is, affect for me is the plane on which any individual (persons and practices are the two most obvious forms of individuation) is empowered to act in particular ways at particular places. Affect is the term I use to describe the observable differences in how practices matter to, or are taken up by, different configurations of popular discourses and practices – different alliances (which are not simply audiences). But perhaps this makes affect sound too mental, for affect is both psychic and material; it demands that we speak of the body and of discursive practices in their materiality. This foregrounding of affect is also probably connected with my reading of Stuart Hall's 'founding' insight in the first issue of the *New Left Review* (1960): 'The task of socialism is to meet people where they are – where they are touched, bitten, moved, frustrated, nauseated – to develop discontent and at the same time, to give the socialist movement some direct sense of the times and the ways in which we live.' I am interested in the various ways popular discourses can empower and disempower specific groups and practices, in the ways different cultural alliances operate in and produce different 'mattering maps'.

In that sense, I think popular culture cannot be limited to those practices that we might normally locate within the circumscribed (modernist) region of culture. For many generations and for many people, religion was itself within the popular. It served not as an exact body of knowledge, but as an affective structure, one that helped make sense of the world by producing the feeling that the world was a totality, that life must have a meaning. The nature of that meaning may be less important than the confidence that the world, despite its contradictions, still makes sense. The popular, in the narrower sense of popular culture, can still serve this function, but it can rarely do so by producing a stable and enduring affective horizon.

The question of empowerment is a crucial one. On the one hand, for me, empowerment has never been intrinsically political; rather I think of empowerment as involvement and investment, as a matter of vectors of energy connecting positions in space. And as such, it is a necessary condition for the possibility of agency, of any form of action or commitment. However, to leave it at that – at what some writers have called the level of micropolitics (but this is not the Foucauldean sense) or what others describe as everyday life (again, not my sense) – is to render it impotent and irrelevant. For the question is always how structures of empowerment are themselves articulated to and by other forms of practices and effects. It cannot be thought of simply as the articulations between micro and macro levels of politics, but rather, of the articulations between different practices and effects which, taken together, make the politics of everyday life and the politics of 'politics' (both of which exist at both the micro and the macro levels) inseparable.

The popular articulates everyday life as a structured mobility by constructing the spaces and places of everyday life, the spaces within which, and the places in which, people live their everyday lives. In other words, popular culture is constantly enacting and enabling specific forms and trajectories of movement (change) and stability (agency). It defines certain formations of practices as the possible sites of individual investments, sites at which subjects and identities are constructed. It defines the vectors by which people and practices can or cannot move between, and connect, such investments. And it defines particular practices as billboards or guideposts along these vectors. In this way, popular discourses empower and enable specific forms of agency and action in everyday life, and they become crucial sites of both the appeal to authenticity and the construction of authority. Admittedly, then, my conclusion – that the new conservatism is an affective struggle to change the maps of what matters through the operating logics of specific popular formations,[11] that it is producing a particular structured mobility (what I have called a disciplined mobilization (Grossberg, 1994)) that is articulated in significant ways to and by the struggles of contemporary capitalism – is as much a result of the choices I have made as it is a 'description' of an empirical reality. Yet the question is not, is this an accurate representation, but rather, does this open up new political strategic possibilities?

It is in the context of this larger project that I would like to position my own researches on rock music: the attempt to analyse the new conservatism's articulation with the popular requires not only that we find a way of understand the functioning of popular discourses in terms of their operating logics, but also that we describe the specific operating logics that are being deployed in this hegemonic struggle. It is these questions that have defined my interest in rock (although my faith that rock is at the centre of the relevant formations is probably more the result of my own position as a fan, and my particular generational identity as a babyboomer, heavily invested, in different ways at different times and places, in rock).

Thus, my research questions about rock have always been about its political possibilities rather than about any judgement of its aesthetic quality or cultural authenticity, about its effects on everyday life (and its potential deployments into larger hegemonic struggles) rather than about any judgement of its immediate impact as containment within or resistance to some abstract structure of ideological power. I was always interested in the ability of rock to interpellate so many people in particular ways, ways that can only be described by saying that rock mattered – people gave it a real power in and over their lives – without becoming the dominant identification in their identity. Being a rock fan has always had significant consequences, but it would be a mistake to assume that interpreting the music or its fans' experience offers an adequate description or account of what drives its fans. Rock seemed to operate somehow as an affective articulatory agent; my question was: how this was accomplished, why and with what effects?

Answering these questions, using a wide variety of research methods (although I must admit, almost always too informally and without the proper care),[12] I have studied rock culture as a configuration of cultural practices and effects that have been organized around rock music, the ways its fans have empowered it and been empowered by it. But I have never thought of myself as studying rock music/culture as an isolatable cultural phenomenon – as a set of texts and audiences and communicative relations. My notion of rock as an object of study has always operated at a particularly high level of abstraction, a level that I have called 'the rock formation'. This phrase is meant to signal a specific material, spatial and temporal identity. Thus, I assumed that rock's identity and effects (whether as a musical genre or a specific text/practice within the genre) depend on more than its specific textuality or sound. To describe rock culture as a formation is to constitute it as a material – discursive and non-discursive – context, a complex and always specific organization of cultural and non-cultural practices which produces particular effects – specific forms and organizations of boredom and fun, of pleasure and pain, of meaning and nonsense. The rock formation cuts across any attempt to divide up the field of popular discourses and practices, bringing together genres, media, styles, etc. To speak of a formation is also to constitute rock culture spatially, as a particular dispersion of practices across time and space. I was never interested in the empirically describable details of various specific organizations of fans and practices (what I have called apparatuses, scenes and alliances) *per se*, but in the more abstract questions of how such assemblages and their effects might be understood. I have never been interested in the concrete as a local, empirical phenomenon (that I leave to better critics and analysts than myself), but in the formation of rock culture at the broadest level (i.e. as a particular organization of American popular culture); my disinterest in any concrete instance (geographically and temporally) of rock culture has been defined (and to my mind justified by) my interest in the concrete context of American political hegemony. I have never championed the local; rather I have always argued that political projects define the appropriate definition of contexts and objects of analyses. For, given my project, the particular articulations and manifestations of the rock formation were less important than its existence across practices, time and space.

At the same time, the rock formation has a temporal extension and boundary: it is an historical event and production, which emerged at a particular moment, made possible by and in response to specific conditions of possibility, conditions which enabled rock culture but also constrained it, which defined it but also opened up its trajectories of transformation, which empowered it but also set limits on its shapes and effects. But if the rock formation is an event, it must also have the possibility of an end, which explains my obsession with the notion that rock is dead, again not as a judgement I want to make about particular musical practices or variants of rock culture, but as a discursive haunting within the rock formation and, of course, as a possible eventual reality. That is, I simply assumed that, if the rock formation emerged as a response to particular conditions, eventually, when those conditions changed, and the effects of the discourses within the formation changed (not necessarily in some simple corresponding way), then whatever music sounded like (perhaps even exactly like some of the music in the rock formation), the set of relations and effects articulated around it would not be the same. In fact, they would be so different as to be no longer usefully described as another variant of the rock formation. The discontinuities would be more significant than the continuities.

Understanding this formation involves trying to map the conditions and effects of its emergence, understanding why this particular formation appeared rather than another. What sort of forces and dimensions constituted the context of the emergence of the rock formation? How have these conditions – and the relations among them – been transformed over the course of recent American history? Obviously, it is impossible to know in advance what conditions are the most pertinent, which have the greatest purchase and the greatest reach. But I believe one can put together a sense of the context of the rock formation by describing at least the following aspects: the economic and political terrain; the structural position of youth and generations; the state of play of the various axes that articulate power and identity; the dominant structures of feeling; the media economy (the availability and popularity of various media with different audiences); the state and structure of the music technology and industry; the availability (to youth audiences) of images and discourses of alienation and rebellion; and finally, the emergent structures of feeling (including that of youth in its various articulations).

But the real work begins when one tries to describe the effects of this context, and the ways in which particular cultural practices and formations emerge and function as responses to and transformations of that context. But even to put it this way is to risk the danger of falling back into a model of culture representing an external social and political reality. Instead, what we are attempting to do is to redescribe the context, to fabricate another map which enables us to see better the contradictions, fault lines and struggles that are already at work in the context, either as actualities or as possibilities. If people make the world, but in conditions not of their own making, then we must move from a description of the social context as a structure of social relationships and experiences to another description of the context as a field of forces. My own critical investment in the popular leads me to understand such a field in terms of, and as constituted by, a struggle over the production and distribution of operating logics – modes of articulation by which particular organizations of practices are able to produce particular organizations of effects. That is to say, if we assume that context everyday life is not a static structure, but an active configuration of possibilities, of mobilities and stabilities, of the spaces and places at which forms of agency become available, then popular formations define possible ways of producing and navigating one's way within and across the spatial field of everyday life, even as they constitute that field.

This theoretical apparatus developed as I attempted to describe the logics – what I have called the politics – of the rock formation and how they have changed over the past forty years (and eventually, how they have played into the new conservative hegemony). Doing so requires us to lay out the effective geography of the rock formation as it has moved across the various configurations of everyday life (i.e. the first description of the context). This 'geometry' describes a functioning apparatus that is transformed by its conditions even as it transforms itself. It is a matter of material effects and agencies which need not be consciously experienced or represented. It describes the possibilities – the forms and locations of empowerment and disempowerment – which the rock formation makes available to those placed within its logics.

Given the lack of any available vocabulary for describing the forms, quantities and organizations of affect, this geography or operational logic cannot be described directly, but the parameters and possibilities of its articulatory power can be laid out at least schematically. The only significant continuity I 'discovered' in the process of mapping out the conditions of the emergence of the rock formation is a certain 'postmodern vector' operating at the intersection of the rock formation and everyday life in postwar America.[13] For me, the postmodern is a very specific and restricted (always local, partial and temporary, although also mobile and increasingly powerful) rearticulation of everyday life (or experience, as long as experience is not reduced to the ideologically constructed realm of meaning, knowledge and subjectivity). It involves the proliferation of sites in everyday life where the relation between ideology and affect is attenuated. At such sites, there seems to be a gap or a distance between the ways we make sense of our lives and the investments we make in them. That is, if affect and ideology are usually tightly articulated together – otherwise there is a psychological and emotional crisis – the postmodern points to those places where our taken-for-granted systems of meaning and value, and our affective structures of mood and volition, are disarticulated and fly apart. The result is an inability to find places where meanings matter, or where we can make sense of what does seem to matter.

And this vector is rearticulated into the popular logics of the rock formation – although its importance, pertinence and power have varied significantly over time – where it defines the affectivity of the formation itself. The result is a new articulatory logic and a rapid movement, into the centre of contemporary cultural life, of two figures of this affective logic: sentimentality (affect without any claim to represent real lives) and an ironic cynicism in which the very claim to self-representation (authenticity) is denied. Confronting the postmodern vector of everyday life produces an increasing tendency to stop in places (e.g. taking on particular cultural identities or taking up forms of agency), while self-consciously questioning, limiting and perhaps even challenging the investment in them: authentic inauthenticity (or 'in-difference') is a popular logic which refuses to distinguish between the authentic and the inauthentic, between boredom and terror – and a set of practices which celebrates the affectivity of investment while refusing to discriminate between different forms and sites of investment – as the only viable response to contemporary conditions. I want to make clear that I do not think that this logic and the vector which it rearticulates constitute a crisis in so far as they are both constructed at the intersection of the popular and everyday life. It is only when they are themselves deployed within and linked to specific hegemonic struggles that the postmodern becomes a crisis of sorts.

But perhaps more importantly, I have tried to describe the changing shape of the rock formation over time, in different contexts, according to the following dimensions: the *rock terrain,* which describes the internal differentiation of the alliances within the formation itself (e.g. mainstream, countercultural, undergrounds, alternatives, etc.); the *affective machine,* which describes the primary register of rock's productivity (e.g. fun, lifestyle, style/fantasy, attitude); the *ideologies* of the formation (e.g. liberalism, anarchic utopianism, self-conscious commodification); the articulation of rock as a *differentiating machine* (whether differences in taste do matter, whether they are articulated to generational, social and political differences, and to identities); the *politics of fun,* which describes both the antagonism around which the formation is structured (fun versus boredom, insanity, reality or despair) and the primary sites of investment (youth, movement, pleasure, experimentation, body, pain, style, reflexivity, entertainment, etc.); the *politics of everyday life,* which describes different projects in relation to the conditions of possibility of everyday life (relative deterritorialization, the fantasy of absolute deterritorialization, reterritorialization, polemological struggle); the *geometry of affect,* which describes where rock locates itself in the formation and everyday life (e.g. as topical it has a place of its own; as panoptical it is everywhere; as heterotopical it is only in others' places; and as atopical it is a space without a place, which is to say, at the border); *affective differences,* which describes the nature of its borders with the dominant culture (independent, alternative, oppositional); and *affective alliances,* which describes the nature of its self-positioning (experiential, utopian, critical). Together, these dimensions might enable us to describe rock's politics of empowerment, its operational logic as different ways of allowing people to navigate their way through and even to respond to their lived context. I have always thought of rock as a practice which helps us make it through the day. These dimensions, taken together, can be used, I think, to chart the trajectory of the rock formation, and to mark the point of its possible disappearance.

If I am right that the rock formation is coming to an end or at least being replaced by something different enough that it must be recognized as such, if I am right that the rock formation is no longer as powerful a site of agency and articulation as it has been for the past forty years, then both the tiers for analysis and the political stake in such studies will have to be rethought. I think this partly explains the increasing professionalization and disciplinization of popular music studies, a development with which, I must admit, I have limited sympathy, and in which I have no interest.

I have tried to suggest throughout this chapter something about my project – about its contextual and strategic approach – but equally impor- tant, I have tried to suggest that it is as much a collective project as it is my own. After all, cultural studies is itself an intellectual practice which not only claims to belong somewhere, but also claims to belong within a collective intellectual enterprise. It challenges not only the boundaries between the disciplines, but more importantly, the boundary between the academy and the world outside. Much like rock, I have always found it empowering and enabling, and like rock, I have always found it to be fun. But also like rock, I have always taken its challenge seriously: in a struggle in which the dominant mattering maps are being restructured – when the individual and the concrete matter so much more than the general and the abstract, when the freedom of the market matters so much more than caring for the people – the political intellectual has no choice but to enter on to the terrain of the popular. When the very possibility of political struggle is being erased – not because the scene of politics (or the public sphere) has disappeared in some postmodern apocalypse, but because there is an active attempt to use popular discourses to restructure the possibilities of everyday life – then the political intellectual has no choice but to enter into the struggle over affect.

If particular cultural formations and historical events come to an end, then some old political possibilities may no longer be possible. We may lament such closures, but we would be better advised to ask what new political possi- bilities have become imaginable. That is, my interest in the death of rock is actually an interest in the possibility of rock becoming something else, in an attempt to ask what a new popular politics might look like, and how it might be discursively constructed. In fact, it seems to me that the disappearance of any progressive political movement (not as an institutional organization, but as an organization of spaces and places) has been actively constructed, for particular fractions of the populace, at three sites, all being actively constructed through rearticulations of postmodernity and the operating logic of the rock formation: first, the impossibility of investing in the political (i.e. whether in the government or 'the people' as agents of change or some utopian field of political and ethical values); second, the active discourage- ment of any investment in the possibility of political community (i.e of rethinking the relation of the individual to the group, and of identity to struggle); and third, the impossibility of articulating a theory and practice agency (of reconsidering how people make history, but not in conditions of their own making). These are, in the first instance, problems of everyday life, constructed in struggles in and over the popular. They are also problems at the intersection of everyday life and the tendential forces struggling to deter- mine it. But they are also challenges for the intellectual, and we will have failed if we cannot find ways to address them outside of the limits of our own theoretical and political positions; if we cannot speak, as intellectuals, through the popular, in order to connect everyday life with the very real struggles and sufferings of economic and political injustice.

Notes

1   For example, I began teaching courses in cultural studies in the early 1970s, gave my first public lecture on it in 1976, and published my first article on cultural studies in 1977. Of course, other scholars in the USA, most especially James Carey, were talking about cultural studies even earlier. Obviously, courses in popular culture have a much longer history, but even when combined with cultural studies, even implicitly, their history goes back into the 1960s. Again, I began teaching courses in popular culture in the early 1970s; my first public presentation on popular music was in 1981 (although I began teaching classes on popular music in 1977) and my first publication was in 1983.

2   Habermas is the clearest example, although I would also describe the particular appropriation of poststructuralism and postmodernism which became dominant in the USA in these terms.

3   Meaghan Morris has been arguing something like this for some time now.

4   I use 'everyday life' in a very specific sense. It is not merely daily life, but an organization of routinized structures under capitalism. That is, everyday life is already a product of power rather than an escape from it. Thus I do not think that everyday life can be equated with Foucault's description of micropolitics and discipline. My own view is taken from Lefebvre (1984), but would not have been possible without the help of Meaghan Morris.

5   I have always been opposed to carving up the field of popular culture into a series of new disciplines: film studies, television studies, popular music studies, etc. To my mind, none of these makes sense and none remains true to the political practice of cultural studies. However, I do not mean to suggest that every moment of work in cultural studies has to be saturated, as it were, in political intentionality. Rather, the issue is the way one articulates any analysis of popular culture to political projects and possibilities.

6   My work, both theoretically and politically, has been most strongly influenced by Stuart Hall and Meaghan Morris. I have always attempted to bring together two different theoretical perspectives, two different practices of cultural studies: a modernist theory of articulation and hegemony (Gramsci, as read through Stuart Hall) and a radically non-modernist theory of effectivity, spaciality and machinics (Michael Foucault, Gilles Deleuze and Felix Guattari, often as read through Meaghan Morris). I do not mean to make either Stuart or Meaghan responsible for my work, but to acknowledge my personal debt to and my admiration for both of them. Both of them have rather dispersed bodies of work, but good starting points are Morley and Chen (1996) and Morris (forthcoming).

7   Obviously, I am making sweeping generalizations about what are often diverse and sophisticated bodies of work. I do not mean to dismiss the contributions of each of these practices, or to ignore the fact that the best critics are often those who can push the limits of their theoretical positions.

8   Often, this involves conflating notions of decoding and articulation. But the former assumes agency and context, while the latter problematizes both.

9   This is probably not the best metaphor. Now that I have a child, I think 'Lego' provides a better image.

10 Obviously, most work on popular culture starts with the visible and the legible, a move which often foregrounds the relationship between popular and 'high' culture.

11 I am not claiming that my work has described all of the ways in which the new conservatism depolys popular operating logics. For example, there is clearly a logic of conspiracy involved in the success of this hegemonic struggle. Such a logic of conspiracy can be embodied in a variety of forms and sites of conspiracy theories, from the individual intentionality of control narratives as in the work of Tom Clancy, to the collective intentionalities of the system in many popular conspiracies (e.g. Nowhere Man or the Illuminati). I am grateful to Jim Hevia for raising this with me.

12 But then I don't think that cultural studies has ever been particularly concerned about methodological rigour.

13 I have sometimes been described as a postmodernist, although I must admit that I am not sure what the various authors of such descriptions have intended by the phrase.

References

Bourdieu, Pierre (1984) *Distinction: A Social Critique of the Judgement of Taste*, trans. R. Nice, Cambridge, MA: Harvard University Press.

Deleuze, Gilles, and Felix Guattari (1977) *Anti-Oedipus: Capitalism and Schizophrenia*, New York: Viking.

(1987) *A Thousand Plateaus: Capitalism and Schizophrenia* Trans. B. Massumi, Minneapolis, MN: University of Minnesota Press.

Grossberg, Lawrence (1994) *We Gotta Get Out of This Place: Popular Conservatism and Postmodern Culture*, New York and London: Routledge.

Hall, Stuart (1960) 'Editorial', *New Left Review*, no. 1, p. 1.

(1981) 'Notes on deconstructing "the popular"', in R. Samuel (ed.), *People's History and Socialist Theory*, London: Routledge and Kegan Paul.

(1988) *The Hard Road to Renewal: Thatcherism and the Crisis of the Left*, London: Verso.

Lefebvre, Henri (1984) *Everyday Life in the Modern World*, trans. S. Rabinovitch, New Brunswick: Transaction.

Morley, David and Kuan-Hsing Chen (1996) *Stuart Hall: Critical Dialogues in Cultural Studies*, London: Routledge.

Morris, Meaghan (1988) *The Pirate's Fiancee*, London: Verso.

(forthcoming).

Shiach, Morag (1989) *Discourse on Popular Culture*, Stanford, CA: Stanford University Press.

Index

Note: page numbers in *italic* refer to endnotes.